P9-CCK-524

PART I
HOW TO GET STARTED TODAY AS A PROFITABLE REAL ESTATE INVESTOR

What you need to know about the real estate bubble babble
in the media. • Why this may turn out to be the *Golden Age*
of real estate investing in America. • Why you shouldn't
start out in the real estate investment business as a full-
time investor. • How you can double your annual income by
investing in real estate on a part-time basis. • How you can
use my nine-step process for buying and selling real estate.
• How to contact the most accessible real estate author in
America right now.

What every investor must possess to succeed in the real
estate investment business today. • Why you must obtain
your real estate knowledge from reliable sources. • How to
avoid doing business with incompetent real estate service
providers. • What you need to know about real estate
investment clubs. • What you need to know about your
perceived competition. • How to use this book to become
your own real estate investment expert.

Why it's always best for real estate investors to maintain a
low profile. • The four types of insurance coverage that all
real estate investors should carry. • Sixteen ways that you
can reduce your annual insurance premium payments. •

CONTENTS

PART II
FIVE REALISTIC INVESTMENT STRATEGIES
THAT YOU CAN USE TO MAKE MONEY
FROM REAL ESTATE TODAY

The No-Nonsense Real Estate
Investor's Kit

THE NO-NONSENSE REAL ESTATE INVESTOR'S KIT

How You Can Double Your Income by Investing in Real Estate on a Part-Time Basis

THOMAS J. LUCIER

John Wiley & Sons, Inc.

Published by John Wiley & Sons, Inc., Hoboken, New Jersey.
Published simultaneously in Canada.

For general information on our other products and services or for technical support, please contact our Customer Care Department within the United States at (800) 762-2974, outside the United States at (317) 572-3993 or fax (317) 572-4002.

Wiley also publishes its books in a variety of electronic formats. Some content that appears in print may not be available in electronic books. For more information about Wiley products, visit our web site at www.wiley.com.

Library of Congress Cataloging-in-Publication Data:

Lucier, Thomas J.
 The no-nonsense real estate investor's kit : how you can double your income by investing in real estate on a part-time basis / Thomas J. Lucier.
     p. cm.
  Includes index.
  ISBN-13: 978-0-471-75653-8
  ISBN-10: 0-471-75653-9
  1. Real estate investment—United States. 2. Real
property—Purchasing—United States.   3. House buying—United States.   4.
  House selling—United States. I. Title.
  HD255.L8286 2006
  332.63′240973—dc22

                                                          2005034024

Printed in the United States of America.

10 9 8 7 6 5 4 3 2 1

To my good friend and
fellow real estate entrepreneur,
Lucas Hoppel,
keep on keeping on!

real estate transactions are so closely scrutinized by closing agents and lenders.

Why vacant properties can be a bonanza for savvy real estate investors. • How I made a $30,000 profit from a vacant building full of pigeon droppings. • How to quickly find the owners of vacant properties. • The 10 telltale signs that a property is probably vacant. • What to check for when looking over a vacant property. • How to make an unsolicited offer to purchase a vacant piece of property. • Vacant property checklist. • Letter to vacant property owners.

The three most common types of code violations. • How the code enforcement process works in most jurisdictions. • Where to find your local code enforcement regulations online. • How to get the addresses of all the condemned properties in your city or county. • How to effectively deal with local code enforcement bureaucrats. • How to contact the owners of condemned properties. • Letter to condemned property owners.

Why being a serial home buyer may be the ideal real estate investment strategy. • Five types of properties that qualify as a principal residence. • Six factors the IRS considers to determine a home owner's principal residence. • How married couples can earn up to $500,000 tax-free every two years. • How single and joint home owners can earn up to $250,000 every two years. • How to use real estate options to keep houses in the pipeline for future purchase.

The four most profitable types of problem properties to buy. • Why you must know the difference between correctable and non-correctable property problems. • The four most efficient ways to find problem properties. • How to find solutions to property problems. • How to contact

problem property owners. • Letter to problem property
owners.

The three largest groups of underserved tenants in America
today. • How to profit by providing rental housing to
tenants with physical disabilities. • How to make money
renting to responsible pet owners. • What you need to
know about the Housing for Older Persons Act. • Pet
application. • Pet agreement.

PART III
THE FUNDAMENTALS OF REAL ESTATE INVESTING

Where to find your state's civil statutes online. • What you
need to know about practicing real estate without a license.
• The 13 federal statutes that pertain to real estate
investing. • Where you can find federal statutes and
regulations online. • Why there's nothing illegal, unethical,
or immoral about flipping property.

The two types of security instruments that are used to
secure real estate loans. • The three types of residential
real estate loans. • The difference between assuming a
loan and buying subject to. • What you need to know about
the due-on-sale clause that's contained in residential loans.
• What you need to know about the assumption rules for
FHA and DVA loans. • How to take title to property subject
to existing loans. • What you need to know about equity
skimming and other forms of loan fraud.

What you must know about the Real Estate Settlement
Procedures Act (RESPA). • Why it's best to hire a board-
certified real estate attorney to close your transaction. •
Finding a board-certified real estate attorney in your area.
• What you need to know about title insurance. • How an

owner's title insurance policy protects property owners. •
How title insurance rates are calculated. • Everything you
need to know about HUD 1 Settlement Statements. •
Closing checklist.

PART IV
NINE-STEP PROCESS FOR BUYING
AND SELLING REAL ESTATE

Four effective ways to find owners, who are willing to sell
you their property below market value. • Why you must
look for owners, who are experiencing problems, situations,
and circumstances that they can't handle. • Why owners
are willing to sell their property below market value. •
Where to find the names of all of the property owners in
your county. • How to determine an owner's level of
motivation during your initial telephone conversation. •
Letter to small residential rental property owners. •
Property tracking worksheet.

Where to obtain property information from the public
records. • Where to search for property records online. •
What to do when your county's property records aren't
available online. • Sixteen types of liens to check for when
searching property titles. • What to search for when
performing preliminary due diligence. • Area selection
checklist.

How to locate a competent building inspector. • When to
have the property inspected. • Why you must be on the
lookout for any nonpermitted work that's been done on a
building. • Eleven potential problems to check for when
inspecting a property. • Phase one environmental audit
checklist. • Twelve property inspection checklists.

The difference between tax-assessed value and appraised
value. • The three common methods used by appraisers to

CONTENTS

should hire retired tradesmen and contractors. • What you
need to know about your state's construction lien law. •
How you can reduce your fix-up costs. • Why you must
keep track of your expenses on a daily basis.

Four methods to market your property to prospective
buyers. • How the resale value of a property is calculated.
• What to include on your property's information sheet. •
How to advertise your properties for sale online. • Where
to advertise your property for sale online. • How to avoid
wasting your time with nonqualified prospective buyers.

To download the forms contained in *The No-Nonsense Real Estate Investor's Kit,* type the exact same URL or web site address that is clearly printed below each form in this book into the browser window on your computer.

PART I

HOW TO GET STARTED TODAY AS A PROFITABLE REAL ESTATE INVESTOR

How You Can Double Your Annual Income by Investing in Real Estate on a Part-Time Basis

First things first: If you're looking for some sort of magic real estate formula, that's guaranteed to catapult you into the ever-growing ranks of America's real estate millionaires, you won't find it here. I want to warn you right upfront, that the real estate investment business is full of four-letter words such as: hard, work, risk, and loss. I also want you to know that investing in real estate isn't an exact science, and as a consequence, things don't always turn out the way that you expect them to. And that's exactly why this business is best suited for serious-minded, hard-working people, who have the "stick-to-itiveness" to overcome obstacles and finish what they start. In other words, real estate isn't for namby-pamby types, who want everything handed to them on a silver platter, and cringe at the thought of breaking into a sweat. But if you're an intelligent, reality-based, goal-driven, and action-oriented adult, who's willing to take calculated risks, and you're not afraid to roll up your sleeves and bust your buns, you've come to the right place. After you read, study, and thoroughly understand the contents of this book, you'll have the equivalent of a graduate level degree on how to be a successful do-it-yourself real estate investor. You'll be armed with the specialized knowledge that you need in order to hold your own and not get taken to the cleaners when you go up against seasoned professional investors in your local real estate market. But if you're sitting on the fence and waiting around for everything to be just right in your world, before you get started in the real estate investment business, you're probably going to be waiting for the rest of your life. And the same holds true for all of the overly superstitious people reading this book, who insist on waiting until the stars are in perfect alignment with their universe, before they dare to make a move.

Finally, I have just one word for all of you worrywarts who have been hesitant about taking the plunge into real estate investing because of an unfounded fear of losing your shirt when the so-called real estate bubble bursts: Relax. And stop listening to all of the Chicken-Little types in the media, who are chockfull of what makes the grass grow greener. The truth is that real estate is one of the safest investments in America, and if you always abide by the following two rules, you'll be insulated from the economic fallout of a bursting real estate bubble:

1. Never pay market value for property.
2. Never buy property that doesn't provide immediate positive cash flow.

What You Need to Know about the Real Estate Bubble Babble in the Media

Most of the journalists in the print and electronic media didn't see the tech stock bubble that finally burst in late 2000 coming. They were apparently out to lunch and totally oblivious to what was happening at the time! And a fear, bordering on paranoia, of getting caught off guard again is probably what has fueled the constant bubble babble about the imminent demise of the real estate market ever since early 2001. For example, the September 3, 2001, issue of *Forbes* magazine contains an article entitled, *What If Housing Crashed?* But to date, nothing has happened and that question that was posed in the article, back in 2001, is yet to be answered. From reading news and business magazine covers alone, uninformed members of the general public could get the impression that the real estate market nationwide is on the verge of collapse, and that every real estate investor in America is headed straight to hell in a hand basket when the real estate equivalent of a tsunami hits the market. However, based on the reality of the real estate marketplace, this is just another of many stories that the media has gotten awfully wrong. And it's no wonder, when you consider that almost all of the journalists in the so-called financial press and electronic media, mainly use stockbrokers, salespeople, and analysts as their sole sources for information, insights, and advice on investing in real estate. But the problem with using these people as sources for real estate expertise is twofold: First, their collective knowledge about investing in real estate wouldn't fill a thimble. How many of these self-professed real estate experts have ever actually been a principal in any type of real estate transaction? Second, Wall Street is extremely envious of the bullish real estate market, and those who work there are getting more desperate by the day, and they'll say and do virtually anything to try and lure the hundreds of thousands of investors, who have pulled their money out of an underperforming stock market to invest in real estate, back to the stock market. Right now, it is investors' mistrust and fear of being ripped-off, again, that's keeping them from going back to Wall Street. They're worried, and rightfully so, that they'll end up being swindled out of their life's savings, by the likes of Bernie Ebbers and Dennis Kozlowski. As I stated in my letter to the editor, which was published in the June 27, 2005, issue of *Fortune* magazine, when compared to investing in the world's largest crapshoot, better known as the stock market, investing in real estate looks sane.

The Chances of a Nationwide Residential Real Estate Market Meltdown Are Zero

I don't profess to be some sort of real estate swami or prognosticator, but I can state with complete confidence, that the odds that the United States will experience a nationwide residential real estate market meltdown, are right around zero. That's because unlike the stock market, which is a single national market, the so-called real estate market is comprised of thousands of local markets, nationwide. Granted, there are a few overvalued real estate markets in some states along the East and West Coasts, which may eventually experience corrections that could possibly see a 10 to 20 percent decrease in residential property values. But that's a far cry from the colossal financial calamity that the media have been predicting for many real estate markets nationwide since late 2000.

Why This May Turnout to Be the *Golden Age* of Real Estate Investing in America

Unless you've been living under a rock in Outer Mongolia for the past few years, you can't help but notice the real estate mania that seems to have swept most of the country. And in spite of the constant bashing that real estate has taken over the years from the doom and gloom media and jealous Wall Street types, it's still the investment of choice for most Americans. In a nutshell: Americans are very bullish on real estate. I don't think that it would be too far-fetched to believe that we may be living in a period of time right now that could possibly go down in history as the *Golden Age of Real Estate Investing* in America. In no previous time in our history has there been such a steady rise in property values, in so many markets, over a longer period of time. For example, in the county where I live, Hillsborough County, Florida, the single-family residential housing market has had a history of being undervalued. But over the past five years, there has been a steady increase in property values. And as a result of this market correction, real estate prices here are now right about where they should be. Overall, the robust real estate market has been the driving force behind the nation's economic growth for the past several years. Six key factors that have fueled the real estate boom are:

1. An almost insatiable demand for real estate.
2. Historically low interest rates.
3. Lax loan underwriting standards.
4. A huge infusion of money into real estate markets nationwide from former stock market investors who got burned when the dot-com bubble burst in late 2000.
5. Foreign investors buying American real estate in order to take advantage of a weak U.S. dollar.
6. The tax advantages that real estate has over other types of investments.

It's Never Too Late to Get Started

In spite of what some uninformed and overly negative skeptics may want you to believe, it's never too late to get started as a real estate investor. So don't let anyone talk you into believing that you've somehow missed the boat and that all of the really good deals have already been bought up. Case in point: In 1982, right after I had left the army and returned to Tampa, I was approached by a real estate know-it-all, who told me that it was no longer profitable to buy and fix-up rundown properties in Tampa. This naysayer went on and on about how all of the good deals had been snatched up and now the cupboard was bare. At first, I thought that maybe he was telling me this tale of woe because he viewed me as a potential competitor and was trying to discourage me from entering the market. Needless to say, I totally ignored his unsolicited advice and went on my merry way. In 1985, we both happened to own rental houses on the same street in South Tampa, near MacDill Air Force Base. I was getting $625 per month in rental payments, while he was only getting $475 a month, for the same size house. I know this because he stopped me on the street one day and asked me if I thought it was a good idea for him to raise the rent to $500 per month, when his current tenant's lease expired. At this point, it dawned on me, that this guy was caught in a 1970s time warp. And our initial conversation, in 1982, now made perfect sense to me. I found out that this guy was a real nutcase who hadn't bought any property since 1976. He had loaded up on precious metals instead and was waiting for Armageddon, when the Soviet Union nuked the United States back into the Stone Age. I guess he figured that he would survive a nuclear attack and use the silver and gold that he had been hoarding to barter for property. Thankfully for Planet Earth, things didn't turn out the way this guy had envisioned they would!

Why You Shouldn't Start Out in the Real Estate Business as a Full-Time Investor

Here's one surefire way for you to quickly end up broke and unemployed: Quit your day job and blindly jump into the real estate investment business as a full-time investor, without a viable game plan or a financial safety net—cash reserves and lines of credit to keep you afloat financially for at least six months. Yet, this is exactly what happens when "wannabe" investors naively enter the real estate business under the false assumption that all they have to do is just stick a few "I Buy Houses" signs in the ground, or place a "property wanted" ad in their local newspaper and killer deals will start rolling in overnight. But these aspiring real estate mavens soon experience a very rude awakening when things don't go according to script and the expected avalanche of telephone calls fails to materialize. Then reality sets in and life suddenly gets awful dicey in a hurry, when there's no money coming in and the bills keep piling up, and the downward spiral toward financial ruin, rapidly picks up speed. So, unless you've got deep pockets or the equivalent of a real estate sugar daddy who doesn't mind subsidizing your foray into the business, I would forgo starting out as a full-time investor. The smart thing to do is to keep your current source of income and work in your real estate investment business on a part-time basis, until you're in a position to live off your real estate income. Trust me; real estate investing can be stressful enough without the added burden of having to worry about how you're going to scrape up the money to pay your living expenses while you're struggling to get your business up and running. And the best way to scuttle a real estate business in its infancy is to make decisions while you're stressed-out and in a panic mode. This desperate mind-set usually results in investors making bad buying decisions that are extremely hard to recover from financially. By a "bad buying decision," I mean that an investor pays more for a property than it's worth in its current condition. And once an investor is upside down in a property, they have two choices: They can sell the property at a loss or they can hold out and hope that marketwide property appreciation bails them out.

Earn Full-Time Profits as a Part-Time Real Estate Investor

Unlike most other types of businesses, which generally require full-time participation from their owners in order for them to work well, a real estate investment business can be operated on a part-time basis and still be very profitable. And for savvy investors who are knowledgeable, well-organized, and know how to manage money, time, and people, real estate can be a part-time business that yields full-time profits. The trick is to work smart so that your business always operates at maximum efficiency and profitability. You'll get the lowdown on how to run a tight ship in Chapter 4. Some of the most successful real estate investors I know are part-time investors who have outside sources of income. In fact, I know several real estate millionaires, who probably never made more than $50,000 a year at their day jobs and invested in real estate on a part-time basis, and over a 10- to 15-year period, they became financially independent. To me, real estate is the ideal type of business for small business owners who operate home-based businesses, or other types of businesses that don't have walk-in customers or set business hours, to run as a side business. For example, over the years, I've operated my real estate investment business in conjunction with home repair, commercial pressure-washing, and publishing businesses. All three businesses have provided me with a steady source of income while allowing me the freedom to invest in real estate at the same time. In fact, both the home repair and pressure-washing businesses put me into direct contact with a lot of property owners with rundown properties that were either in dire need of repair, or desperately needed an industrial strength cleaning. And the $64,000 question, which I always asked every property owner who I gave a written estimate to was: "What do you plan on doing with the property, once it's fixed up/cleaned up?" Luckily for me, roughly 3 out of 10 times, the owner responded that they wished they could just sell the property the way it was, without having to go through the hassle of fixing or cleaning the place up. Needless to say, that type of a response was music to my ears, resulting in some of my best property buys.

It's How You Spend Your Time as a Real Estate Investor That Really Counts

First off, I want to clarify a popular misconception among most novice real estate investors who have been misled to believe that if they can earn $25,000 a year as a part-time investor, they can surely double their income simply by becoming full-time real estate investors. Sorry, but that's not exactly how things work in the real world of real estate investing. First off, at any given time, in any real estate market nationwide, there are only a certain number of properties that are worth pursuing. And being at the right place at the right time to scoop up bargain properties is more about which type of property search techniques you use than the amount of time that you have available to look for properties. As you'll soon learn in Chapter 4, it isn't about how much time you spend working as a real estate investor that counts, it's about what you're able to accomplish with the amount of time that you have as an investor, that's important. In other words, what good is it to be a full-time real estate investor, if you don't know what you're doing and you end up squandering your time away, without ever buying a single piece of property.

The Internet Has Leveled the Playing Field between Part-Time and Full-Time Investors

I consider the Internet to be the single most important invention for individual real estate investors in America. I feel this way because before the

Internet (a period of time that I refer to as BTI), whenever a real estate investor needed to research a property, they had to go traipsing downtown to where their local government is headquartered, and then go from office to office begging surly, bored and often incompetent civil servants, for real estate related information. But today, thanks to the Internet, any investor with a personal computer and Internet connection can have instant access to just about *every* type of real estate related record, 24 hours a day, 7 days a week, right in the comfort and privacy of their home or office. And for part-time real estate investors, who previously had to risk life and limb in a mad dash to government offices after their day job ended and before the office closed at 5 P.M., the Internet has leveled the playing field between part-time and full-time investors.

Real Estate Service Providers Can Perform Tasks for You during Business Hours

Nowadays, there are a slew of real estate service providers who offer every conceivable type of real estate related service to the public. For example, in most areas, there are mobile notary public services that will come to your home or office and notarize documents for real estate and loan closings. There are also freelance title researchers who you can hire to do title searches at your county's public records library. And these real estate professionals can perform tasks for you during business hours when you're not able to do them yourself. In Chapter 2, I give you step-by-step instructions on how to check out real estate service providers so you don't end up hiring a dud.

Most People Have Never Calculated How to Earn a Million Dollars in a Year

I've often wondered how many wannabe real estate investors have ever actually sat down and run the numbers and calculated exactly what it would take to earn a million dollars a year (before taxes). In case you haven't crunched the numbers yet, for you to earn one million dollars over a 12-month period, you would have to take in $2,740 per day ($1,000,000 divided by 365 days equals $2,740) or $19,231 per week ($1,000,000 divided by 52 weeks equals $19,231) or, $83,333 per month ($1,000,000 divided by 12 months equals $83,334). When a million dollars is broken down this way, aspiring real estate investors can see exactly what they need to make on a daily, weekly, and monthly basis to earn a million dollars in a year, before taxes. As you can see from the calculations that I've done here, earning your first million dollars in real estate isn't going to be quite the cakewalk that the get rich quick in real estate crowd, makes it out to be. In fact, a successful, hard working, full-time real estate investor, with average luck, would be hard pressed to earn a million dollars after taxes, within a five-year period. An investor would have to net $200,000 per year, for five years. In order to accomplish this, an investor would have to do 10 $20,000 deals or four $50,000 deals, or any other combination of deals, which equaled $200,000 a year. I don't care what those slick-talking real estate hucksters on TV say; earning $200,000 for five consecutive years in a row, as an individual real estate investor, is difficult to pull off in any market. The only possible way for the average successful investor to earn a million dollars in less than five years would be to buy a million dollar income-producing property and substantially increase its net operating income and hold it until its value increased enough for the investor to pocket a million dollars after taxes.

Your Goal as a Part-Time Investor Should Be to Double Your Annual Income

First things first: The reason why state lotteries are such a rousing success financially is because most Americans—more than 51 percent—worship the trappings of wealth and are constantly daydreaming about becoming millionaires. And the average person generally views winning the lottery as their only chance of ever grabbing the brass ring and living high on the hog. I am by no means a goody two-shoes, but I've never purchased a lottery ticket in my life. In lieu of squandering my hard-earned money on lottery tickets, I've chosen to make regular contributions to the pension fund of the hardworking Germans, who slave away at Beck's Brewery in Bremen, Germany. At least this way, I always get to enjoy the "fruits" of my labor. Don't get me wrong, I happen to think that a serious, "I want to be a millionaire mentality," is one of the prerequisites for making it big in real estate. But as I just told you, most people have no real concept of what it takes to actually earn a million dollars. And that's exactly why your initial financial goal, as a part-time real estate investor, must be a dollar amount, such as your annual income, which you can easily relate to. For example, if your annual income is $50,000, your goal should be to earn $50,000 in real estate, which would give you a combined annual income of $100,000. I realize that $50,000 may be chump change to aspiring real estate wheeler-dealers, who spend the majority of their time sitting around fantasizing about doing million dollar deals. But as far as I am concerned, thinking that you're going to earn a million dollars your first year out as a real estate investor isn't just a matter of being overly optimistic, it's downright delusional and a classic example of the pie-in-the-sky logic that fuels unrealistic expectations on the part of so many beginning investors.

How You Can Double Your Annual Income by Investing in Real Estate Part-Time

Over the past 26 years, I've observed many knowledgeable and hard-working investors who were able to double their annual income, year after year, by investing in real estate on a part-time basis. And these were mostly people, who weren't born with silver spoons in their mouths. In fact, many of them weren't even born in the United States. But the one thing that they all had in common was a burning desire to succeed and the persistence and dogged determination to keep going when most people would've called it quits and thrown in the towel. And when it comes right down to brass tacks, whether or not you're going to be able to double your annual income as a part-time real estate investor, really depends on:

1. Your desire to be a successful real estate investor.
2. Your ability as a real estate investor.
3. Your financial resources.
4. The amount of time and energy that you have to dedicate to your real estate investment business.
5. Where you're located geographically.
6. The size of your local real estate market.

7. Local real estate market conditions.

8. The segment of your market that you decide to invest in.

The number of real estate transactions that you'll need to complete in order to double your annual income will mainly depend on your geographical location, number 5 in the list. For example, if you're located in Yazoo City, Mississippi, it may take you five $10,000 deals, to make $50,000. On the other hand, if you're in Bellingham, Washington, you could probably earn $50,000 from just two $25,000 transactions. And if you happen to live in a super expensive real estate market, such as Southern California or Northern Virginia, you could probably make a $50,000 profit from buying and reselling a single property. You must also understand that just as there are no guarantees in life, all real estate investors aren't going to experience the same type of results. And due to the learning curve, many investors will be hard pressed to double their annual income their first year in business. But so what if you "only" earn half of your annual income during your first year in business. That's money that you otherwise wouldn't have had if you weren't involved in real estate. And I am willing to bet an ice-cold case of my favorite adult beverage that most of the people reading this book could put a 50 percent increase in their annual income to very good use, especially if it enabled them to payoff their bills and become debt free.

Buy 3 Out of 10 Properties That You Make Offers on and You'll Be a Success

I realize that it's much easier said, than done, but in reality, all you have to do in order to be successful in the real estate investment business is to buy 3 out of every 10 properties that you make offers on. That's right, if you're able to close roughly a third of the deals that you attempt to do, you'll never have to worry about where your next meal is coming from. To illustrate my point, I'll use the analogy of a major league baseball player, with a career batting average of .300, which means that he got 3 hits for every 10 times he went to bat. Or put another way, he failed to get a hit, 7 out of every 10 times at bat. And in major league baseball today, an excellent all-around player with a career batting average of .300 or above has a realistic shot at being inducted into the Baseball Hall of Fame. For example, I buy properties directly from owners during the *preforeclosure* stage of the foreclosure process. And to date, I am batting right around .400, which means that I buy 4 out of every 10 preforeclosure properties, that I make offers on. I also specialize in buying small—2 to 12 unit—mismanaged residential rental properties from burnt-out landlords. So far, I am hitting a solid .300, by buying 3 out of every 10 rental properties, that I put offers on.

How You Can Use My Nine-Step Process for Buying and Selling Real Estate

Over the past 26 years, I have developed and refined a nine-step process for buying and selling real estate. In Part IV of this book, you will learn the details of how to use my nine-step process and avoid the pitfalls and problems that plague most uniformed and unsuspecting novice investors just starting out. Here's a summary of my nine-step process, along with a brief description of each step:

Step 1: Find Property Owners Who Are Willing to Sell Their Property below Market Value

In Chapter 15, you'll learn how to use the Internet, property-wanted ads, bird dogs, finder's fees, and direct mail to locate the owners who are most likely to sell you their property below market value.

Step 2: Perform Preliminary Due Diligence on the Property

You'll receive step-by-step instructions on how to perform preliminary due diligence on a piece of property in Chapter 16. You'll also learn all of the nitty-gritty details on how to use your personal computer to access the numerous real estate public records that are available on the Internet in order to find current information on a property and its owner.

Step 3: Conduct a Thorough Pre-Buy Property Inspection

After you've finished Chapter 17, you'll know how to avoid being bamboozled by unscrupulous owners who are trying to unload a lemon of a property. This chapter also comes with 12 ready-to-use checklists, which you can use to conduct your own pre-buy property inspections.

Step 4: Accurately Estimate the Property's Market Value

The single most important aspect of the entire buying process is accurately estimating the market value of a piece of property, so you don't end up paying more than what its worth. And that's exactly what you're going to learn how to do in Chapter 18.

Step 5: Prepare a Purchase Agreement That Protects You

In Chapter 19, you'll learn, how to prepare purchase and sale agreements that protect your rights and interests during a real estate transaction. There's also a sample purchase agreement that you can use as a template, when you're having your own agreement drawn up.

Step 6: Negotiate the Best Possible Deal for Yourself

To be a successful real estate investor, you must know what to say and how to act, during face-to-face negotiations with buyers and sellers. And in Chapter 20, you'll learn how to negotiate the best possible deal for yourself.

Step 7: Obtain Financing to Purchase the Property

Chapter 21 is filled with ways that you can finance your real estate investments, even when you don't have a six-figure income, a hefty bank account, or an 850 FICO score. You'll learn about a myriad of loan programs that are available to real estate investors.

Step 8: Fix Up the Property for Maximum Curb Appeal and Resale Value

In Chapter 22, you'll learn how to fix up a piece of property so that you're able to maximize its curb appeal and resale value. You'll also get the inside scoop on how to finish the job on schedule and within budget, without getting ripped off by tradesmen and contractors.

Step 9: Package, Market, and Resell the Property for Maximum Profit

Savvy real estate investors make their profit upfront when they buy a property, but they don't actually get paid, until they resell the property. And in

Chapter 23, you'll learn how to package and market a property, so that it can be resold for maximum profit.

How to Contact the Most Accessible Real Estate Author in America Right Now

Unlike 99 percent of all real estate authors in America, there isn't a phalanx of gatekeepers between me and my readers. I answer my own telephone and e-mail and I am fully wired to communicate from anywhere within the United States. You can e-mail me directly at tjlucier@ thomaslucier.com. Or, you can call me direct at my office in Tampa, Florida, at (813) 237-6267. If there's something that you still don't understand, after reading this book twice, please feel free to e-mail your questions to me and I promise to get an answer right back to you. No other real estate author in America offers readers this type of free one-on-one personal service! However, if for whatever reason, you fail to read and study this book, please don't expect me to spoon feed the contents to you. My web site, www.thomaslucier.com, is the companion resource for *The No-Nonsense Real Estate Investor's Kit* and has direct links to all of the web sites that are listed throughout this book. I also offer telephone consultations to investors who are seeking in-depth advice on real estate investing. To learn more about my telephone consulting service, log onto my web site at: www.thomaslucier.com/consultations.html. After you've finished reading my book, I would greatly appreciate you taking a few minutes of your valuable time, to write a review of *The No-Nonsense Real Estate Investor's Kit*, at your favorite online bookstore.

CHAPTER 2

What It Takes to Be a Successful Real Estate Investor in Today's Competitive Market

Thanks in large part to the record increases in property values that have occurred in many markets nationwide over the past six years, many Americans are under the misconception that it's a snap to make money in real estate today. But in reality, nothing could be further from the truth. I hate to come across as some sort of real estate killjoy, but making a bundle in today's competitive real estate market just might be a little harder to pull off than what you've been misled to believe. Real estate investing can either be your ticket to financial independence or a trip to the poor house. And how it turns out is entirely up to you. The fact of the matter is that investing in real estate is hard work and to be successful at it, you must be willing to go out and bust your buns and do whatever it takes, within legal and ethical bounds, to get deals done. In addition, it takes leadership skills and the ability to manage money, time, and people. There's also an excellent chance that it will take much longer than you ever imagined before you get to join the ranks of the seven-figure net worth club. That's because success in the real estate investment business very seldom happens overnight. Instead, it's usually a get-rich-slow process that takes place over a number of years. To make it big as a real estate investor in today's competitive market, you must:

1. Have a positive mental attitude.
2. Control your fear of failure.
3. Have the courage to take action.
4. Never, ever quit.
5. Be a leader who can manage money, time, and people.
6. Have good English language skills.

7. Obtain specialized real estate investment knowledge from reliable sources.

8. Know the reasons why most people fail to make it as real estate investors.

My Description of the Ideal Candidate to Be a Successful Real Estate Investor

If I were looking for an apprentice to be my understudy and learn how to become a successful real estate investor, the ideal candidate would be a smart, aggressive, personable, confident, determined, adaptable, resourceful, innovative, disciplined, commonsensical, imaginative, visionary, and a self-starter who can get along with people, think on his or her feet, and who possesses the ability to quickly analyze problems and come up with fast and inexpensive solutions.

The Only Person Who Can Make You a Successful Real Estate Investor Is You

Americans are notorious for blaming everyone but themselves for their own screw-ups. And from the looks of civil court dockets nationwide, it seems as though the "blame game," as evidenced by the mind-boggling number of lawsuits filed annually, has surpassed baseball as the national pastime. You must understand right from the get-go that the only person who can make you a successful real estate investor is you. And if you're not willing to educate yourself and put in the time and effort that's required to be successful in this business, there's absolutely no one that you can legitimately blame but yourself. Every once in awhile, I'll get an e-mail from a wannabe investor lamenting about their lack of success and hinting that it's somehow my fault because, for whatever reason, they weren't able to put the information in one of my books to practical use. I always answer these e-mails by explaining to the wannabe investor that they're ultimately responsible for their own successes and failures in life, and until they're willing to accept it, they have little to no chance of ever getting their real estate investment career off the ground. At the end of the day, whether or not you're a successful real estate investor, really has very little to do with this book. But it does have everything to do with your ability, attitude, desire, determination, and persistence.

Success Can Be Boiled down to Decisions, Priorities, and Action

Over the years, I've given a lot of thought as to why some people succeed while others fail miserably. And I've come to the conclusion that success can be boiled down to three simple things: decisions, priorities, and action. For example, people who routinely make bad decisions, have misplaced priorities, and fail to take action are generally relegated to failure. However, people who exercise sound judgment, set priorities based on importance, and take action are usually successful. And the same holds true for aspiring real estate investors, who decide that real estate investing is their number one priority—outside of taking care of their family—and take the action that's necessary to make it a reality. The point that I am making here is that success isn't going to just fall into your lap as a result of wishful thinking or divine intervention. Instead, you must choose to be successful. And if you're really serious about being a successful real estate investor, you must make a conscientious decision to do so, set your priorities accordingly, and then follow everything up with action.

It Takes a Positive Mental Attitude to Be Successful

First off, I realize that in this day and age, a healthy dose of skepticism is the first line of defense that people have against the numerous fraudsters who perpetrate various types of scams against the American public on a daily basis. However, an overdose of skepticism can have a chilling effect and end up sabotaging your chances for success. It is a fact of life that it takes a positive mental attitude for a person to be successful. For you to be a successful real estate investor, you're going to have to fight a daily battle against the rampant negativism that is so prevalent in today's society. I have observed that most people are their own worst enemy and their biggest obstacle to achieving success. And the sooner you're able to convince the person that you see every time you look into a mirror that you'll be successful, come hell or high water, the sooner you'll start achieving success. Success is a mental state of mind and one success tends to breed another success and, eventually, being successful becomes a way of life. And that's exactly why people who have a track record of being successful, expect to succeed at everything they do.

Don't Let Fear of Failure Keep You from Being Successful

The number one reason why most aspiring real estate investors never get beyond the wannabe stage is because they're paralyzed by an uncontrollable fear of failure. All human beings have self-doubts and fears but it's how we humans overcome our self-doubts and keep our fears in check that counts. And unless you're able to control the fear of failure that you're harboring in your mind, you'll never get your real estate investment business off the ground. Granted, you may never be able to completely conquer your fear of failure but you can learn to control it so that it doesn't take over your life and stop your quest for success, dead in its tracks. I use my own fear of failure as a form of self-motivation to stay focused on the task at hand until it's complete.

Action Is the Key to Achieving Success

I learned at a young age that there are three types of people on Planet Earth: People who make things happen; people who watch things happen; and people who wonder what happened. Action is to success, as water is to plants. Success can't happen without action and plants won't grow without water. And if you don't get anything else from this chapter, please make certain that you get this: Action is the keystone to your achieving success as a real estate investor! You can have all of the real estate investment knowledge in the world, but it's worthless if you don't use it and put it into action.

Never Quitting Is 99 Percent of Being Successful

Quitting is a natural human reaction to adversity, but the urge to quit and throw in the towel can be overcome by persistence and a dogged determination to succeed. And persistence and determination are what stoke the fire that burns in the belly of every successful real estate investor in America. I've never been one who subscribes to the theory that people succeed because they're destined to. Instead, it has always been my experience that people succeed because they're determined to. And that's why, to my way of thinking, never quitting is 99 percent of being successful. You must understand that as a real estate investor, there are always going to be potholes, roadblocks, and other obstacles on the road to success, which can make for very rough sledding. In order to see things through to completion, you're going to have to have the "stick-to-itiveness," that's required to stay the course and finish what you start. As a Marine, I was taught from the day that I stepped onto the yellow footprints at Parris Island, South Carolina, on October 3, 1969, that I must do whatever it took, come hell or high water, to overcome any obstacles that stood between me and accomplishing the mission, or die trying. Our motto in the infantry was FIDO: Forget it; drive on. Quitting wasn't an option because the word "quit" wasn't part of our vocabulary. I have taken the same never-quit, can-do attitude that was honed in the Marine Corps and applied it to my real estate investment business. A fellow Vermont native and the thirtieth president of the United States, Calvin Coolidge, aptly summed up the power of dogged determination and persistence, when he so eloquently stated that: *"Nothing in the world can take the place of persistence. Talent will not; nothing is more common than unsuccessful men with talent. Genius will not; unrewarded genius is almost a proverb. Education will not; the world is full of educated derelicts. Persistence and determination alone are omnipotent. The slogan, 'Press on,' has solved and always will solve the problems of the human race."*

Leadership Skills Are Needed to Be a Successful Real Estate Investor

As far as I am concerned, the old Marine Corps maxim of *lead, follow, or get the hell out of the way* should be the mantra of every real estate investor in America. That's because, to succeed in today's competitive real estate market, you must be a leader who can grab the bull by the horns, take control of a real estate transaction, and do whatever it takes, within legal and ethical bounds, to get the deal done. And to do this, you must build lasting business relationships with honest competent professionals who can help you achieve your financial goals. But you must also understand that no one is going to look after your interests as well as you are. You can delegate tasks to the people that you hire to do them, but ultimately, you're responsible for what happens and you're the one who's going to suffer the financial or legal consequences if the job gets botched or doesn't get done at all.

Good English Language Skills Are Essential

In spite of what some people seem to believe, English is the official language of business in America. And it's also the international language of business the world over. To effectively communicate with buyers, sellers, and real estate service providers, you must possess good English language skills. One of the biggest turn offs in the business world is poorly written communications, such as e-mail messages, letters, and agreements, that are riddled with grammatical and spelling errors. The same holds true for people who speak using poor grammar. We are all judged on a daily basis by the way in which we speak and write the English language. If your written and verbal English language skills are lacking, I highly recommend that you invest the time, effort, and money that's necessary to upgrade these skills. If English isn't your native language, I recommend that you spend the time and effort necessary to become proficient in speaking, reading, and writing English. I never get involved in real estate transactions in which the principals don't comprehend the English language. To me, real estate transactions can be difficult enough, without the added stress and aggravation of not being able to communicate clearly with the other party.

Specialized Real Estate Investment Knowledge Is a Prerequisite for Success

I hate to burst your bubble, but you're not going to become the next Donald Trump simply by attending an overpriced two-day seminar in some fancy hotel ballroom! The fact of the matter is that most beginning real estate investors go through a crawl, walk, and run learning progression. And in this business, the difference between what you think you know, and what you really know, can end up costing you a bundle of money and a ton of grief. Case in point: As far as I am concerned, one of the few people, who are more dangerous than a newly minted MBA with no real-world hands-on work experience; or a newly commissioned U.S Army second lieutenant with a map, is a so-called wannabe real estate investor, with just a teensy-weensy bit of knowledge. The MBA has the potential to run a business straight into the ground; the second lieutenant will most likely get lost every time he or she ventures out into the field on a training exercise. But the wannabe real estate investor can muck up a real estate deal beyond all recognition while wreaking financial havoc upon themselves and getting sued in the process. And when this happens, it can take a very long time for anyone to recover from the effects of this type of a triple financial whammy. But luckily, this type of financially devastating ignorance can be overcome by acquiring in-depth specialized knowledge in a myriad of subjects, such as:

1. Finance.
2. Accounting.
3. Marketing.
4. Real estate, landlord and tenant, and tax law.
5. Negotiations.
6. Zoning and land use.
7. Building, fire, and safety codes.
8. Building construction.
9. Demographics.
10. Environmentally hazardous materials.
11. Indoor air quality.
12. Indoor mold.

You Won't Learn How to Be a Successful Real Estate Investor in College

I am rather proud of the fact that I've never taken a college level real estate investment course in my entire life. What I am writing about in this book is based on my actual hands-on experiences, and not on the usual theory that's taught in business college classrooms across the country. Many professors teaching real estate investing at the undergraduate and graduate levels have never been a principal in any type of commercial real estate transaction. It has been my observation that the standard MBA approach to business is not well suited for investing in real estate, which is more entrepreneurial in nature. An MBA refers to a master's degree in business administration from an accredited college or university. It does not mean that this individual has any practical experience in the real estate field.

Why You Must Obtain Your Real Estate Knowledge from Reliable Sources

I have found that many investors' knowledge about investing in real estate is superficial, at best. And they lack the in-depth nuts-and-bolts knowledge that's required to put a real estate transaction together from start to finish. I attribute this lack of in-depth knowledge to the fact that, for whatever reason, many people rely solely on the real estate, legal, financial, and accounting advice that they're able to get for free from Internet message boards, friends, coworkers, next door neighbors, in-laws, soothsayers, and psychics. The problem with obtaining free information from dubious sources is that it's almost always wrong. A word of warning: If your "knowledge" about investing in real estate has been gleaned from reading Internet message boards, or if it's based on the sayings of Uncle Elmo, instead of reliable sources such as competent, licensed professionals, there's an excellent chance that you'll suffer severe financial consequences for being ignorant.

Avoid Doing Business with Incompetent Real Estate Service Providers

Your success as a real estate investor will be tied directly to the people you choose to hire. There are a slew of incompetent real estate service providers working within the real estate industry nationwide. These are people who, when left to their own devices, would screw-up a soup sandwich! Inept real estate service providers run the gamut from title and escrow agents, attorneys, lenders, mortgage brokers, real estate agents, building inspectors, to insurance agents and property appraisers. The ideal way to avoid being victimized by incompetent real estate service providers is to never do business with them in the first place. But because most investors usually don't do their homework before they hire a service provider, they usually don't know that they're dealing with an incompetent person, until it's too late and the damage has already been done. Granted, there's no foolproof method for screening out incompetent people, and whenever you hire anyone, there's a certain element of risk, but you have a much better chance of ferreting out the bad guys when you take the following basic precautions before you ever hire any real estate service provider:

1. Verify the status of professional licenses with the government agencies that issued the licenses.
2. Verify membership and professional designations with professional associations.
3. Verify proof of errors and omissions insurance policies with the insurers who issued the policies.
4. Check the public records for complaints and lawsuits.
5. Require verifiable references from past customers.
6. Do an Internet name search using the Google search engine.

What You Need to Know about Real Estate Investment Clubs

Ideally, real estate investment clubs should provide a setting where like-minded people can gather to share ideas, information, resources, and experiences, and network with fellow members and learn the ropes from knowledgeable local real estate professionals in an environment that's devoid of hucksters using hard-sell tactics to hawk overpriced real estate courses and seminars. However, that's generally not what happens at most—more than 51 percent—real estate club meetings. Instead, members are usually inundated with sales pitches from the numerous real estate carnies who travel the real estate investment club circuit and make their living from selling everything from $150 books, to $250 DVDs, to $1,500 courses, to $10,000 seminars. And if that's not bad enough, then there are the local sharks who view new members as fresh meat and try to unload their overpriced properties on the unsuspecting beginners. Or, the club meetings end up being nothing more than a bullspit festival where blowhards tell real estate war stories to an audience that's mostly made-up of gullible wannabe investors who don't know a deed from a promissory note. Another problem with most real estate investment clubs is that they have a tendency to attract more than their fair share of people who have unrealistic expectations, no money, and lousy credit, and are looking for an easy way to make a fast buck in real estate. Also be on the lookout for real estate club junkies, who regularly attend meetings and talk a good fight but have never actually been a principal in any type of real estate transaction. Needless to say, these aren't exactly the types of people that you should seek out to help you advance your career as a real estate investor. I suggest that you avoid these types of people like the plague. The best advice that I can give you about real estate investment clubs is to:

1. Never bring your credit cards to a meeting.
2. Attend at least three meetings before you buy an annual membership.
3. Avoid doing business with any of the local sharks who regularly attend monthly meetings.

Federal Trade Commission Brochure on Seminar Scams

Predatory seminar promoters rip off the public to the tune of tens of millions of dollars annually, by fraudulently misrepresenting the worthless information and advice they peddle as being valuable. The Federal Trade Commission (FTC) has published a brochure entitled, *The Seminar Pitch: A Real Curve Ball,* that warns consumers about the various get-rich-quick seminar scams that are perpetrated against the American public. The FTC brochure is available online at: www.ftc.gov/bcp/conline /pubs/invest/seminar.pdf.

Use This Book to Become Your Own Real Estate Investment Expert

I wrote *The No-Nonsense Real Estate Investor's Kit,* so that you can use it to become your own real estate investment expert. You can avoid being at the mercy of so-called real estate experts who, more often than not, know little about the inner workings of the real estate investment business. I've learned the hard way that in this business you just can't afford to blindly rely on the advice that's given to you by supposed experts. You must always be able to verify that everything you're told is 100 percent accurate and on the up and up. And if you can't confirm that what you're being told to do is correct, there's an excellent chance that you'll end up being what I call a "mushroom investor"—

an investor who's kept in the dark and fed a lot of bullspit by their advisors! And unless you want to become a member of the mushroom club, I very highly recommend that you adopt my real estate investor motto of: *"Assume nothing, verify everything, and be prepared for anything."*

My Recommended Reading List

The best, fastest, and least expensive way to acquire the specialized knowledge that you're going to need to be a successful real estate investor is to read books that contain reliable how-to information and practical no-nonsense advice. You can rest assured that my recommended reading list doesn't contain any books that are packed with nothing but hyperbolic get-rich-quick rhetoric, and are best suited for lining birdcages and wrapping garbage in. The problem that I have with most of the information that's contained in the majority of real estate investment books being published today is that it's incomplete, unreliable, and not very useful. Personally, I wouldn't want to be caught dead in the same room with most of the people in the real estate investment information and advice business today. But if you happen to be one of the many shortsighted people in America who are hesitant to invest in themselves, please ponder these immortal words of wisdom from former Harvard University President Derek Bok, *"If you think education is expensive, try ignorance."* And don't make the colossal mistake of allowing the cost of a few essential books to come between you and success, especially when you can buy most of them used at online bookstores on the Internet. The following is a listing of 31 books—in no particular order—that every serious real estate investor should eventually have in their reference library:

1. *Realty Bluebook* by Robert de Heer
2. *The Magic of Thinking Big* by David J. Schwartz
3. *Real Estate Principles* by Charles J. Jacobus
4. *The Complete Guide to Your Real Estate Closing* by Sandy Gadow
5. *How to Win Friends and Influence People* by Dale Carnegie
6. *Fundamentals of Real Estate Appraisal* by William J. Ventolo Jr. and Martha R. Williams
7. *How I Turned $1,000 into Five Million in Real Estate* by William Nickerson
8. *If You Want to Sue a Lawyer* by Kay Ostberg

9. *How You Can Become Financially Independent by Investing in Real Estate* by Albert Lowry
10. *Barron's Real Estate Handbook* by James Harris and Jack Friedman
11. *Real Estate Finance and Investment Manual* by Jack Cummings
12. *Real Estate Quick and Easy* by Roy Maloney
13. *U.S. Master Tax Guide* published annually by CCH, Inc.
14. *Timing the Real Estate Market* by Robert M. Campbell
15. *Land Trusts for Privacy and Profit* by Mark Warda
16. *IRA Wealth* by Patrick W. Rice and Jennifer Dirks
17. *The Millionaire Next Door* by Thomas J. Stanley
18. *Failing Forward* by John C. Maxwell
19. *Using a Lawyer* by Kay Ostberg
20. *The 80/20 Principle* by Richard Koch
21. *The Millionaire Mind* by Thomas J. Stanley
22. *Goals: How to Get Everything You Want—Faster than You Ever Thought Possible* by Brian Tracy
23. *The E Myth Revisited* by Michael E. Gerber
24. *Everybody's Guide to Small Claims Court* by Ralph Warner
25. *Think and Grow Rich* by Napoleon Hill
26. *Business Lessons for Entrepreneurs: 35 Things I Learned before the Age of Thirty* by Mark D. Csordos
27. *Little Red Book of Selling: 12.5 Principles of Sales Greatness* by Jeffrey Gitomer
28. *Earl Nightingale's Greatest Discovery* by Earl Nightingale
29. *Cash Copy: How to Offer Your Products and Services so Your Prospects Buy Them Now* by Jeffrey Lant
30. *How to Get Control of Your Time and Your Life* by Alan Lakein
31. *A Message to Garcia* by Elbert Hubbard

My 10 Rules for Success

To me, success is doing what you want to do, how you want to do it, when you want to do it, and where you want to do it. Success is all about calling your own shots in life and doing things on your own terms, without ever having to answer to anyone but yourself. Over the course of my lifetime, I've found that lasting success can be achieved by following these 10 basic rules:

Rule 1: Know what you don't know.

Rule 2: Anticipate situations before they become problems.

Rule 3: Don't let other people make their problems your problems.

Rule 4: Concentrate on doing what you do best.

Rule 5: Set a goal, make a plan, and work hard.

Rule 6: Accept full responsibility for your own actions.

Rule 7: Understand that agreements are only as good as the people who sign them.

Rule 8: Assume nothing, verify everything, and be prepared for anything.

Rule 9: Learn from your past mistakes and don't repeat them.

Rule 10: Do what you say you're going to do when you say you're going to do it.

Twenty Reasons Why Most People Fail to Make It as Real Estate Investors

You should be able to tell by now, that I am not exactly your typical cash-in-a-flash real estate author, who's going to promise to make you a millionaire in 30 days or less. I am a straight shooter who doesn't mince words and sugarcoat the truth. The fact of the matter is that the real estate investment business is a tough business to be in. I know from firsthand experience just how hard it can be at times to succeed in this business, and I am not about to try to tell you otherwise. And that's exactly why I am telling you here and now that most people—more than 51 percent—fail to make it as successful real estate investors. I am not telling you this to discourage you, but rather to warn you about the consequences of investing in real estate, without having your eyes wide open and your head screwed on right. In large part, I attribute this relatively high failure rate to the fact that the real estate investment business doesn't have any of the so-called barriers to entry that many other businesses have. In other words, there isn't any background, educational, competency-testing, licensing, insurance, or capital requirements to set up shop as a real estate investor. Anyone can enter the business at anytime, without the slightest clue as to how to operate a profitable real estate investment business. As a result, most people usually fail to make it as real estate investors, for one or more of the following reasons:

Reason 1: Pay above market value for property.

Reason 2: Lack of persistence.

Reason 3: Lack of organizational skills.

Reason 4: Lack of local real estate market knowledge.

Reason 5: Inability to stay focused on a single objective.

Reason 6: Failure to act in a timely manner.

Reason 7: No clearly defined exit strategy.

Reason 8: Lack of capital and credit.

Reason 9: Lack of clearly defined investment goals.

Reason 10: Unrealistic expectations.

Reason 11: Bad advice from unreliable sources.

Reason 12: Lack of planning.

Reason 13: Poor record keeping.

Reason 14: Lack of self-discipline.

Reason 15: Lack of basic real estate investment knowledge.

Reason 16: Lack of patience.

Reason 17: Lack of mental toughness.

Reason 18: Inability to manage time.

Reason 19: Failure to perform adequate due diligence inspections.

Reason 20: Failure to prioritize tasks in accordance with their importance.

Don't Let Family and Friends Keep You from Being Successful

The two biggest obstacles that most aspiring real estate investors must overcome are ignorant family members and friends who'll try and do everything within their power, to discourage anyone from bettering themselves financially. And the best way that I know of to keep family and friends from undermining your real estate investment career before it ever gets off the ground is to keep mum about what you're doing. In other words, keep your own counsel and never, ever:

1. Discuss your business with family and friends.
2. Hire family and friends to work for you.
3. Become involved in any type of real estate transaction with family and friends.

My Real Estate Investor's Aptitude Test

My real estate investor's aptitude test is the Rorschach test equivalent for wannabe real estate investors. So before you take the plunge and buy any property, please do yourself a huge favor, and take this short 26-question aptitude test, to see if you have what it takes to be a do-it-yourself real estate investor. Please be completely honest with yourself and don't cheat when answering the following yes or no answer test questions:

1. Are you a self-starter?
2. Can you think on your feet?
3. Do you handle rejection well?
4. Are you willing to accept financial responsibility for your actions?
5. Do you have a hard time making decisions?
6. Do you find it hard to say "no" to people?
7. Do you allow other people to make their problems your problems?
8. Does the thought of getting your hands dirty make you cringe?
9. Do you feel comfortable speaking with complete strangers?
10. Do you maintain self-control when dealing with unreasonable people?
11. Do you act as a rational, reasonable, intelligent adult in tense situations?
12. Do you know what you don't know?
13. Do you anticipate situations before they become problems?
14. Do you know how to quickly analyze and solve problems?
15. Do you procrastinate when faced with an unpleasant task?
16. Do you make good decisions when you have only limited information?
17. Do you have the self-discipline to be self-employed?
18. Do you use good judgment when put in stressful situations?
19. Do you have the time, energy, and desire to work nights and weekends?

20. Do you have the mental toughness to overcome numerous obstacles in order to finish what you start?

21. Do you have a paralyzing fear of failing?

22. Do you know how to prioritize tasks in their order of importance?

23. Do you have realistic expectations about your ability to earn money from real estate investments?

24. Do you know how to manage your time so that you can achieve your financial goals in life?

25. Do you have the financial resources that are usually necessary to be a successful real estate investor?

26. Do you have a burning desire to be a successful real estate investor?

If you answered all 26 questions honestly and didn't lie to yourself, you should have a gut feeling, as to whether or not, you're cut out to be a successful do-it-yourself real estate investor.

What You Need to Know about Your Perceived Competition

One of the biggest unfounded fears that most wannabe real estate investors have, is that there's already too many other investors in their local market. They wrongly believe that all of the best deals must have already been scarfed up by their competition. And as a result, many beginners end up talking themselves right out of this business without ever trying their hand at it. But in reality, most competition is more perceived than real. I've found that most newbie investors fall into the trap of confusing interest with competition. Granted, record numbers of people are interested in real estate investments, but the vast majority of them will never act on their interest. Keep in mind that probably less than 10 percent of all the people who buy books and attend seminars ever actually put what they learn into action. And then there's the so-called 80/20 rule, which is formally known as the Pareto Principle, which states that 80 percent of all results are derived from 20 percent of all effort. And the 80/20 rule, as it applies to real estate investors, can be best summed up in this corollary: 80 percent of all real estate investment deals are done by 20 percent of all investors. In other words, 8 out of every 10 transactions are completed by just 20 percent of the total number of investors in any given real estate market. And as a few of you will soon learn, most of your perceived competitors are clueless flakes, who are no competition for a knowledgeable, savvy, aggressive, and hard-working investor with a can-do attitude and a never-quit mind-set.

In the course of writing this book, I received a telephone call from a wannabe real estate investor who claimed to be a stock analyst for a well-known Wall Street firm in New York City. During our one-sided telephone conversation, this stock-jockey went on and on about all of the reasons why he didn't think he could make any money as a real estate investor in New York City's competitive real estate market. I listened to his whining for three minutes, before I finally cut him off; and told him that he was absolutely correct, and that he should stay out of the real estate market and to have a nice day. He immediately called back and asked me if "I was joking?" I assured him that I was as serious as a heart attack and asked him to please refrain from calling me in the future! I guess this guy expected me to waste my valuable time on the telephone, trying to talk him into becoming a real estate investor. The lesson here is very simple: The hardest person to convince that you can accomplish any goal in life is you! And if you don't have any confidence in your own abilities, how do you expect anyone else to believe in you? So please be forewarned: If you call me up and start telling me all the reasons that you believe you can't do something, don't be surprised when I completely agree with you and then abruptly terminate the telephone call!

Take the Time to Bask in the Glory of Your Success and Savor the Moment

Finally, if you're able to accomplish what 90 percent of all wannabes fail to do and you actually become a successful real estate investor, you'll experience a sense of self-satisfaction and a mental peace of mind that no amount of money can ever buy! For you will have done what most people have been trained to believe is impossible to do and become a successful real estate investor who started at the bottom rung of the real estate investment ladder and through education, hard work, persistence, and dogged determination became the ruler of your destiny and fate. When this golden moment arrives and you're standing in the winners' circle, be sure to take the time to bask in the glory of your hard-earned and well-deserved success, and pause to savor the moment to the fullest.

CHAPTER 3

How to Reduce Your Risk and Limit Your Liability as a Real Estate Investor

Let's face it: We live in the most litigious society on Planet Earth. Nowadays, thanks to predatory plaintiffs' attorneys, many people view lawsuits as a way to achieve the so-called American Dream without having to work for it. In America, anyone can be sued by anybody, for any reason, at anytime. I don't know about you, but to me, it makes absolutely no sense for anyone to bust their buns as a real estate investor and acquire properties only to end up losing everything because they failed to understand how to protect themselves from financially ruinous lawsuits. And that's exactly why real estate investors must take precautions to protect themselves, so they don't end up being roadkill in today's sue-happy society.

Here are four ways that real estate investors can reduce their risks and limit their personal liability:

1. Maintain adequate property and casualty insurance coverage on all investment properties.
2. Maintain adequate general liability and umbrella liability insurance coverage to limit personal liability.
3. Form a separate business entity to hold the title of each investment property.
4. Practice sound risk management principles to reduce the possibility of lawsuits.

It's Always Best for Real Estate Investors to Maintain a Low Profile

In spite of the threat of lawsuits and other risks that are inherent to the real estate investment business, there are still many real estate investors who strut around town with the words "sue me" figuratively tattooed on their foreheads in bright fluorescent colors. And they do some really dumb things like flaunting their wealth in front of the public by listing the addresses of all the properties they own on their web site. Or worse yet, they're the willing subject of a feature article in their local newspaper that outlines their "road to real estate riches" and lists the street addresses of all the properties they own. These Donald Trump wannabes also drive around in exotic automobiles and wear expensive designer clothes and have flashy jewelry draped all over their bodies. And they brag incessantly to everyone they come into contact with about how much real estate they own and how much money they have in the bank. Ironically, these same people are usually woefully underinsured and totally clueless when it comes to knowing how to reduce their risks and limit their personal liability as real estate investors. A word to the wise: If you don't want to end up being a target for all of the legal sharpshooters in your town, maintain a low profile. By maintaining a low profile, I mean that you should operate your real estate investment business in a low-key manner that keeps both you and your business under the radar screens of jealous tenants, overzealous government officials, snooping members of the media, and sue-happy plaintiffs' attorneys representing professional defendants who are looking to make some quick cash in court. Please understand that I am not telling you to forego enjoying the fruits of your labor, I am just telling you to be careful about where and how you do it. For example, if you're a residential landlord, I don't recommend that you show up to collect rental payments from tenants while driving a late-model luxury automobile and all decked out in your Armani suit or high-fashion dress. Nor do I recommend that you pull into the driveway of a property owner in foreclosure in your brand spanking new Mercedes Benz and try to buy their equity for fifty cents on the dollar. The point that I am making here is that there's a time and place to show off your trappings of wealth. But it's not when you're collecting rent from your tenants or trying to negotiate the discounted purchase of a property from an owner in foreclosure. Almost all tenants and property owners in distress are usually resentful of anyone who they feel is taking advantage of them and rubbing their noses in it. So, unless you want to make your tenants jealous and alienate property owners who are struggling financially, I very highly recommend that you keep your fancy car parked in the garage and hang your designer clothes up in the closet. My "work vehicle" is an 11-year-old pickup truck with 165,000 miles on the odometer. And my work clothes are bought off the rack at JCPenney.

Four Types of Insurance Coverage That Real Estate Investors Should Carry

First off I am no fan of the insurance industry, but I do consider insurance to be a necessary evil. I feel this way because I know that adequate insurance coverage is a real estate investor's first line of defense against possible financial ruin. So, I pay my insurance premiums in the hopes that I'll never have to file a claim. And I highly recommend that all real estate investors carry the following four types of insurance coverage on their property:

1. *Property and casualty or hazard insurance:* Covers property owners from losses resulting from fire, storm, earthquake, or other catastrophic acts that could damage or destroy their property.

2. *General liability insurance:* Covers property owners in the event they're liable for compensating a third party for bodily injury or property damage that occurred on their property.

3. *Umbrella insurance:* Personal or commercial umbrella insurance provides property owners with liability insurance coverage beyond the limits provided for in a standard general liability insurance policy.

4. *Flood insurance:* Available for properties that are located in designated flood plains in communities that participate in the National Flood Insurance Program. The federal government administers the National Flood Insurance Program and private insurance companies issue the policies.

Insurers Now Use Credit-Based Insurance Scores to Calculate Policy Premiums

It shouldn't come as any great surprise, that in today's credit conscious society, a person's credit history is the key element of credit-based insurance scores that insurers use to calculate insurance policy premiums. According to insurers, independent studies have shown a link between credit history and insurance losses. And this strong correlation between financial instability and the probability of a loss is the main reason insurers cite, when they explain to insurance regulators, why so much emphasis is put on a person's credit history when calculating policy premiums. Personally, I think that credit-based insurance scoring is great. I happen to be a financially responsible adult who has excellent credit, and I feel very strongly that people who do the right thing and play by the rules should be rewarded. I also firmly believe that people who are financially irresponsible should be held accountable for their actions and pay the consequences. The following web site has answers to questions that consumers frequently ask about credit-based insurance scoring: www.insurancescoringinfo.com.

Adequate Insurance Coverage Can Be Expensive

Unless you've been living on Mars for the past few years, you should know that the cost of any type of insurance nationwide has gone through the stratosphere. And depending on where you're located, the insurance rates for property and casualty and general liability insurance coverage for residential and commercial property can be quite expensive. Insurance carriers have also made their policy terms and conditions more stringent than ever before. Today, real estate investors nationwide have to contend with greedy insurance carriers who continually:

1. Increases rates.
2. Refuse to write new policies.
3. Exclude certain coverage.
4. Require higher deductibles.
5. Refuse to write umbrella policies with high limits.

Consider Hiring a Risk Consultant

I am usually not a big fan of consultants. And that's probably because I happen to believe that there's a lot of truth to the old joke: "A consultant is someone who uses your watch to tell you what time it is and then charges you for it." However, it may make financial sense for you to hire a so-called risk consultant, on a flat fee basis, to do an in-depth analysis of your insurance needs, and then recommend the best and least expensive types of coverage that would protect you from possible financial ruin. To find a risk consultant in your area, look in the online version of your local *Yellow Pages* under risk management or insurance.

Sixteen Ways That You Can Reduce Your Annual Insurance Premium Payments

Today, the cost of adequate insurance coverage can represent a significant portion of a property's annual operating expenses. And if you're frugal like me, you don't want to pay a penny more than you absolutely have to for any type of insurance coverage. Here are 16 ways that you can reduce your annual insurance premiums:

1. Compare insurance coverage and costs between a minimum of five insurers.
2. Take advantage of group rates offered by professional, business, and trade associations.
3. Buy all of your insurance coverage from the same insurer.
4. Take advantage of all the discounts that your insurer offers that you're eligible for.
5. Take the highest deductible amount that your insurer offers.
6. Don't carry comprehensive insurance coverage on older vehicles that are owned free and clear.
7. Don't over insure your property and vehicles with coverage that's not needed.
8. Practice preventive maintenance to keep your property well maintained.

9. Require your tenants to purchase renters' insurance.

10. Don't allow tenants to keep vicious breeds of dogs on your rental property.

11. Maintain a good credit score.

12. Drive responsibly.

13. Check your insurance premiums to make certain that you're not being overcharged or charged for coverage that you didn't request.

14. Maintain accurate insurance records, so that you don't end up with multiple policies for the same property and vehicle.

15. Avoid filing insurance claims for small losses.

16. Maintain a smoke-free policy for all of your properties.

Take the Highest Deductible Amount That Your Insurer Offers

When calculating insurance premium payments, insurers always take the amount of the deductible into consideration. The term *deductible* refers to the amount of an insurable loss that a policyholder must pay before their insurer reimburses them for the loss. This means that the higher the amount of the deductible, the lower the cost of the insurance premium. And that's exactly why I always take the highest deductible amount that my insurer offers.

Demand That Everyone Working on Your Property Show Proof of Insurance

To reduce your general liability insurance premiums, require that all tradesman and contractors working on your property provide certificates of insurance, proving that they carry adequate liability coverage and workers' compensation insurance. For example, I require that all trades-man and contractors working on my property have a minimum of one million dollars in liability insurance coverage. As a result, if a tradesman or contractor causes a loss while working on my property, their insurer pays for it instead of mine.

Don't Allow Tenants to Keep Vicious Breeds of Dogs on Your Rental Property

Please don't get me wrong, I am not some sort of dog hater, but for insurance and liability purposes, I never allow tenants to keep so-called "vicious breeds" of dogs on my rental property. The breeds of dogs that most insurers consider to be vicious are named in Chapter 11. And these are breeds of dogs that most insurers refuse to insure through homeowner and liability insurance policies. That's because, insurers are fearful of lawsuits that could be caused by vicious breeds of dogs attacking and possibly killing people on the insured property. Such an incident could result in the insurer being ordered by a court, to pay the victim's estate millions of dollars in damages.

Require That All of Your Tenants Purchase Renters' Insurance

As part of your risk management program, I very highly recommend that you include a clause in your rental agreement that requires all tenants to provide proof of renters' insurance coverage, prior to taking possession and occupying your rental property. A renters' insurance policy generally provides coverage against fire and theft to personal property, and personal liability coverage for injuries and damages caused by tenant neglect. And best of all for you, requiring tenants to purchase renters' insurance, will help to reduce your overall insurance costs. The following web sites have information about renters' insurance:

Geico Renters' Insurance: www.geico.com/home/renters

Insweb: www.insweb.com

NETQUOTE: www.netquote.com

Avoid Filing Insurance Claims for Small Losses

One surefire way that you can keep your property and casualty and liability insurance premium payments from going through the roof is to avoid filing insurance claims for small losses. What constitutes a small loss usually depends on the amount of your deductible. I always take the highest deductible that an insurer will allow, so to me, a small loss is any loss that's less than the amount of my deductible. The reason for not filing claims for small losses is because insurers use a property owner's loss history when calculating insurance premium payments. Loss history refers to the number of claims that an owner has filed for a particular property within a specified period of time. For example, a property owner who has filed five insurance claims within the past five years will most likely be denied coverage altogether, or be charged a much higher premium than a property owner who has filed just one claim over the same period of time.

Maintain a Smoke-Free Policy for Your Properties

Contrary to popular belief, Americans don't have an unalienable right to smoke tobacco products on other peoples privately owned property. There is no state or federal statutes protecting the so-called rights of smokers. Smoking materials such as lighters and matches are two of the leading causes of fires and fire-related deaths nationwide. And as far as I am concerned, tenants who smoke tobacco products in and on rental property pose a potential fire hazard. But it's a potential fire hazard that can be eliminated by implementing a smoke-free policy in and on your rental property. And that's exactly what I recommend you do to help reduce your property and casualty insurance premium payments.

Insist on a 60-Day Cancellation Notice Clause in All of Your Insurance Policies

In today's unstable insurance market, investors need as much protection as possible from fickle insurance carriers, who it seems, will cancel an insurance policy at the drop of a hat. In most states, insurers are required to give property owners a 30-day notice of their intent to cancel an insurance policy. And that's why you must always insist that a 60-day cancellation notice clause be included in all of your insurance policies. Trust me; as a real estate investor, there are few things worse than getting a 30-day cancellation notice from your long-time insurance carrier a month before the beginning of hurricane season in Florida. And believe me, once your insurance policy has been cancelled on short notice for whatever reason, you're pretty much at the mercy of the swell folks who run insurance companies and you'll end up paying an arm and a leg for basic coverage.

How Insurers Classify Residential Rental Property for Insurance Purposes

For insurance purposes, property and casualty insurers generally classify residential rental properties into the following two classes:

1. One- to four-unit properties to include single-family homes are classified as rental properties.

2. Five or more unit properties are classified as multifamily rental properties.

Most so-called landlords' rental dwelling policies are designed for residential landlords owning rental properties with one to four units. These types of property and casualty insurance policies generally provide landlords with a broad range of coverage at relatively inexpensive rates.

Buy Replacement Cost Property and Casualty Insurance

In case you didn't know it, the cost of building materials, especially lumber, concrete, roof shingles, and drywall, has gone through the roof over the past couple of years. And that's exactly why I very highly recommend that you only buy replacement cost property and casualty insurance. Replacement cost insurance compensates residential and commercial property owners for losses by paying the cost of replacing the improvements on the property, minus the cost of the land. Damaged or destroyed buildings are replaced by using building materials, mechanical equipment, and construction methods that are similar in cost and quality to the original structure, with no deduction for depreciation. Insurance replacement costs are calculated on a per-square-foot basis, by dividing the total number of square feet in the building by the per-square-foot construction cost. For example, a 2,000 square foot building, that cost $275,000 to build, would have a replacement cost of $137.50 per square foot ($275,000 divided by 2,000 equals $137.50). Replacement costs are calculated by using the insurer's replacement cost formula, which is based on the property's geographical location and its:

1. Street address.
2. Age.

3. Type of construction.
4. Number of stories.
5. Type of roof.
6. Current use.
7. Heating and cooling system.
8. Square footage.

The $1,200 Lesson That I Learned from Not Having Replacement Cost Insurance

I learned an expensive lesson about not having replacement cost insurance many years ago, when I was young and dumb and my former insurance broker talked me into purchasing what's known in the insurance business as a cash value policy, to supposedly "save money" on insuring a rental house that I owned at the time. Well, lo and behold, six months later a so-called no-name storm blew through the part of Tampa where the house was located and pretty much peeled off most of the 10-year-old roof shingles. And because my cash value insurance policy didn't cover depreciation, I ended up getting reimbursed for the cost of replacing 10-year-old roof shingles. In other words, because of 10 year's worth of depreciation on roofing shingles with a 20-year lifespan, I was paid half of the cost to replace the roofing materials. So, instead of saving money, I ended up paying over $1,200 out of my pocket—the hip national bank—to have the roof replaced. Needless to say, just as soon as I cashed my insurance reimbursement check, I fired my insurance broker and cancelled all of my policies with him. And I've been insuring my properties with replacement cost insurance ever since.

Why You Must Carry Adequate General Liability Insurance Coverage

To help reduce your risk and limit your personal liability as an investment property owner, you must maintain adequate general liability coverage on each one of your properties. In a nutshell, general liability insurance provides coverage for the cost of defending lawsuits stemming from accidents that cause bodily injury or property damage to third parties on rental property. For example, if a trip hazard on a walkway on your rental property causes a guest of one of your tenants to trip and fall, and break their ankle, and the injured guest turns around and sues you for being negligent for having a trip hazard on your walkway, your liability insurance would cover the cost of the lawsuit to include paying for any damages, up to the policy limit, that's awarded to the injured guest by the court. In addition to general liability insurance, you must also purchase an umbrella insurance policy to give you added liability coverage, beyond the limits of a standard liability insurance policy.

How to Use an Umbrella Insurance Policy to Provide Added Liability Coverage

One of the best and least expensive ways for real estate investors to protect themselves from a myriad of unforeseen accidents, which can take place in automobiles and at personal residences and rental property, and result in serious injury, long-term physical impairment, psychological damage, or death, is to purchase a personal umbrella insurance policy. Personal umbrella insurance protects policyholders from lawsuits by providing additional liability coverage—in one to five million dollar increments—above the liability limits that are contained in standard home owners' and automobile owners' insurance policies. However, as a general rule, insurers will only issue personal umbrella insurance coverage to existing customers, who have purchased their home and automobile insurance through them. Umbrella insurance is designed to kick in when the liability coverage on other policies has been exhausted, or to cover claims that may be excluded under standard liability policies to include:

1. Injuries suffered by guests visiting personal residences.
2. Injuries suffered by tenants and their guests on rental properties.
3. Libel lawsuits.
4. Slander lawsuits.

Just so you know: A commercial umbrella insurance policy works the same way that a personal umbrella insurance policy does. It provides liability coverage above the standard liability limits contained in commercial general liability, automobile liability, and employer liability policies. Commercial umbrella insurance coverage is available in amounts ranging from 1 million to 100 million dollars.

What You Must Know about the
Vacancy Exclusion Clause in Insurance Policies

As a real estate investor, you need to know that virtually all property and casualty insurance policies contain what is called a vacancy exclusion clause, which excludes coverage for properties that have been vacant for 30 to 60 days. Each insurance carrier has its own vacancy exclusion period, which is supposed to be in accordance with state insurance statutes. For example, most insurance policies generally have a vacancy exclusion period of 30 days. This means that the insurer could not be held liable, for any losses that occur to a property that has been vacant for longer than 30 days. This vacancy exclusion clause is important to real estate investors, because it usually takes from 30 to 120 days to resell a property. In the meantime, the property is excluded from insurance coverage, which means that the property owner has violated the terms of their mortgage or deed of trust loan, by failing to carry adequate insurance coverage. Plus, the investor risks losing all of their equity, if the property were to become a total loss, while vacant and waiting to be resold.

How You Can Use Builders' Risk Insurance
to Insure Vacant Buildings

The only practical way that I know to obtain insurance coverage on a property that's going to be vacant for an extended period of time is to purchase what's known as a builders' risk insurance policy. Builders' risk insurance is what lenders, investors, builders, and contractors use to insure vacant buildings during construction and renovation to provide coverage against:

1. Theft of tools, equipment, and building and landscaping materials.
2. Breakdown of plumbing, electrical, and mechanical systems.

3. Backup of water and sewer drains.
4. Vandalism, malicious mischief, and riots.
5. Water damage.
6. Fire and explosions.
7. Collapse.

Information about builders' risk insurance is available at the following two web sites: Zurich North America: www.zurichna.com and the International Risk Management Institute: www.irmi.com.

What You Need to Know about the Comprehensive Loss Underwriting Exchange

The Comprehensive Loss Underwriting Exchange (CLUE) is an insurance claim history information data exchange that insurance companies use to calculate insurance premiums when underwriting policies. According to the CLUE web site, their service: "Provides loss history to help insurers qualify applicants and properties for homeowner coverage and helps insurers maximize premiums and minimize expenses." It's the insurance industry's method of pulling the equivalent of a consumer credit report to determine how many insurance claims have been filed against a property within the past five years. And just like consumer credit reports, not all of the information contained in CLUE reports is accurate and up-to-date. In some reports, claims are erroneously reported for damages that were never claimed or paid as a loss by the insurer. But regardless of whether the report is accurate, any property with more than two claims within a five-year period may not be eligible to be insured at the market rate for comparable properties within the same area. To learn more about CLUE, log onto the following web site: www.choicepoint.net and click on the CLUE report tab.

Obtain a Commitment for Insurance Coverage before You Offer to Buy Property

If you don't get anything else from this chapter, please make certain that you get this: Never make a written offer on any type of property until you have obtained some form of written commitment from a reputable insurer guaranteeing insurance coverage at the market rate for the location and type of property being insured. I am appalled at how many real estate investors wait until a day or two before their scheduled closing date, before they try and obtain adequate insurance coverage from a reputable insurer. Please heed the very sage advice that I am dispensing here and don't treat insurance as an afterthought.

Eight Steps That You Must Take When You Have an Insured Loss on Your Property

Today, it's not at all unusual for insurance carriers to stall and try to cheat their customers out of a fair settlement. And if you doubt what I am telling you here, just ask any one of the hundreds of thousands of Floridians, whose property got run over by six hurricanes during the hurricane seasons in 2004 and 2005, what they think about the tactics that their insurance company used on them. In many cases, it ended up taking property owners more than six months before their insurers even got around to making an offer to settle. And to add insult to injury, when many insurers finally did make property owners a settlement offer, it was for far less than their actual losses. However, in some cases, that was because property owners had failed to properly document their losses, and to take the necessary precautions to protect their property from the hurricanes that followed. And in the end, they were forced to accept far less than they would have gotten from their insurer, if they had taken the following eight steps to fully protect their rights and financial interests as the insured party:

Step 1: Immediately notify your insurance company of your loss.

Step 2: Take detailed photographs or videos of all the damage to your property before you begin cleaning up and making temporary repairs.

Step 3: Make temporary repairs to protect your property from further damage.

Step 4: Document your losses by using a detailed inventory, receipts, cancelled checks, credit card receipts, and photographs and videos.

Step 5: Consult with a reputable public insurance adjuster and have the adjuster on standby just in case your insurer tries to settle your claim by making a lowball offer.

Step 6: Obtain replacement cost estimates from a minimum of three licensed contractors.

Step 7: Maintain a claim logbook to record all of the details associated with your claim.

Step 8: Don't accept your insurance company's final offer to settle your claim, until you've confirmed that it's a fair and equitable offer with a reputable insurance claim's expert.

Where to Find a Public Insurance Adjuster

To find a public insurance adjuster in your area, log on to the National Association of Public Insurance Adjusters' web site at: www.napia.com /search/index.asp.

What You Must Do When an Insurer Handles Your Claim in Bad Faith

Property owners purchase insurance policies in good faith and with the clear expectation and belief that their insurance carrier will honor its commitment and provide reimbursement for insured losses. So, when property owners file a legitimate claim with their insurer to be reimbursed for a bona fide insured loss, they have every right to expect that their claim will be handled in a fair and expeditious manner. But many times, that's not what happens. Instead, too many insurance companies drag their feet and act in bad faith by making lowball offers to settle claims or by denying claims altogether. State courts nationwide have long recognized that insurance companies have a special relationship with their policyholders. The courts have also ruled that insurers have a legal obligation to deal with their policyholders fairly and in good faith. If you believe that your insurance company has acted unfairly and in bad faith by making a below market value offer to settle your claim, or wrongfully denying your claim, you can file what's called a *declaratory judgment action lawsuit* against the insurer, requesting that the court order the insurance carrier to pay all necessary costs associated with your claim.

Tax-Deductible Business Losses Caused by Casualty, Disaster, and Theft

Business losses caused by casualty, disaster, and theft may be tax deductible. Internal Revenue Service publications 547, *Casualties, Disasters, and Thefts* and 584B, *Business Casualty, Disaster, and Theft Loss Workbook,* cover business losses caused by casualty, disaster, and theft, and are available at the following web site: www.irs.gov/formspubs/index.html.

Best to Use an Independent Insurance Agent Who Represents Many Insurers

As I see it, the main problem with buying insurance from one of the so-called brand name insurance companies, is that their agents can only sell policies that are underwritten by the company whose name appears on their door. In the insurance industry, they're known as *captive agents,* because they can only sell policies that are underwritten by the insurer they represent. So when you buy insurance through them, it's pretty much a take it or leave it proposition. But unlike so-called captive insurance agents, independent insurance agents represent many insurance carriers. Independent insurance agents work a lot like a mortgage broker, who shops a loan application around to numerous mortgage lenders to try and obtain the best interest rate and loan terms available at the time. An independent insurance agent shops an insurance application to property and casualty and liability insurance carriers to get the best coverage at the lowest annual premium. To locate an independent insurance agent in your area, log onto the following web site: www.iiaa.org and click on the "find an agent" tab.

Information on Insurers Available Online

The following web sites have an extensive listing of property and casualty and liability insurance carriers nationwide:

Property and Casualty Insurance Carriers: www.ultimate-insurancelinks
.com

Property and Casualty Insurance Buyer's Guide: www.propertyandcasualty
.com/ buyersguide

Verify the Rating of an Insurance Company

As in any industry, all insurance companies aren't the same. And just because you pay an insurer for adequate insurance coverage doesn't mean that you'll be reimbursed in the event that an insured loss occurs. It's up to you to make certain that the insurance carrier you select to insure your property has the financial wherewithal to reimburse you for insured losses. You can verify the rating of an insurance company by logging onto the following web sites that provide insurance company rating services:

A.M. Best Company: www.ambest.com

Standard & Poor's: www.standardandpoors.com

Insurance Information Available Online

The following web sites have insurance information available online:

Insurance Institute: www.iii.org

A.M. Best Company: www.ambest.com

National Underwriter Company: www.nationalunderwriter.com

National Association of Public Insurance Adjusters: www.napia.com

State Insurance Departments: www.naic.org/state_web_map.htm

Independent Insurance Agents and Brokers of America: www
.independentagent.com

Standard & Poor's: www.standardandpoors.com

Form a Separate Business Entity after
You Become an Investor

I have never been one to advise aspiring real estate investors, who have never done a deal, to run out and form a separate business entity to buy property. Probably less than 10 percent of the people reading this book will ever actually buy any property. And as far as I am concerned, it is a total waste for anyone to go to the expense of forming any type of business entity before they even know if they're cut out to be a real estate investor.

Use a Separate Business Entity to Hold the Title to Your Property

As I've been telling you throughout this chapter, owning investment property in present day America can be risky business. Accidents can and do happen. And when people get injured or killed on someone else's property, the injured party or family members of the deceased frequently sue the property owner for damages. This is why I very strongly suggest that you form a separate business entity such as a subchapter S corporation or a limited liability company (LLC) to hold the title to each one of your investment properties. It's one of the best and least expensive methods available to help to reduce your risk and limit your personal liability as a real estate investor. This way, there's a clear legal delineation between your personal and family assets, and the assets held by your corporation or LLC. And, in most cases, any liability incurred by the business entity would be limited to the business entity's assets. In most states, the cost to form a business entity is inexpensive when compared to the amount of money that could be lost if all of your assets were taken as a result of a lawsuit. For example, in Florida, the total cost to form a LLC is $125.

Information on How to Form Business Entities Available Online

To obtain information on the various types of business entities that are available for use in your state, log onto your state's secretary of state web site and click on the division of corporations or a similar name for the instructions, forms, and fees required to form a corporation or limited liability company. For example, in Florida, all of the forms that are necessary to form a corporation, partnership, or limited liability company can be completed and filed online.

How to Form a Business Entity in Your State

In spite of what the members of state bar associations want the public to believe; it doesn't take a legal genius to form a business entity in most states. Nowadays, most states make all of the forms that are necessary to form a business entity available online. For example, in Florida, all of the paperwork that's necessary to form a business entity can be completed online at the Florida Secretary of State's web site, including paying the filing fees. Here's a sequential outline of the steps that are necessary to form a business entity in most states nationwide:

1. Check the availability of the name that you want to use for your business online at your state's secretary of state web site.
2. Fill out the forms that are necessary to establish a business entity online at your state's secretary of state web site.
3. Apply for a Federal Employer Identification Number (FEIN) for your business entity by filling out IRS Form SS-4 at the following Web page: IRS Form SS-4: www.irs.gov/pub/irs-pdf/fss4.pdf.
4. Apply to have your business entity treated as a subchapter S corporation for tax purposes by completing IRS Form 2553 at the following Web page: IRS Form 2553: www.irs.gov/pub/irs-access/f2553_accessible.pdf.
5. Order a Black Beauty corporate kit for your business entity online from Blumberg Excelsior legal supplies at the following web site: www.blumberg.com/corporate/outfit_details.html.

Always Verify the Identity of the People with Whom You Do Business

Identity theft is now the fastest growing crime in America. Identity theft occurs when a criminal assumes another person's identity and then uses their social security account number, bank account number, credit card number, or driver's license number to commit various types of financial related crimes. And unless you want to run the very real risk of being flim-flammed by some sleazy identity thief, posing as a legitimate businessperson, you must verify the identity of all the people you do business with.

The best way to verify that the person you're dealing with is who they claim to be and not an imposter is to do what I do when I meet with any businessperson for the first time: Show them your driver's license, and ask the other party to do likewise. As I show the person my Florida Driver's License, I matter-of-factly explain that I am doing this, because of the rampant spread of identity theft. And if for whatever reason, the person I am about to do business with refuses to identify themselves by showing me some form of government-issued photo identification, I politely explain to them that we won't be doing any business together. I generally find a lot of people who are doing business without having a valid Florida Driver's License. And to me, that raises a huge red flag because it's one of the telltale signs that a person has no intention of taking up permanent residency in Florida and he or she is probably a fly-by-night operator.

Shred All Personal, Financial, and Business Documents That Are No Longer Needed

I don't know how you're wired, but just the thought of some sleazy weasel stealing my personal identity or using my credit to run up tens of thousands of dollars in fraudulent charges is enough to nearly put me into a fit of rage. And because of my fear of becoming a victim of the rapidly growing crime of identity theft, my wife Barbara and I are very vigilant when it comes to protecting our personal, financial, and business-related mail and documents from would-be identity thieves. According to law enforcement officials who specialize in identity theft, the first line of defense against identity thieves is to keep all of your personal, financial, and business-related documents under lock and key. The second line of defense is to immediately shred all mail and documents that you no longer need. I learned quickly, that when it comes to paper shredders, you get exactly what you pay for. The first paper shredder I bought was an inexpensive model that the manufacturer claimed would shred up to 10 sheets of paper at a time. Well, it turned out that the shredder would jam whenever I tried to shred more than three sheets of paper at one time. So, I promptly returned my lemon of a paper shredder and obtained a full refund in the process. Today I use a Fellowes OD1500 high-performance personal strip-cut shredder that I bought on sale at the Office Depot for $180, to shred all of my personal, financial, and business-related mail and documents that I no longer have a use for.

Claim Your Personal Residence as Your Homestead

A very inexpensive form of asset protection that is often overlooked is the homestead protection for personal residences that many states provide to their residents. If you're a legal resident of a state that allows its residents to claim their personal residence as their homestead property, make certain that you file for homestead exemption status with your county's property appraiser or assessor's office. For example, here in Florida, the Constitution of the State of Florida allows for legal residents of Florida, who claim homestead exemption on their personal residence, to have $25,000 of the tax-assessed value of their personal residence to be tax-exempt from property taxes. It also protects property owners who claim their personal residence as a Florida homestead from having their property sold at a forced sale to satisfy creditors. Article X, Section 4 (a) of the Florida Constitution states that: *"There shall be exempt from forced sale under the process of any court, and no judgment, decree or execution shall be a lien thereon, except for the payment of taxes and assessments thereon, obligations contracted for the purchase, improvement, or repair thereof, or obligations contracted for house, field, or other labor performed on the realty."*

CHAPTER 4

How to Set Up and Operate Your Real Estate Investment Business for Maximum Efficiency and Profitability

As far as I am concerned, one of the primary reasons the washout rate for real estate investors is so high is because too many investors fail to place enough emphasis on getting the maximum return on every dollar and hour that they put into their real estate investment business. Instead, they seem to be more concerned about frivolous stuff like the color of their business cards. In this business, a lack of focus, coupled with the inability to prioritize tasks, is a recipe for failure. So, too, is the type of complacency that breeds an "if it ain't broke, don't fix it" mentality, which usually results in a stagnant business that's barely able to keep its head above water. That's why to my way of thinking, the catch-phrase "easier, faster, and cheaper" should be the mantra of every real estate investor in America. I say this because I've learned the hard way that for me to consistently achieve the highest possible rate of return on the money and time that I invest in my business, I must continually analyze, refine, and tweak every aspect of my operation, to make it easier, faster, and cheaper to run. Nowadays, I think of my business as a high performance automobile engine, which must be finely turned and calibrated to run at its optimum speed and maximum efficiency. I can tell you from experience that in order to operate a real estate investment business at maximum efficiency and profitability, it takes:

1. Personal and financial discipline.
2. Organizational skills.
3. Management know-how.
4. Meticulous planning and attention to detail.

5. Prioritization of tasks according to their profit potential.

6. Maximum use of available technology.

7. Accurate record keeping.

8. Maximum use of all the tax benefits that are available to business owners.

It Takes Discipline to Operate a Business at Maximum Efficiency and Profitability

It takes a combination of personal and financial discipline to operate a real estate investment business at maximum efficiency and profitability. First, you need to have the initiative and self-discipline that's required to be successfully self-employed. You must work smart, so you don't waste your valuable time doing grunt-type tasks that can be hired out. In other words, don't spend your time cleaning up trash around a property when you should be out searching for your next deal. Second, you need to possess the financial discipline that's necessary to operate your business at maximum profitability. The only way that you're ever going to be able to keep your spending under control is by:

1. Adopting a bottom-line mentality that's totally focused on maximizing the profitability of your business.

2. Operating your business on a bare-bones budget by buying all equipment, supplies, and services at the lowest available prices in your area.

3. Keeping close track of operating expenses by carefully reviewing all invoices for errors, overcharges, and bogus charges.

Prioritize Tasks according to Their Profit Potential

The number one question that you must continually ask yourself when you're working in your real estate investment business is: Is what I am doing right this minute the most profitable use of my time? A lot of people fail in this business simply because they're never able to prioritize tasks according to their profit potential. They end up never getting a deal done because they couldn't distinguish between what's important and what's trivial. As a general rule of thumb, I consider any business function that doesn't contribute directly to my bottom line to be low priority and best left for after business hours. In other words, if the task at hand isn't part of the process of completing a real estate transaction that'll eventually end with me going to the bank, I put it off until later in the day. I divide my workday into primetime and downtime. Primetime—6 A.M. to 6 P.M.—is when I operate at peak efficiency and spend all of my time working on deals. I handle everything else in the evening after 6 P.M.

Obtain the Maximum Return on Each Hour That You Invest in Your Business

There are exactly 168 hours in a week, and time is the single most valuable asset that any human being possesses. Time is irreplaceable and once it's gone, you can never get it back. How you spend each waking hour of your adult life has a profound impact on how much you'll accomplish. In other words, if you decide to squander your valuable time on nonproductive pursuits, such as constantly watching mind-numbing television programs, there's an excellent chance that all you'll have to show for your time spent in front of the aptly named boob tube is a limited intellect and a bulging belly. For real estate investors who operate an inefficient business in which they waste most of their valuable time performing mundane tasks that contribute absolutely nothing to their bottom line, there's an excellent chance that they'll go broke without ever doing a single deal. The often-heard expression "time is money" is ever so true for self-employed real estate investors. Unless you want to end up working for subminimum wages or, worse yet, for nothing at all, you must first learn how to get the maximum return out of each hour that you invest in your real estate investment business. The trick to running a real estate investment business at maximum efficiency is to spend at least 90 percent of your valuable time on money-making endeavors such as finding, negotiating, buying, and selling property. This way, you'll receive the maximum return from each hour that you spend working. This is crucial to your success, especially when you're investing in real estate on a part-time basis, and time is a precious commodity.

Avoid Reinventing the Wheel Every Time You Need to Complete a Routine Task

Whatever you do, don't fall into the trap of reinventing the wheel every time you need to complete a routine task. The term, *reinventing the wheel*, refers to re-creating something from scratch. An example of reinventing the wheel would be retyping standard documents, such as purchase agreements, over and over again, instead of storing them in a Microsoft Word document file where they can be printed out as needed. The point here is to work smart by making your operation as streamlined as humanly possible.

Maintain a "Deal Book" Whenever You're Working on a Real Estate Transaction

Whenever, I am working on putting a real estate deal together, I always keep all of the paperwork that's associated with the transaction in what I call my "deal book." My deal book is an inch thick, clear overlay, three-ring binder. I like using overlay binders because the front and back covers and spine have clear pockets, which are open at the top and allow me to insert the property's street address on the front cover and spine of the binder for quick reference. All of the paperwork is placed in document protectors, which are hung on the rings in the binder. This way, I have everything about the transaction available at my fingertips and I don't have to rummage around my office looking for it. And when I meet with sellers, lenders, attorneys, and closing agents, I don't have to haul around a bulky file full of loose-leaf papers that could fall out and become lost. Once I close on the transaction, the deal book then becomes the property's records book for as long as I own it.

Operate Your Real Estate Investment Business on a Bare-Bones Budget

One surefire way to fail in the real estate investment business is to run your operation in a slipshod manner with no financial controls in place to keep your operating costs from going through the roof. The best way to keep your overhead expenses in check is to establish a bare-bones budget, which provides the basic essentials that are necessary to operate your business at maximum efficiency. And a bare-bones budget is just that— bare bones. It's a lean, no-frills budget that doesn't include nonessential items, such as expensive electronic gizmos and gadgets, or fancy office furniture and high-tech telephone systems, which do absolutely nothing to contribute to the overall profitability of your business. Case in point: Over the past 26 plus years, I have seen more than a few wannabe big-shot real estate investors here in Tampa make the financially fatal mistake of renting expensive office space, which they decked out with high-end furniture, state-of-the-art computers, and the most up-to-date telephone system. And much to my astonishment, every single one of these wannabe real estate mavens did all of this before they had ever done deal one. The upshot of this colossal lack of business acumen was that virtually all of their businesses went belly-up in less than six months time, and most of them never did get a deal under their belt. I guess these hapless beginners were too preoccupied with their fancy surroundings to ever venture out of their offices and actually buy a piece of property. What really surprised me about these fledgling investors was that most of them had a college education and experience working in a corporate business environment. And three of these greenhorns even had MBA degrees from big-name universities. They should've known better than to squander their operating capital on frivolous stuff and, after reading this, you should too.

Do a Cost-Benefit Analysis before You Make a Purchase

I suggest that you do what I always do, before I ever part with any of my hard-earned money, and ask yourself this very poignant question: How exactly is this—(fill-in-the-blank)—going to have a direct impact on the profitability of my business? Unless you can justify to yourself why the purchase under consideration will immediately contribute to your bottom line, you should hold onto your money. This type of decision-making process is referred to in business schools as "cost-benefit analysis," which means that if the cost outweighs the benefit that'll be gained from purchasing an item, it shouldn't be bought. Keep this in mind the next time that you get the urge to splurge.

How I Operate My Real Estate Investment Business on a Low-Cost Budget

I am a parsimonious old Yankee from New Hampshire who strictly adheres to Northern New England philosophy: Use-it-up, make-it-do, wear-it-out, or do-without. So when it came to equipping my home office, I did what I always do, and shopped around to get the best value for my money. I bought a Compaq 7550 personal computer at Sam's Club for under $600. My computer came with a Microsoft 2003 Windows XP operating system. I use Microsoft Word 2003 word-processing software that I also bought at Sam's Club for $245. My laser printer is a Hewlett Packard LaserJet 1300, which I purchased at Sam's Club for under $400. I use a six-year-old Qualcom dual-band cell phone that I bought from Sprint PCS for less than a $100. My total equipment cost was right around $1,345, which I wrote off as a business expense for tax purposes. My cell phone bill is less than $40 a month, and I spend under $50 a month for a high-speed cable connection to the Internet through Bright House Networks. And it costs me $25 a month to have my web site on the Internet. My total monthly fixed operating costs are less than $115. Most Americans spend more than that a month on fast-food alone. So for a grand total of $2,725, I equipped my office and paid my fixed operating costs for a year. That works out to roughly $227 a month, when broken down over a 12-month period. Granted, this figure only covers fixed operating costs, and doesn't include advertising and mailing expenses. But they too can be controlled by using sound business principles. You can see from my example that it's possible to set up shop and operate your business without having to go into debt.

What You Should Have When You Set Up Shop as a Real Estate Investor

I am willing to concede that an investor could possibly run their real estate investment business without any of the basic amenities of a modern high-tech office at their disposal. However, it would be a very inefficient operation, and I am willing to bet that most investors, in this type of work environment, would end up spending much of their time performing tedious tasks such as retyping the same documents over and over again. I don't know about you, but I've never met anyone who has typed their way to real estate riches. As far as I am concerned, every beginning real estate investor, who's really serious about consistently making money in this business, should have the following six items when they set up shop:

1. Telephone service and a prepaid telephone calling card to make calls on the road from pay phones.
2. Personal computer with Microsoft Windows operating system.
3. Microsoft Word software.
4. Internet connection.
5. Black-and-white laser or inkjet printer.
6. Financial calculator.

Nice-to-Have Stuff That You Really Don't Need to Do Your First Few Deals

Granted, the stuff listed below would probably make your life as a real estate investor a little easier. But they're strictly nice-to-have items, which you don't need in order to buy and sell your first few properties. So don't use the fact that you don't happen to have any of the following nice-to-have items as an excuse for why you haven't done any deals:

1. Separate home office.
2. Web site.
3. Digital camera.
4. Facsimile machine.
5. Cellular telephone.
6. Laptop computer.
7. Personal digital assistant.
8. Global positioning system for your vehicle.

It's Hard to Succeed in a Digital World Using Horse-and-Buggy Technology

Computer technology is here to stay, and, if you want to make it as a successful real estate investor in today's digital world, you had better embrace the latest technology and learn how to use it to your advantage. So if you happen to be computer illiterate, the very best advice that I can give you is to buy an inexpensive personal computer (PC) and then jump in with both feet and learn how to use it. If someone with a nontechnical background like me can use a computer, anyone can. To get the best deal on a personal computer, I recommend that you first do some comparison shopping by using a friend's or relative's computer, or a computer at your local public library, to log onto the following store web sites:

Dell: www.dell.com
Hewlett Packard: www.hp.com
Sam's Club: www.samsclub.com
Best Buy: www.bestbuy.com
Costco: www.costco.com
Office Depot: www.officedepot.com
Staples: www.staples.com
Office Max: www.officemax.com

What It Takes to Run a Real Estate Investment Business at Maximum Efficiency

According to the Small Business Administration (SBA), 80 percent of all new small businesses fail within five years of opening their doors. More often than not, the cause of failure can be directly attributed to an appalling lack of organization and planning on the part of business owners. I hate to come across as some sort of real estate killjoy, but you just can't throw a business together without any organization and planning and expect it to be an efficient operation. It takes meticulous planning and attention to detail to set up a real estate investment business so that it operates at maximum efficiency. The only way that you're ever going to have a smooth running business is by doing the little things right, such as:

1. Maintaining a master to-do checklist to run your business.
2. Computerizing all business documents and records.
3. Setting up your business so you avoid re-creating anything from scratch.

4. Organizing your office so that everything you need is available at your fingertips.

5. Mapping out trips so that you don't waste time and gasoline driving in circles.

Business Start-Up Information Available Online

For detailed information on how to get your business up and running, log onto the following web sites:

Small Business Administration: www.sba.gov/starting_business /startup/basics.html

CCH Tax and Accounting: www.toolkit.cch.com/tools/tools.asp

Small Business Resource Guide: http://apps.irs.gov/businesses/small /page/0,,id=7128,00.html

Use a Master To-Do Checklist to Run Your Business

To keep your business operating at maximum efficiency, I recommend that you do what I've done for the past 20 plus years, and maintain a master to-do checklist. I keep my checklist on my computer in a Microsoft Word file. It serves as a combination checklist and appointment calendar. For example, each entry that I make on my checklist, lists the task or appointment along with the completion or meeting date. This way, nothing slips through the crack and tasks are completed on time and appointments are kept.

Map Out Your Trips in Advance to Save Time and Money

To avoid wasting your valuable time and expensive gasoline driving around in circles while you're lost, you must map out your trips before you get behind the wheel of your car or truck. But instead of using an expensive global positioning system for your automobile, do what I do and obtain free written driving directions online from one of the following web sites:

MapQuest: www.mapquest.com

MapBlast: www.mapblast.com

Yahoo Maps: http://maps.yahoo.com

Maps: www.maps.com/DriveSolo.aspx?nav=DD

It's Cheaper to Hire Independent Contractors instead of Hourly Employees

To me, it has always made more sense financially to hire independent contractors and pay them by the job than to hire hourly employees and maintain a payroll. For example, my real estate investment business consists of one person—me. I work alone and have no hourly employees at my beck and call. When I need something done, I hire it out to an independent contractor, who charges me by the job. This way, I avoid all of the rigmarole that goes along with babysitting hourly employees and dealing with the following state and federal government agencies that regulate employers:

1. The U.S. Occupational Safety and Health Administration.
2. The U.S. Department of Labor.
3. The Internal Revenue Service.
4. The Social Security Administration.
5. Florida Department of Labor and Employment Security.

Deduct Your Home Office as a Business Expense

In order for a home office to qualify as a business deduction for federal tax purposes, it must be used regularly and exclusively for business purposes. For example, if you're a part-time real estate investor and a full-time school teacher, who has a home office that you claim as a real estate investment business expense, but you use your office for both your real estate investment business and for grading student papers, your home office deduction would be disallowed if you were ever audited by the Internal Revenue Service (IRS). The IRS would do this because your home office isn't being used exclusively for business purposes. The best way to make certain that your home office will pass muster with the IRS is to regularly use the space you're claiming as your home office exclusively as your principal place of business. I comply with the IRS home office use rules by having a home office that's located in a separate building behind my home—approximately 40 steps one way—and used exclusively for business purposes. My compact home office measures a measly 10 feet long by 10 feet wide and is a scant 100 square feet in size, but it serves its purpose quite well. I like this arrangement, as it allows me to separate my business from my personal life. For more information on how to deduct your home office as a business expense, read IRS Publication 587, *Business Use of Your Home*, which is available online at the following Web page: www.irs.gov/pub/irs-pdf/p587.pdf.

Keep Your Desk from Becoming a Cluttered Mess

When it's on TV, I watch the so-called reality show, *The Apprentice*. I do this for comedic relief and a one-hour escape from reality. I very seriously doubt that I would ever hire any of the contestants to mow my lawn, but I did learn about something of value from watching Donald Trump's minions that I want to share with you. In one of the mind-numbing segments, the two teams of would-be tycoons were tasked with designing a desk organizer for Staples—the office supply chain. Staples has turned the winning design into an excellent desk organizer aptly named the *Desk Apprentice*. This compact desk organizer is made of durable plastic, is rectangular shaped, and has large vertical file-like pockets attached to all four sides and rotates 360 degrees, just like a lazy Susan. The center is open and has a narrow sliding tray on top to store small office supplies like paperclips. The outside dimensions of the *Desk Apprentice* are approximately 16 inches in width by 12 inches in height. Those of you who have read my other books know that I would never be accused of being a spendthrift. So when I tell you to breakdown and spend $34.99 for a *Desk Apprentice*, you can bet that it's worth every penny, but, more important, it will help you keep your desk organized. And for investors who don't have the luxury of having a separate office, the *Desk Apprentice* can serve as a desk in a box that can be easily stored away while it's not being used. Finally, to the overly skeptical people reading this, no, I am not on Trump's payroll, nor did Staples pay me a fee for mentioning one of its office products in my book. This is what's known in marketing circles as an "unsolicited product testimonial."

Keep Your Office on Wheels Well Organized

If you're really serious about being a real estate investor, you're going to be spending a lot of time behind the wheel of your vehicle searching for properties, conducting drive-by property inspections, and driving to appointments. This means that the front seat of your vehicle is going to have to double as an office on wheels. The best way that I know to stay organized while you're on the road, is to use the *Cab Commander* that's available from the Duluth Trading Company. The *Cab Commander* is what building contractors and law enforcement officers use to keep their front seat offices organized. It comes complete with a heavy duty adjustable strap that fits around car or truck seat headrests and doubles as a shoulder strap that lets you carry it in and out of your vehicle. Again, this is strictly an unsolicited product testimonial on my part. To checkout the *Cab Commander,* log onto the following web site: www.duluthtrading.com/items/96720.asp.

Accurate Record Keeping Is an Integral Part of Running an Efficient Business

Maintaining accurate records is an integral part of running any type of successful business. Yet, it's probably the most overlooked aspect of the real estate investment business. For many investors, record keeping is a last minute ritual that's performed annually around 8 P.M. on the fourteenth of April, and forgotten about the other 364 days of the year. Needless to say, this is definitely not the smart way to run business. Here's a listing of the five types of records that real estate investors must maintain in order to have a smooth and efficiently running business:

1. *Income records:* Income records include monthly income and expense statements, bank statements, and accounting records documenting all of the income generated by your real estate investment business.

2. *Expense records:* Expense records include paid invoices, bank statements, cancelled checks, and accounting records documenting all of the expenses associated with operating your business.

3. *Property records:* Property records include mortgages, deeds of trust, promissory notes, grant and warranty deeds, surveys, purchase

agreements, property appraisal reports, closing documents, easements, blueprints, certificates of occupancy, construction warranties, building material warranties, equipment warranties, building inspection reports, termite and pest inspection reports, and utility services account information.

4. *Insurance records:* Insurance records include property and casualty insurance policies, title insurance policies, workers' compensation insurance policies, flood insurance policies, liability insurance policies, umbrella insurance policies, automobile and truck insurance policies, pest control insurance policies, and equipment insurance policies.

5. *Tax records:* Tax records consist of property tax assessment notices, property tax payments, federal tax returns, federal withholding-tax payments, state tax payments, and county and city occupational license fee payments.

Store Original Copies of Records and Documents in a Safe Deposit Box

I recommend that you photocopy or scan all of your important property related records and documents onto a CD-ROM and store all of the original copies in a safe deposit box. This way, you'll have all of your original records and documents in a safe, secure, off-site location where they can be easily located in case of an emergency.

Use Generally Accepted Accounting Practices to Maintain Financial Records

Over the past couple of years, there have been a slew of court cases involving fraudulent accounting practices in which CEOs and other corporate higher-ups "cooked the books" to prop up the value of their company's stock. Unless a stay at a "Club Fed" facility appeals to you, it's best that you stick with generally accepted accounting practices instead of using creative accounting methods, which are based on fuzzy mathematics. In basic accounting jargon, the term *generally accepted accounting practices* (GAAP) refers to accounting principles and practices that are standard in a certain industry. The best way that I know to keep bookkeeping straight is to use an off-the-shelf computer software accounting program such as QuickBooks financial software. This way, all you have to do is enter your financial data and the software does the accounting functions and balances the books and makes it easy for you to:

1. Identify the source of receipts.
2. Keep track of tax-deductible expenses.
3. Document expenses claimed on tax returns.
4. Prepare tax returns.

Maintain a Separate Checking Account for Your Real Estate Investment Business

For record-keeping and tax purposes, you must maintain a separate checking account for your real estate investment business that you can deposit checks into and pay expenses from. One of the criteria that the Internal Revenue Service uses to determine if a business is legitimate, and not a sham, is bank accounts. A business that claims expenses, losses, and depreciation on federal tax returns but doesn't maintain a checking account is going to be suspect and have a very hard time trying to document expenses if it's ever audited by the swell folks at the Internal Revenue Service.

Pay All Expenses with Business Checks or Business Credit Cards

The best method for documenting and recording expenses is to pay them with checks written on your real estate investment business checking account or with a credit card issued in the name of your real estate business. This way, you'll be able to easily distinguish between personal and business expenses. The same holds true for using business credit cards to charge business expenses.

Deduct All Business-Related Travel Expenses

Make certain that you deduct the cost of all travel expenses related to running your real estate investment business. The Internal Revenue Service requires that taxpayers maintain automobile mileage logs to document business-related mileage that's claimed on federal tax returns as a business expense. The standard mileage rate that can be deducted from federal taxes for the cost of operating a vehicle on business-related travel changes each tax year.

Depreciate All of the Equipment Used in Your Real Estate Investment Business

In order for your real estate investment business to earn a maximum profit, you must take full advantage of all of the depreciation allowed under the Internal Revenue Code. To do this, make certain that you claim the maximum depreciation allowed on all of the equipment used in your business to include:

1. Office furniture and equipment such as computers, printers, and facsimile machines.
2. Software programs for accounting and word processing.
3. Cellular telephones, telephones, and telephone answering machines.

How to Prepare Your Tax Returns

For years, I've advised real estate investors to hire a tax professional, such as a certified public accountant, board-certified tax attorney, or an enrolled agent, who is licensed to represent taxpayers before all administrative levels of the Internal Revenue Service to prepare their tax returns. I made this recommendation because of the very real possibility that an unreported glitch in an off-the-shelf tax preparation software program could cause an investor's tax return to be audited. And then the investor would be on their own, as no one from the tax preparation software company is going to represent them in front of the Internal Revenue Service during an audit. However, I've had a change of heart after using the *Turbo Tax Business* tax preparation software program, which is made by Intuit, Inc., to prepare my 2004 and 2005 federal tax returns. I've found *Turbo Tax Business* to be relatively easy to use and a fast, safe, and economical way for me to prepare my tax returns in the privacy and comfort of my home office. And it's the same tax preparation program that the enrolled agent, who previously prepared my tax returns, uses. I very seriously doubt that the chance of my taxes being audited has been significantly increased by preparing my own returns. But if you're not comfortable preparing your own tax returns, I recommend that you hire a licensed tax professional to do it for you. For more information on the *Turbo Tax Business* tax preparation software program, log onto the following web site: www .turbotax.com.

The Difference between a Certified Public Accountant and an Enrolled Agent

Certified public accountants are licensed to practice accountancy by state boards of accountancy. Enrolled Agents are licensed by the federal government and authorized to represent taxpayers before all administrative levels of the Internal Revenue Service. The following web sites have information on licensed certified public accountants and federally licensed enrolled agents:

> American Institute of Certified Public Accountants: www.aicpa.org
>
> National Association of Enrolled Agents: www.naea.org

Use the *U.S. Master Tax Guide* as a Guide

I highly recommend that you use the *U.S. Master Tax Guide* as your tax reference guide. It's published annually by CCH Tax and Accounting and is available for purchase online at the following web site: http://onlinestore .cch.com/default.asp?ProductID=2883

Internal Revenue Service Forms and Publications

Internal Revenue Service forms and publications are available online in PDF format at the following Web page: www.irs.gov/formspubs/index .html.

The following Internal Revenue Service publications pertain to running a real estate investment business:

Publication 334: *Tax Guide For Small Business.*

Publication 535: *Business Expenses.*

Publication 583: *Starting a Business and Keeping Records.*

Publication 587: *Business Use of Your Home.*

Publication 1779: *Independent Contractor or Employee.*

CHAPTER 5

How to Choose Real Estate Investment Strategies That Will Work for You

Before you begin to read Part II of this book and learn about five realistic investment strategies, that you can use to make money in real estate today, I want to tell you how to choose real estate investment strategies that will work for you. However, you must first understand that because each real estate investor's background, interests, personality, and life experiences are different, there isn't a single cookie-cutter type of real estate investment strategy that will work for every single investor across America. One of the most common mistakes that many beginning real estate investors make is that they jump headfirst into their local real estate market and buy property without thinking it through beforehand. This lack of forethought often results in novice investors trying to use real estate investment strategies, which they don't have the temperament, knowledge, experience, or financial resources to pull off. For example, most people aren't cut out to be residential landlords. The average person doesn't have the temperament that's required to run a successful rental housing business in this day and age. The overly rambunctious novice investors, who blindly jump into the landlord business, usually end up falling flat on their faces. What's worse is that many neophyte investors don't learn from their initial mistakes. In other words, they never wise up to the fact that maybe being a landlord just isn't their cup of tea. Instead, they go out and repeat the same mistake over and over again and wonder why the results never change. To me, this type of behavior is a form of insanity, which eventually leads greenhorn investors to committing financial suicide by overdosing on a gargantuan amount of debt. When you're starting out in this business, you must take your time and carefully analyze a real estate investment strategy and take into account the:

1. Temperament, knowledge, skill, and experience needed to implement the strategy.
2. Amount of cash and credit needed to finance the strategy.
3. Amount of time and energy needed to complete the strategy from start to finish.
4. Potential risks and pitfalls associated with the strategy.
5. Segment of the local real estate market where the strategy will work best.
6. Barriers to entering the real estate market where the strategy will work best.
7. Level of competition from other individual investors using the same strategy.
8. Transaction costs associated with the strategy.
9. Exit plans for the strategy.
10. Tax efficiency of the investment strategy.

Trust Your Gut Instinct When Choosing Investment Strategies

Another factor that you must not overlook when choosing investment strategies is your gut instinct. I've learned the hard way, not to ignore that little voice in the back of my head. The voice that we all have and that occasionally screams out to warn us when we are about to do something really stupid, which deep down in our gut, we know is wrong. In other words, don't let anyone talk you into using a real estate investment strategy that's outside of your comfort zone. For example, if you consider yourself to be a type-B personality, who's pretty laid-back and easy going, you may have a real hard time dealing with tenants and feel very uncomfortable in the role of landlord. Investing in residential rental properties probably wouldn't be a good investment strategy for you to pursue.

Know Your Tolerance Level for Risk and Don't Exceed It

When it comes to risk, the world is made up of three types of people: Those who are risk takers, those who are risk adverse, and those somewhere in the middle. At one extreme, there are high risk takers, such as daredevils and thrill seekers, who seem to have no qualms whatsoever about laying their lives on the line when performing death-defying type stunts. At the other extreme, there are the severely risk adverse, who seem to be petrified of taking any chances at all and want everything they attempt to do to somehow have guaranteed results. But I've found that most people have a tolerance for risk that falls somewhere in the middle of both extremes. The trick, to achieving mental peace of mind as a real estate investor, is to stay within your tolerance level for risk. For example, I know a long-time investor in Orlando, Florida, who did extremely well investing in single-family houses. At one time, he had a portfolio of 45 rental houses worth several million dollars and a five-figure monthly cash flow from the rental income. But he allowed one of his sons to talk him into buying a hotel near Disney World. Almost overnight he went from being a relaxed, easygoing guy to a nervous wreck, who worried day and night about something bad happening at his hotel. That's because buying the hotel had exceeded his tolerance level for risk, and, as a result, he lost his mental peace of mind in the process. The lesson here is twofold: Stay within your risk comfort zone and do what makes you happy. In real estate, bigger isn't necessarily better.

Include a Worst-Case Scenario When Analyzing Investment Strategies

I consider myself to be a pragmatic realist. I fully understand that there's always a 50-50 chance that something bad could happen when using any investment strategy, which could take the wind out of my sails and knock me for a financial loop. So when I am analyzing a real estate investment strategy, to determine if it's suitable for me, the very first question that I always ask myself is: What is the absolute worst thing that could go wrong with this investment strategy, and could I survive it? And if I come up with a financially devastating worst-case scenario that has a much better than 50-50 chance of occurring, I take a pass on the strategy. For example, awhile back, I had the opportunity to buy a 20-pad mobile home park in the small agricultural town of Wimauma, Florida. I've never owned a mobile home park, and after doing my research, I probably never will. The majority of tenants in this particular park were illegal aliens, who worked on local farms and spent their evenings and weekends drinking, or fighting among themselves. To make matters worse, there was no other potential pool of tenants in town. In other words, if I had bought the park, I would have been stuck renting to that class of tenants. My idea of being a mobile home park owner didn't involve alcohol, drugs, firearms, domestic violence, and filling out police reports. To me, this place was nothing but a powder keg of problems, just waiting to explode, and I very quickly decided, that the mobile home park investment strategy wasn't for me.

My Definition of a Realistic Investment Strategy

To me, a real estate investment strategy is realistic if it has a better than 50 percent chance of working, and it can be successfully implemented by the average investor. In other words, it can't be one of those "creative real estate investment strategies" that you're going to read about in Chapter 6, which will only work on the fourth Thursday of February during leap years and when there's a full moon.

You Must Have More Than One Investment Strategy in Your Repertoire

In spite of what the real estate fairy-tale authors and slick seminar promoters are constantly telling the public, it's hard to be a successful real estate investor, when you're a one-trick pony, who's limited to a single investment strategy. In order to maximize your chances of being successful in this business, you must be able to take advantage of various types of investment opportunities the moment they become available. To do this, you're going to have to master more than a single investment strategy. As an example, I use four basic investment strategies. I buy:

1. Properties directly from owners in foreclosure.
2. Small mismanaged residential rental properties.
3. Properties with correctable problems.
4. Options on undervalued properties with immediate resale profit potential.

Real Estate Is a Multifaceted Business with Numerous Opportunities for Investors

Real estate is a multifaceted business that's comprised of the following five types of properties, which provide savvy investors with numerous investment opportunities nationwide:

1. Residential.
2. Commercial.
3. Office.
4. Industrial.
5. Land.

In Part II of this book, you're going to learn about five realistic real estate investment strategies that you can use to profit from real estate today. But just about every real estate investment strategy is a variation of the following two tried-and-true basic strategies:

1. Buy and hold.
2. Buy and resell.

Four Main Ways That Real Estate Investors Can Profit from Owning Property

The four main ways in which real estate investors can profit from owning property are:

1. *Appreciation in value:* Property can increase in value through improvements, a change in use, or from market-wide appreciation.
2. *Depreciation for tax purposes:* Depreciation is an income tax deduction that property owners can claim annually to recover the cost of wear and tear, deterioration, or obsolescence of their property.
3. *Cash flow from rental income:* Rental income from property provides owners with cash flow.
4. *Equity buildup from repaying loans:* Equity buildup occurs when the balance of an amortizing loan is reduced through repayment of the principal.

My Real Estate Investment Modus Operandi

I prefer investment strategies, which allow me to get in and out of a piece of property in a relatively short period of time. My real estate investment business is based on the time-tested BLASH—buy low and sell higher—

Principle. I target undervalued properties, which have immediate resale profit potential. This way, I almost always make most of my profit upfront when I buy a piece of property well-below market value. I specialize in financially and physically distressed problem properties, which belong to owners, who have a compelling reason to sell. In other words, I look for property owners, who need to sell to me worse than I want to buy from them. I provide distressed property owners with immediate debt relief and allow them to avoid:

1. Dealing with real estate brokers and paying sales commissions.
2. Making costly and time-consuming property repairs.
3. Putting up with the hassles and inconvenience that are a part of marketing property to the public.

Use Your Million-Dollar Mind to Develop Your Own Investment Strategies

First things first: Stop wasting your million-dollar mind on the mundane minutiae of everyday life. Instead, use your mind to develop real estate investment strategies, which take full advantage of your knowledge, skills, experiences, and the things that you like best in life. To get your creative juices flowing, spend at least 30 minutes a day in deep thought. Do what I do and think about what you want to achieve as a real estate investor. I do my best thinking in the early morning hours, just before dawn, when it's quiet and there are no interruptions from family, friends, and the outside world. Sit down in your favorite chair, lean back, close your eyes, exercise your million-dollar mind, and picture yourself as a successful real estate investor. In addition to deep thinking, partake in brainstorming sessions with your spouse or a like-minded friend and write down everything that's discussed on a legal pad. During one of your brainstorming sessions, you could experience one of those rare times in life, when a one-million-watt light bulb comes on in your mind and a brilliant idea is hatched. After you've finished batting ideas around, have your spouse or friend play devil's advocate, and run a bunch of what-if scenarios by you, to try and find any gapping holes in your ideas. Once you come up with a workable investment strategy, develop a written plan of action that outlines exactly how you're going to implement the strategy in your local real estate market.

Your Real Estate Investment Strategies Must Be Goal Oriented

The one thing that all successful real estate investors have in common is that they write down their investment goals and develop a detailed step-by-step plan of action for achieving them. In the immortal words of the father of time management, Alan Lakein: *"Failing to plan is planning to fail."* As far as I am concerned, novice investors who fail to establish goals as part of their overall real estate investment strategy are setting themselves up for failure. Lately, I've noticed that many wannabe investors, who consider themselves to be members of the hip just-do-it crowd, pooh-pooh goal setting as being old-fashioned, a waste of time, and somehow below their exalted status as millionaires in the making. The just-do-it mind-set may be fine for people who are contemplating whether they should order octopus in a swanky restaurant but, for wannabe real estate mavens, this kind of careless spontaneity can end in financial ruin. Unless you want to spend your time as a real estate investor running around in circles like a chicken with its head cutoff, your investment strategies must be based on achieving financial goals, which are clearly spelled out and include:

1. A beginning date.
2. A detailed plan of action for accomplishing the goal.
3. A financial objective stated in a specific dollar amount.
4. A completion date.
5. An exit plan.

Develop Multiple Exit Plans for Each One of Your Investment Strategies

As far as I am concerned, the most crucial part of any real estate investment strategy is the part that describes exactly what's supposed to happen to a property after it has been purchased. From what I've seen, most real estate investors never really put much time or forethought into developing any type of exit plan before they buy a property. Most investors' idea of an exit plan is to place a "for sale" sign on the property and hope that someone makes an offer. To me, not including multiple exit plans in a real estate investment strategy is an invitation to failure. That's why I've developed exit plans A, B, and C for each one of the investment strategies that I use. This way, if plan A doesn't pan out, I can fall back to plan B and, if that doesn't workout, then I can resort to plan C. For example, if your investment strategy is to buy and turn around small, mismanaged residential rental properties, your exit plans should be to:

A. Resell the property 13 months from the date of purchase, take advantage of the long-term capital gains tax rate, and find a buyer who provides their own financing and cashes you out of the property.

B. Resell the property within 13 months from the date of purchase, take advantage of the long-term capital gains tax rate, and do an installment sale by providing a seller-financed mortgage or deed of trust loan to a qualified buyer.

C. Refinance the property in order to pullout the money that you've invested in it, so you can buy and turn another property around.

You Must Prepare a Written Plan of Action for Achieving Your Goals

To me, if you're not willing to put pen to paper and write a detailed step-by-step plan of action, which outlines exactly how you're going to accomplish your investment goals, you might as well not bother setting any goals in the first place. What good are goals, if you have no idea how you're going to turn them into reality? A well-written plan of action is to a successful real estate investor what a:

1. Blueprint is to a carpenter.
2. Road map is to a truck driver.
3. Flight plan is to a pilot.
4. Lesson plan is to a teacher.

Know What Type of a Real Estate Market You're Investing In

The very first thing that you must do, before you choose investment strategies, is learn the type of real estate market that you're going to be investing in. In other words, you must know if you're investing in a balanced market, a buyers' market, or a sellers' market. For example, in a balanced market, the supply and demand for a particular type of property is pretty much even. In a buyers' market, there's an oversupply of property, which tends to keep prices flat, while in a sellers' market, the demand for property exceeds the supply, which causes prices to spike. If you don't have a handle on what's going on right in your own backyard and are oblivious to local real estate market conditions, you're not going to last very long in this business. The driving force behind any real estate market is supply and demand. But in any market, the supply and demand for various types of properties changes over time. That's why you must become an expert on the dynamics of your local real estate market, so that you know how to recognize trends and adjust your investment strategies to take advantage of market conditions. You can get a feel for your local real estate market by:

1. Reading local business and real estate related publications.
2. Logging onto local government, college, chamber of commerce, business, and real estate related web sites.
3. Listening to and watching local business and real estate related news broadcasts.
4. Attending networking functions with local business and real estate professionals.

Don't Fall Victim to the "It Won't Work in My Real Estate Market" Mind-Set

As far as I am concerned, one of the biggest mistakes that any investor can make is to automatically dismiss an investment strategy, with the comment, "it won't work in my real estate market," before they've ever even given it a try themselves. Yet, it seems to me, that more and more investors, in today's competitive real estate market, are falling victim to this self-defeating mind-set. Instead of blowing off an investment strategy, investors need to adopt the Marine Corps mantra "improvise, adapt, and overcome" as part of their investment philosophy and start thinking in terms of how an investment strategy can be modified to work in their marketplace and stop dwelling on all the reasons why they assume it won't work in their area. The point that I want to emphasis here is to keep an open mind and be receptive to new ideas and different ways of solving problems. After all, the human mind is like a parachute, and it works best when open.

Maintain a Balance between Your Family and Your Real Estate Business

When starting out, many real estate investors go hog wild and end up breathing, eating, sleeping, and dreaming real estate. This is fine and dandy for investors who are single, but, if you're married, it can be very difficult at times to maintain a balance between your real estate investment business and your family. That's because, on one hand, you want your family to achieve financial security, but, on the other hand, you want to spend quality time with your spouse and children. This can cause internal conflicts, which can have a detrimental effect on an investor's health and family. The best way that I've found to maintain a balance between family and business is to designate times during the week, which are set aside strictly for family activities. Doing this is especially important when children are young and in the formative years of their lives. This way, your spouse won't feel like a real estate widow, and your children won't feel neglected and like they're playing second fiddle to your real estate business. After all, what's the sense in busting your tail to get ahead financially, if your obsession with real estate causes irreparable damage to your relationship with your spouse and children? In a nutshell, always put your family first and real estate second.

Most Real Estate Investment Partnerships Don't End Well

I would think long and hard before I ever entered into any type of real estate investment partnership. Over 20 years ago, I made the near-fatal mistake of investing in real estate with four so-called partners and nearly lost my shirt in the process. The real estate partnership that I was in failed for two very good reasons: All of the partners didn't have the same level of real estate expertise, nor did they all have an equal amount of drive and determination. It took me awhile before I finally realized that the other four partners weren't wired like me. In the beginning, they all talked a good talk, but not a one of them had an entrepreneurial bone in their body. And after that very unpleasant and costly experience, I made a solemn vow to myself that I would never again enter into any type of partnership, with anyone other than my wife Barbara.

No Real Estate Investment Strategy on Earth Will Work Unless You Do

At the end of the day, whether you become a successful real estate investor really has very little to do with this book. But it does have everything to do with your ability, attitude, desire, determination, and persistence. There isn't a real estate investment strategy known to mankind that will work, unless you're willing to get up off your keister and put in the time and effort to make it work. Let me put it to you this way: You can sit around on your hands, do nothing, and complain about your life, or you can turn off the TV, get up from the couch, and start doing something productive, which can change your financial circumstances. The choice is entirely up to you.

FIVE REALISTIC INVESTMENT STRATEGIES THAT YOU CAN USE TO MAKE MONEY FROM REAL ESTATE TODAY

CHAPTER 6

Why Most of the Creative Real Estate Investment Strategies Being Taught Today Seldom Work Well

The all-time favorite catchphrase of the get rich quick in real estate crowd is "creative real estate." It's a takeoff from the popular term *creative financing* that came into vogue during the late 1970s and early 1980s when the interest rate for a 30-year fixed-rate conventional mortgage peaked at 17.48 percent in January 1982. Home owners and real estate investors alike had to come up with nontraditional or so-called creative ways to finance the purchase of properties. Nowadays, most creative real estate seminar hucksters, use the slogan "no money or credit required" to lure the public into attending overpriced seminars, where self-professed real estate experts babble on and on about how anyone with a pulse can quickly make a million bucks with their "cutting-edge" creative real estate investment strategies without using a dime of their own money or credit. This ad slogan has turned out to be a sort of clarion call for every wannabe real estate investor in America who's dead broke and has lousy credit. The creative real estate hustlers have used this deceptive advertising hook to give a false sense of hope to a group of people who aren't financially, or otherwise, suited for real estate.

During the year, I receive over 3,000 e-mails and telephone calls from the readers of my books. And a lot of the cockamamie ideas, which are being pushed by creative real estate types, are run by me by the people reading my books. For the most part, these are "strategies" that'll only earn a profit in some wannabe investor's dreams. I can tell you from first-hand observation that most of the people I've watched try their hand at various types of creative real estate investment strategies, usually ended up spinning their wheels and quitting in disgust. It wasn't because they didn't try hard and give it their best shot. They failed because most of the creative real estate investment strategies that are being taught today don't work very well. They're usually quite hard to implement and are seldom profitable. The truth is that most creative real estate strategies just don't work very well outside of the hotel ballrooms where most seminars are held. Creative real estate fanatics often try and dismiss critics, such as myself, by saying that we don't fully understand the nuts and bolts of how their strategies work. Bullspit. I know all too well how these strategies are supposed to work, and, in this chapter, I am going to give you the inside scoop on the following five popular creative real estate investment strategies and tell you exactly why they very seldom work well:

1. Buying property without making a down payment to the seller.
2. Selling property through the use of lease options.
3. Taking title to property subject to existing loans.
4. Double closings where property is bought and sold at the same time.
5. Receiving money back from the seller at closing.

Most Creative Real Estate Strategies Involve High-Risk, Low-Profit Deals

The main reason I am not a fan of the creative real estate investment strategies that are being taught today is because they involve high-risk, low-profit deals. As far as I am concerned, the risk versus reward ratio for most creative real estate investment strategies is way out of whack. The potential risks that are associated with these strategies far outweigh their profit potential. To me, there are just too many things that can go wrong with these types of deals. For example, during the time that a property is under a lease-option agreement, a tenant-buyer could commit a wanton act of malicious vandalism and destroy the leased property and skip town, while leaving the investor holding the bag and responsible for thousands of dollars in needed repairs. There's just not enough of a profit margin in most creative real estate deals, to make them financially worthwhile, once the following costs are taken into account:

1. Acquisition costs.
2. Transaction costs.

3. Closing costs.
4. Repair costs.
5. Holding costs.
6. Sales costs.

In most transactions, what appears to be a profit on paper really isn't, when all out-of-pocket rent and loan payments and other costs, which can never be recouped, are factored into the equation. It's usually at this point that investors come to the sad realization that they've been working for minimum or subminimum wages. I can't get too excited about the prospect of working for minimum wage, as a self-employed real estate investor.

Most Investors Lack the Cash Reserves That Are Needed to Subsidize Their Deals

Although they don't realize it until it's too late, most creative real estate investors, who lack financial resources, are pretty much doomed from the beginning. That's because investors, who are woefully undercapitalized and don't have the deep pockets or cash reserves, which are almost always needed to subsidize creative real estate deals, are usually one rent or loan payment away from going under. This lack of operating capital creates a domino effect whenever an investor experiences any type of financial emergency. For example, when a so-called tenant-buyer in a standard lease-option deal fails to pay their monthly sublease payment, the investor usually doesn't have the money to make the lease payment to the property owner, which forces the owner to initiate eviction proceedings against the investor for nonpayment of rent. Or the owner of an overleveraged property, which was bought for nothing down, can't come up with cash, that's needed to pay the monthly negative cash flow. The term *negative cash flow* refers to the difference between the amount of monthly rental income a property produces and the amount of the monthly loan payment. For example, a property, which generated $1,500 in rental income, with a mortgage or deed of trust loan payment of $2,100, would have a monthly negative cash flow of $600 ($2,100 loan payment minus $1,500 rental income equals $600 negative cash flow). And most investors who are living right on the edge would be hard-pressed to scrape up an additional $600 every month to keep the loan payment current.

The Nothing-Down Strategy

The most popular creative real estate investment strategy by far, is buying property without making a down payment to the seller, better known as "nothing down," which is due in large part, to Robert Allen's best-selling book, by the same title. The nothing-down strategy involves buying property without making a down payment. And now, thanks to the gross exaggerations and outright lies, made by nothing-down fanatics, wannabe investors have been misled into believing that there are droves of desperate sellers in every real estate market nationwide who, at the drop of a hat, will sell their property for no money down and let the investor take over their mortgage or deed of trust loan in the process. In fact, the odds that anyone, with very limited knowledge and no actual hands-on experience as a real estate investor, can buy a piece of property with any upside potential, for no money down, are slim to none. That's because most beginning real estate investors don't have the finesse that's needed to pull off a profitable nothing-down deal. So whenever I hear a novice real estate investor make outlandish claims, about how they bought a million dollar piece of property for nothing down and walked out of the closing with a certified check for $55,000, my internal bullspit detector immediately goes off. The nothing-down crowd likes to ramble on with the usual psychobabble about how "salesmanship" is what's needed to talk property owners into selling their property, to financially irresponsible investors, for no money down. But I happen to think that it's really more about dazzling property owners with bullspit than it is about using good old-fashioned salesmanship to close the deal. And there are two very good reasons why profitable nothing-down real estate deals are very few and far between. First, when you're a real estate investor, who's dead broke and has crummy credit to boot, you're operating at a huge disadvantage when you go up against other investors, who have the cash and credit to put a deal together on their own without having to ask the seller for help. Second, when you have a track record of being financially irresponsible, it's going to be next to impossible for you to convince an astute property owner that you're not going to walk away from the property, when the going gets tough. After all, when you're broke and have really rotten credit and no assets, you have nothing to lose if you do decide to walk away from a property. In situations like this, it's a no-brainer who any intelligent owner is going to sell their property to. On the rare occasion when a financially shaky investor is able to talk a property owner into doing a nothing-down deal, the owner will most likely jack up the selling price way above market value and charge an interest rate that's 6 to 10 percentage points higher than the market rate. This isn't any type of deal that I would want any part of. But when you're inexperienced and strapped for cash and credit, it's about the best that you're going to be able to do on a nothing-down deal. As you'll learn in Chapter 21, it doesn't take a six-figure income, a humongous bank account, and a super high credit score to get started as a real estate investor today. But it does take a certain amount of cash and credit to implement 99 percent of all legitimate real estate investment strategies.

The Lease-Option Strategy

Those of you, who have read my book *How to Make Money with Real Estate Options* know that I have absolutely no use, whatsoever, for the standard lease-option strategy that's being taught today. The standard sublease-option strategy involves leasing a property and then subleasing it to a tenant-buyer. This in turn makes the lessee (tenant) a lessor (landlord) responsible for managing the tenant-buyer. A sublease is also known as a "sandwich lease," which is generally defined as: *A lease agreement in which the lessee (tenant) becomes a lessor (landlord) by subleasing the property under lease to a sublessee (tenant) who takes possession of the property.* Under a typical sublease-option arrangement, an investor signs a lease-option agreement with a property owner and then subleases the property to a third party, known as a tenant-buyer, by using a sublease-option agreement. The following three parties are involved in two separate lease-option transactions:

1. *Lessor-optionor:* The owner of the property being lease optioned.
2. *Lessee-optionee:* The party leasing the property from the owner with an option to buy.
3. *Tenant-buyer:* The party subleasing the property from the lessee-optionee with an option to buy.

The problem with this scenario is that 99 percent of all investors, who get involved in a lease-option transaction, don't know enough about being a residential landlord. As a result, whenever they have any type of a problem with a tenant-buyer, they are clueless about the correct way to solve it.

Although I know of no case nationwide where a residential mortgage or deed of trust lender has declared a loan to be in default because the borrower signed a lease-option agreement on the property securing the mortgage or deed of trust and promissory note, you need to know that the discovery of a lease-option agreement, by a lender, can trigger the due-on-sale clause contained in residential mortgage and deed of trust loans. Also, under the terms contained in a standard lease-option agreement, the relationship between the parties is that of debtor and creditor and not that of lessee-optionee and lessor-optionor. This debtor-creditor relationship is created whenever the terms of a lease-option call for the property owner/lessor-optionor to credit the option consideration and a fixed portion of the monthly lease payment toward the purchase price when the real estate option is exercised. Once this debtor-creditor relationship is created, the tenant/lessee-optionee has an equitable or ownership interest, instead of a leasehold interest in the property being lease optioned. When a lease-option agreement gives the lessee-optionee an equitable interest in the property being leased optioned, it becomes an installment sales agreement and not a lease-option agreement. This means that if the tenant must be evicted, the owner could be forced to file a costly and time-consuming lawsuit to foreclose, instead of an eviction lawsuit.

The Subject-To Strategy

Unlike when a buyer assumes an existing mortgage or deed of trust loan and becomes legally responsible for repayment of the loan, when a buyer takes title to a property subject to an existing loan all they're really doing is taking over the loan payments, without being held personally liable for repayment of the promissory note. The responsibility for repayment of the loan always lies with the last owner assuming the loan, prior to its being taken subject to. However, taking title to a property subject to an existing residential mortgage or deed of trust loan is in direct violation of the due-on-sale clause that's contained in virtually all residential loan documents used by institutional lenders. Contrary to what the subject-to experts may claim, almost all transactions that are made subject to existing loans are eventually discovered by lenders. The discovery usually occurs when the lender receives a hazard insurance policy that has the new owner's name as the insured, instead of the name of the borrower of record, who's listed on the mortgage or deed of trust loan. Buying any property subject to existing loans without the prior approval of the lender can be risky business.

Once a lender discovers that a sale has taken place in violation of their loan's due on sale clause, they can:

1. Call the loan due and exercise their right to accelerate payments and demand that the entire unpaid principle loan balance be paid in full within 30 days.
2. Foreclose on the loan if the new owner fails to pay it off after the lender calls the loan due.
3. Do nothing and let the new owner take over the loan payments.

The Double-Closing Strategy

Another popular creative real estate investment strategy that's being taught today is how to do double closings, which are also known as simultaneous closings, double escrows, or concurrent closings. Under a typical double-closing scenario, buyer A signs a purchase agreement to buy a property from seller B. In the meantime, buyer A turns around and signs a purchase agreement to sell the same property to buyer C at the same time that buyer A buys the property from seller B. And in hotel ballrooms across the country, seminar speakers make double closings sound as easy as boiling water. But in reality, double closings can be very hard to do, especially, when there are lenders involved in the transaction. This is because, nowadays, almost all lenders issue closing instructions to title and escrow agents doing double closings, which require:

1. *The source of title:* The source of title gives the name, date, and recording information of the document that transferred the property's title to the current owner.
2. *The source of funds:* The source of funds provides information about where the money came from to purchase the property. This is done to prevent the end buyer from funding the seller's purchase of the property, from the original owner. In other words, each transaction within the double closing must be funded by each buyer.
3. *Full disclosure:* All three parties involved in the two separate transactions must be made aware of each other.
4. *HUD 1 Settlement Statements:* Properly completed HUD 1 Settlement Statements that accurately document all of the payments, which were

made in each transaction and match the actual checks that were disbursed during each closing.

The Cash-Back-at-Closing Strategy

The cash-back-at-closing strategy, which is often touted on those tacky real estate infomercials that are shown on television, is another creative real estate strategy, that's damn near impossible to pull off. From the way that I've heard it pitched on TV, it sounds to me like the strategy is based on a buyer reneging on the terms of a purchase agreement by threatening not to close on the purchase unless the seller agrees to make what amounts to a cash refund for repairs, closing costs, or some other cockamamie reason. In legal circles, this is known as extortion. I don't know about you, but I would immediately file a specific performance lawsuit against any buyer, who pulled a stunt like that on me at the closing table and refused to honor the terms of our legally binding agreement. Almost all reputable lenders stipulate in their closing instructions that no type of payment, whatsoever, is to be paid to the buyer in conjunction with the closing. Nowadays, almost all closing agents—title and escrow agents and attorneys—require the buyer and seller to sign an affidavit stating that there are no undisclosed side deals or arrangements that are a part of the transaction. In addition, most states now have laws on their books, which strictly prohibit unlicensed parties from receiving any type of payment, sales commission, or rebate in connection with a real estate transaction. In case you didn't know it, making false statements on real estate closing documents can get you into legal trouble in all 50 states. Other cash-back-at-closing schemes, which are told with a wink and a nod at creative real estate seminars, involve various forms of deception that keep lenders in the dark about material facts in a real estate transaction, which if the lender had known about beforehand, they wouldn't have approved the loan in the first place. Making false statements on loan applications and loan documents happens to be a big no-no and is considered a crime in every state in the union. But making false statements in order to obtain any type of government-backed mortgage or deed of trust loan, is an even bigger no-no; it's a federal crime that is punishable by a hefty monetary fine and an extended stay at a secure facility operated by the Federal Bureau of Prisons. Here's a warning that anyone, who may be contemplating doing some under-the-closing-table or side-deal shenanigans, should heed: If you receive any type of payment from a seller at a real estate closing and it's not listed on the buyer's

HUD 1 Settlement Statement and paid out of the proceeds from the closing, there's an excellent chance that you're taking part in some type of fraudulent activity, which could nip your real estate career in the bud and put you away in the slammer for a very long time. So as you can see, the so-called cash-back-at-closing strategy isn't exactly the cakewalk that it's made out to be.

Why Creative Real Estate Transactions Are So Closely Scrutinized

To many of the people, who work in the mortgage lending and title insurance industries, the term *creative real estate* has pretty much become synonymous with fraud. As a result, any sort of real estate transaction that's in anyway out of the ordinary sends up a red flag, and it's put under the microscope and thoroughly scrutinized by reputable title insurers and escrow companies before they'll agree to close the deal. The reason for this intense scrutiny is because title and escrow agents and lenders are constantly on the lookout for fraudulent real estate investment schemes, which cost them millions of dollars annually. In other words, they're especially leery of being the closing agent for any type of real estate transaction, which doesn't meet their standards. That's exactly why it's usually next to impossible for investors employing questionable investment strategies to find a reputable title or escrow company that'll close their deals.

CHAPTER 7

How to Make Money from Vacant Properties That Aren't Advertised as Being for Sale

In every hamlet, village, town, city, and county across the United States, there are various types of properties, which are currently sitting vacant and are not advertised as being for sale. In fact, some of my best buys have come from vacant properties that weren't even for sale when I first came across them. As you'll learn, once you get involved in this business, just because a property isn't advertised as being "for sale" doesn't necessarily mean that the owner isn't willing to sell it. Sometimes it's a matter of the owner not having the stomach for dealing with the public and selling the property themselves. Or it may be a situation where the owner doesn't want to go through the hassle of listing the property for sale through a real estate broker. And other times, it can be a case of "out of sight, out of mind" when a piece of property belongs to an out-of-town owner and selling it doesn't happen to be a very high priority on their to-do list. But the biggest reason that I've found many vacant properties aren't for sale by owner or listed with real estate brokers is because they're in an unmarketable condition, which can make them hard to sell. By an unmarketable condition, I mean the property is derelict looking and in dire need of repairs and an industrial strength cleaning. In a lot of instances, property owners don't have the desire, time, or money to get their property in shape for resale, so the property remains vacant and continues to deteriorate and becomes even harder to sell. It has been my experience that the majority of vacant properties are usually owned by:

1. Private individuals who inherited the property and live out of the area.
2. Private individuals who have tried to sell their property themselves and failed to do so.

3. Private individuals who had listed their property for sale through real estate brokers, who were unable to sell it.

4. Companies that have closed up shop and left town.

5. Companies that acquired the property through the acquisition or merger with another company.

6. Companies that have cut back on the size of their operations.

Vacant Properties Can Be a Bonanza for Savvy Real Estate Investors

Most Americans today are caught up in the notion that new is better and old is passé. So when investors with this mind-set come across a property that has been vacant for an extended period of time, they automatically assume that there must be something wrong with the property. Why on earth would a piece of property sit vacant for a long time without attracting any offers to buy it? The truth is that many vacant buildings have a lot of years of use left in them and can be a bonanza for real estate investors who have the ability to look at a piece of vacant property and visualize it being put to a variety of profitable uses. For example, when most people look at a vacant three-bay gas station, all they see is a vacant three-bay gas station. But when an investor with a creative and resourceful mind looks at a vacant three-bay gas station, he or she can immediately envision a:

1. Produce market.
2. Convenience store.
3. Tool rental store.
4. Pizza parlor.
5. Plant nursery.
6. Small engine repair shop.
7. Set of small office suites.
8. Delicatessen.

Vacant Class "D" Commercial Buildings

Most of the vacant properties that I buy are class "D" commercial build-ings, which are located in areas that are on the upswing and belong to owners, who do not have the time, energy, money, or desire to fix up and market their property to the general public or hire a broker to do it for them. Class "D" properties are older buildings in need of repairs, which have few modern amenities. One of the reasons I specialize in this type of building is because it is usually well below the radar screens of most individual and corporate real estate investors, who generally don't have a nose for deals like this. During a vacant property search, I look for class "D" buildings that:

1. Are in a filthy, neglected, run-down, and unmarketable condition.
2. Can be bought at prices that are at least 20 percent below their current market value.
3. Have immediate resale profit potential, when marketed to a targeted group of prospective buyers.

My "Vacant Property Specialist" Business Card

Here's a copy of the front and back sides of my "vacant property specialist" business card. As you can see, I offer a $500 finder's fee for leads on vacant properties that I buy.

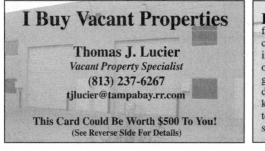

How I Made a $30,000 Profit from a Vacant Building Full of Pigeon Droppings

One of my favorite types of vacant property to buy is a small, run-down commercial property that can be quickly and inexpensively cleaned up. These are what I call "dirty deals." Dirty deals are buildings that are structurally sound but have a filthy, neglected, run-down appearance that's usually an instant turn-off to most people. In other words, these are the type of properties that most other investors wouldn't touch with a 10-foot pole. But that's because most investors can't get past the smell, or look beyond the filth and grime, to see a vacant property's profit potential. The reason I like these dirty deals so much is because they're strictly cleaner-upper properties, which don't require an extreme makeover. All I have to do to spruce them up is to give them an old-fashioned industrial strength cleaning. This way, I don't have any of my own money tied up in costly and time-consuming repairs. My out-of-pocket expenses are limited to the cost of cleaning up the property. I like this particular type of property because I can usually buy it for at least 20 percent below market value and then resell for a hefty profit once the property has been cleaned up.

Case in point: I once bought a vacant, 2,000 square foot, concrete block building in North Tampa from a company located in Houston, Texas, which had acquired the property through a corporate merger. The building had served as a roosting spot for a flock of pigeons for over a year. And I can tell you from experience that a year's worth of pigeon droppings has an acrid aroma that you'll never forget. Pigeon droppings are also acidic and carry diseases and parasites, which can pose a health hazard to humans. So the very first thing that I did, after I became the proud owner of this toxic pigeon coop, was to install one-half inch galvanized wire mesh over the vents of the two gable ends, which the pigeons were using to come into the building. Once the building was pigeon free, I received three estimates to have the droppings removed and the inside of the building disinfected. But the estimates came in between $2,500 and $3,000, which was nearly double the $1,500 that I had budgeted for the interior cleanup. At this point, my internal bullspit detector went off, warning me of a possible impending rip-off. So I decided to cleanup the place myself. I went to my local Home Depot and bought rain gear, a pair of rubber boots, a respirator, a box of heavy-duty plastic bags, and a scoop shovel and rented a pressure washer. Then I went to my local swimming pool supply store and bought four gallons of chlorine. I went back to the building and put on my rubber boots and respirator and scooped up the pigeon droppings and put them into plastic bags. Next, I put on my rain gear and fired up the pressure washer and gave the building an industrial strength cleaning.

Two days later, after everything had dried out, I sprayed the walls, ceiling, and floor with a very strong disinfectant that made the place smell like a hospital. I ended up spending a grand total of $225 and eight hours of my time to get the place into a habitable condition. Three months later, I resold the property to a company that made custom kitchen cabinets and bathroom vanities for a $30,000 profit.

Three Main Reasons Why Many
Commercial Properties End Up Being Vacant

The three main reasons many commercial properties end up being vacant are:

1. *Functional obsolescence:* Occurs when a property loses value due to its architectural design, building style, size, outdated amenities, local economic conditions, and changing technology. Look for properties with design features that would be relatively easy to upgrade or replace. For example, some buildings have facades that include outdated awning type overhangs that can be removed to give the building a more modern appearance.

2. *Economic obsolescence:* Occurs when a property loses value because of external factors, such as local traffic pattern changes or the construction of public nuisance-type properties and utilities, such as county jails and sewer treatment plants, on adjoining property. Seek out vacant but structurally sound properties that adjoin less desirable nuisance-type properties. As an example, a vacant warehouse located next to a sewage treatment plant, which could be used by a manufacturer to store nonhazardous materials.

3. *Physical obsolescence:* Occurs when a property loses value due to gross mismanagement and physical neglect, resulting in deferred maintenance that's usually too costly to repair. Search for properties with only minor structural problems that can be corrected at a cost that's below the property's replacement cost. In other words, don't buy a property that's deemed to be physically obsolescent if it can be rebuilt from scratch for less than it would cost to repair it.

Ten Telltale Signs That a Property Is Probably Vacant

One of the advantages of investing in vacant properties is that they're usually pretty easy to spot, once you know the 10 telltale signs of blatant neglect that usually signal that a property is vacant. For example, when I am in the market for a vacant property, I look for properties that have:

1. Trash-strewn grounds.
2. Overgrown landscaping.

3. Graffiti-covered walls.

4. Broken windows.

5. Missing doors.

6. Boarded-up doors and windows.

7. Peeling paint.

8. Missing roofing material.

9. Overgrown walkways and parking areas.

10. Abandoned vehicles.

What to Check for When Looking Over a Vacant Property

Whenever I come across a vacant property, I always do a quick visual inspection of the outside. I use an inspection checklist like Form 7.1 to try and determine just how long the property has been sitting vacant. I need to know this information because there's usually a direct correlation between how long a property has been vacant and the owner's level of motivation to sell. It has been my experience that the longer a property has been vacant, the better my chances are of negotiating a below market purchase price.

FORM 7.1 Vacant Property Checklist

1. Does the property have an electrical meter? ( ) Yes ( ) No

2. Is there a power line connected to the property? ( ) Yes ( ) No

3. Has the property been cited for code violations? ( ) Yes ( ) No

4. Is the property connected to municipal water and sewer lines? ( ) Yes ( ) No

5. Has the water meter been removed? ( ) Yes ( ) No

6. Are there condemnation notices posted on the property? ( ) Yes ( ) No

7. Are there bodies of standing water on the property that can't drain? ( ) Yes ( ) No

8. Are there any signs that the property is infested with termites or rodents? ( ) Yes ( ) No

9. Are there any signs that nonpermitted work has been done on the property? ( ) Yes ( ) No

10. Are there any visible signs of environmental hazards on the property? ( ) Yes ( ) No

11. Does the property have any visible structural defects? ( ) Yes ( ) No

12. Can the property be insured in its current condition? ( ) Yes ( ) No

---

Never Go Snooping around the Inside
of Vacant Buildings without Permission

A word of warning: Please resist the all-too-human urge to go snooping around the inside of a vacant building without first obtaining the owner's permission. If you fail to heed my sage advice and get caught inside a vacant building, you could end up being charged with breaking and entering or illegal trespassing, which are considered misdemeanor offenses in most jurisdictions. Or, worse yet, you could wind up in cold storage at the county morgue if you went snooping around a building that you somehow thought was vacant, but was actually occupied by an owner who believed in exercising their Second Amendment right to bear arms. That's exactly why I never, ever go inside anyone's property without first getting permission from the owner.

Don't Overlook Vacant Barns and Outbuildings
That Can Be Salvaged and Reused

If you're located in a rural area, don't overlook the vacant barns and other types of farm outbuildings that you most likely drive by every day, which can be dismantled, restored, and reassembled for use as homes, barns, studios, workshops, and a myriad of other uses. For example, if you live in northern New England or upstate New York, or anywhere else where dairy farms once flourished, there should be ample opportunities to buy vacant barns, which can be salvaged and resold to private individuals, builders, architects, and contractors who specialize in restoring "antique buildings." In fact, a hard-working investor, who understands the three basic principles of carpentry—plumb, level, and square—and isn't afraid of getting his or her hands dirty, could make a very good living buying barns locally and reselling them to buyers nationwide. In Chapter 23, you'll learn how to package and market resell properties for maximum profit.

The Smart Way to Buy and Resell
Vacant Barns and Outbuildings

The smart way to work this strategy is to find potential buyers before you ever commit to buying any buildings. And the quickest way that I know to find prospective buyers is to go online and use Google's search engine to locate people who specialize in old barns and outbuildings. To conduct your search, use terms such as *old barns for sale, old barns wanted, old barn boards, old barn timbers, barn restorations, recycled lumber and reclaimed lumber,* or similar words. Once you've compiled a list of prospective buyers from the Internet, send each person a short and right to-the-point e-mail, stating that you specialize in buying vacant barns and are looking for serious buyers who can close on the purchase of a barn, with relatively short notice. There's no hard-and-fast rule on how much you should pay for a vacant barn or outbuilding. The purchase price should be based solely on a building's age, size, and condition. Ultimately, as with all real estate deals, the price that you end up paying will most likely depend on how good of a negotiator you are. In Chapter 20, you'll learn how to negotiate the best possible deal for yourself.

Look for Vacant Lots

In your quest for real estate riches, don't overlook vacant lots. I am telling you this because of all the various types of vacant properties that are available in most real estate markets nationwide, vacant lots are the most overlooked. I suspect the reason for this is because vacant lots aren't very sexy in the eyes of most real estate investors. In other words, a vacant plot of land doesn't have the same appeal that a building does. But I can tell you from experience that vacant lots are nothing to scoff at. For example, I once bought a 200-feet wide by 150-feet deep vacant lot along a river in Riverview, Florida, from an out-of-town owner who worked as a merchant marine. I found the overgrown lot while I was doing repairs on a home on an adjacent lot. Luckily for me, while I was working at the house, a guy driving a tractor with a brush-mowing attachment showed up to mow the lot. From what he told me about the owner, I was able to track him down on an oil tanker operating out of Panama. I bought the lot a month later when the owner came to Tampa on shore leave. I resold it to a custom homebuilder for a $25,000 profit, two months later.

How to Make an Unsolicited Offer to Purchase a Vacant Piece of Property

In every real estate market nationwide, there are vacant properties that aren't generally advertised as being "for sale." Instead, they're bought through what's known in the real estate trade, as an unsolicited offer to purchase. In other words, an investor approaches the owner of a vacant property and makes an offer to buy the property. For example, when I locate a vacant property, which I feel has potential, I obtain the owners name and mailing address from my county's property appraiser's records, which are posted online. How to find out who owns a piece of property is covered in great detail in Chapter 16. Once I know who the owner is, I send them a letter, like Form 7.2, which is short and right to the point. You'll notice that in my letter, I never mention anything about the price that I am willing to pay for the property or any of the terms of the sale. That's because the sole purpose of my letter is to pique the owner's curiosity and arouse any interest they may have in selling the property. The sale price and terms can be hashed out during face-to-face negotiations.

FORM 7.2 Sample Letter to Vacant Property Owners

July 22, 2006

Mr. Paul Costas
2739 West Nile Avenue
Tampa, FL 33606

Dear Mr. Costas,

My name is Thomas J. Lucier, and I specialize in buying vacant properties, in an as-is condition, in the Tampa Bay Area.

The purpose of my letter is to inquire whether you are interested in selling the property that you own at 5609 East Bayside Avenue, in Tampa.

If you're interested, please feel free to call me any time, at (813) 237-6267, or e-mail me at tjlucier@tampabay.rr.com to discuss the sale of your property.

I promise not to waste your valuable time with games, gimmicks, and bullspit.

I look forward to hearing from you soon.

Sincerely,

Thomas J. Lucier

Copyright Thomas J. Lucier, 2006. To customize this document, download it from www.thomaslucier .com/realestateforms.html. The document can then be opened, edited, and printed using Microsoft Word.

Don't Let Your Fear of Rejection
Stop You from Making Unsolicited Offers

Many real estate investors have an unfounded fear of rejection, which stops them from ever making any unsolicited offers on vacant properties. They wrongly assume that they'll be rebuffed by property owners and their offers will be automatically rejected out of hand. But in many cases, nothing could be further from the truth. In reality, it may be the real estate investor who's in the driver's seat when it comes to negotiating the sale price and terms of a vacant property. I say this because of the mind-set that many vacant property owners have. To see what I mean, sit back, close your eyes, and imagine yourself as the owner of a piece of property, in need of repairs that has been sitting vacant for a long time, with no takers in sight. Now, try and picture in your mind how you would react to someone sending you a letter in the mail asking if your unadvertised property is "for sale." I don't know about you, but if you're anything like me, you'd be on the telephone within minutes of receiving the letter to invite the investor over for a look-see and a serious discussion about buying the property. You can hopefully see why, in many situations, you might be the only hope that an owner has on the horizon of selling their vacant property. Keep this in mind the next time you get cold feet and are hesitant to make an unsolicited offer to buy a vacant property because you're afraid the owner will reject your offer.

Some Vacant Properties May
Contain Environmentally Hazardous Materials

In some cases, the reason a property is vacant is because there are environmentally hazardous materials in the building and soil surrounding the property, which the current owner has been ordered by the U.S. Environmental Protection Agency (EPA) or a city, county, or state environmental protection agency to remove or remediate before the property can be sold. For example, here in Tampa, there's an old Honeywell manufacturing plant that's been sitting vacant for a very long time. The trust that owns the property has been in an ongoing battle with Honeywell, the EPA, and the State of Florida over who's liable for cleaning up the property, which is allegedly contaminated with various chemicals that were used in the manufacturing process that took place in the plant. In Chapter 17, I give you step-by-step instructions on how to check to see if a vacant property is on any government list of environmentally contaminated properties. You'll also learn how to have a property inspected for environmentally hazardous materials.

How to Clean Up and Secure a Vacant Property

Once you take possession of a vacant property, you need to clean up around the outside and make the building secure from vandals and squatters. I always start cleaning a vacant property at the front and then I work my way back to the rear property line. The reason you should always start your cleanup from the front is to enhance the property's curb appeal and make it more visible and enticing to prospective buyers passing by. Here is a sequential listing of how you should clean up and secure a vacant property:

1. Cut and remove overgrown brush, grass, and weeds.
2. Trim trees and shrubs and remove cut branches.
3. Rake the grounds clean and remove all trash and debris.
4. Pressure wash asphalt, shingle, and tile roofs.
5. Pressure wash exterior walls.
6. Pressure wash concrete walkways.
7. Sweep the interior of the building and remove all trash and debris.
8. Secure all broken door and window openings with half-inch CDX plywood.
9. Lock the main entry door with a heavy-duty commercial grade Master hasp lock and keyed high security Master padlock.
10. Attach a four-by-eight foot "for sale" sign to the exterior building wall facing traffic that has your telephone number and e-mail address to advertise your property, so that you can also be contacted by police and fire personnel in case there's an emergency on the property.

CHAPTER 8

How to Profit from Properties That Have Been Condemned for Code Violations

Another type of property that's usually under the radar screens of most investors is property that has been condemned by local code enforcement boards for various types of code violations. In my neck of the woods, there's a steady supply of properties that have been condemned for demolition or as being unfit for human habitation. Condemned properties are pretty easy to find once you know where to look for them in the public records. For example, the code enforcement departments for both the City of Tampa and Hillsborough County maintain files on all of the properties that have been cited for code violations. In most areas, when properties are cited for code violations, which is commonly referred to as being red-tagged, brightly colored—usually dark red or orange—placards are conspicuously posted on the property and stick out like a sore thumb to anyone passing by.

What usually puts the code enforcement process into gear is a property in a run-down condition, which in turn generates a code violation complaint call to the local code enforcement agency. Once a code violation complaint is filed, the code enforcement agency sends an inspector to inspect the property. If any code violations are uncovered during the inspection, a written citation is issued to the owner. The owner is generally given between 30 to 60 days to correct the violation or face the prospect of having to pay a hefty daily fine until the property is brought up to code. If the owner does absolutely nothing and fails to correct the code violation before the deadline, the property will usually end up being condemned by the local code enforcement board for building, health, or safety code violations.

The Three Most Common Types of Code Violations

The three most common types of code violations that are cited by code enforcement inspectors are:

1. *Building code violations:* Usually involve broken windows and doors, peeling paint, missing siding and roofing materials, soffit and fascia that need replacing, or structural defects like sagging roofs and floors that need to be shored up.

2. *Health code violations:* Generally range from unsanitary conditions caused by faulty plumbing to infestation of fleas, cockroaches, mice, and other pests, or from pools of standing water, which are caused by a lack of adequate drainage, to toxic mold contamination.

3. *Safety code violations:* Cover unsafe conditions such as doors and windows that can't be properly locked, trees with roots that are rotted and on the verge of collapse, electrical outlets that aren't properly grounded, and broken or missing balcony handrails and stair treads.

Code Violations Usually Stay with a Property until They're Corrected

Contrary to popular belief, in most jurisdictions, code violations remain against a property's title until they're corrected and the property is brought into compliance. This is commonly referred to in the land title industry as "running with the title." This means that when a property with existing code violations is sold, the new owner is responsible for correcting them.

Code Enforcement Is Usually a Complaint-Driven Process

In most towns, cities, and counties, code enforcement is a complaint-driven process in which the local government doesn't take a proactive approach to enforcing local building, health, and safety codes. In other words, nothing happens until someone lodges a complaint against a particular property with the local government agency responsible for enforcing building, health, and safety codes. The City of Tampa was that way until 2003, when a new mayor took over and had the city divided into three areas for code enforcement purposes. Now the department of code enforcement inspectors go through the city block by block, looking for any visible signs of noncompliance such as overgrown yards, accumulations of trash and debris, rundown buildings in need of repairs and painting, and unregistered vehicles.

How the Code Enforcement Process Usually Works

In most areas, code enforcement is a quasi-legal process, which is carried out by local code enforcement boards. Most code enforcement boards are usually comprised of a chairperson, who's an elected official, and board members, who are local citizens appointed by elected officials. To learn all of the nitty-gritty details of exactly how the code enforcement process works in your area, log onto your local government's web site and look under code enforcement. To see the actual code enforcement process in action, attend a public code enforcement board hearing in person, or watch one on your local public access cable television channel. In most areas, the code enforcement process is comprised of the following nine steps:

Step 1: A complaint is filed with the local code enforcement agency against a property for an alleged code violation.

Step 2: A code enforcement inspector performs an inspection of the property to verify the validity of the code violation complaint.

Step 3: If the complaint is valid, the property owner is given written notification by the code enforcement agency that a code violation exists on their property, which usually gives the owner 30 to 60 days to correct the violation and bring the property into compliance.

Step 4: After the time allotted to correct the code violation has expired, a code enforcement inspector performs a follow-up inspection to verify that the code violation has been corrected and the property has been brought up to code.

Step 5: If the property owner fails to correct the code violation within the allotted time, the case is scheduled to be heard before the local code enforcement board.

Step 6: The local code enforcement board hears the case and orders the property owner to bring their property into compliance, within a specified period of time, or face a monetary fine for each day the property remains in violation.

Step 7: If the property owner fails to correct the code violation and bring their property into compliance within the allotted time, the code enforcement board issues a daily monetary fine, which is assessed against the property until the code violation is corrected.

Step 8: After a daily fine has been ordered against the property by the code enforcement board, the case is usually referred to the city or county attorney's office, and the order becomes a lien, which is filed and recorded against the property's title.

Step 9: If the property owner fails to pay the code enforcement lien, the city or county attorney can file a foreclosure action to foreclose on the lien.

How Most Code Enforcement Boards Define a Public Nuisance

Most code enforcement boards define a public nuisance as: *Any nuisance, which is detrimental to the health and safety of humans, whether in a building, on the premises of a building, or on an unoccupied lot, to include abandoned, dismantled, and inoperable motor vehicles, boats, trailers, recreational vehicles, auto parts, scrap tires, machinery, junk, debris, building materials, household trash, appliances, furniture, yard waste, overgrown vegetation, underbrush, and unsanitary conditions, which are dangerous to human health and safety.*

Where to Find Your Local Code Enforcement Regulations Online

Code enforcement regulations are generally part of the local municipal code by which cities and counties are governed. The municipal codes of most cities and counties in the United States are available online at the following web site: www.municode.com/resources/online_codes.asp.

Property Condemned for Being Unfit for Human Habitation

In most jurisdictions, a building is condemned as being unfit for human habitation when it doesn't meet the minimum standards of habitation, due to dilapidation or defects, such as the lack of proper ventilation, sanitary facilities, or other conditions that render the building unsafe and detrimental to the health and safety of the people living or working there. Once a property has been declared unfit for human habitation, its certificate of occupancy is revoked and it must remain vacated until the code violations have been corrected and a new certificate of occupancy has been issued.

Property Condemned for Demolition

Here in Tampa, when a building is deemed uninhabitable and a public danger by the department of code enforcement, due to age, decay, deterioration, structural defects, improper design, an unstable foundation, or termite and fire damage that is beyond repair, it's ordered to be vacated and condemned for demolition. The owner is given a deadline to have the building demolished and removed from the property. If the owner fails to demolish and remove the building within the time limit given, the city hires a private contractor to do it, and places a lien against the property's title for demolition and removal costs.

How to Get the Addresses of All the Condemned Properties in Your City or County

In most states, all code enforcement violations issued by code enforcement agencies and condemnation actions ordered by code enforcement boards are considered public information and made readily available to the public. I suggest that you contact your local code enforcement agency for information on how you can obtain a list of properties that have been condemned in your city or county. For example, in Tampa, the department of code enforcement publishes a monthly *Condemnation List*, which lists all of the properties within the city limits of Tampa that have been condemned. Each listing contains the:

1. Street address of the property being condemned.
2. Owner's name.
3. Owner's mailing address.

4. Property appraiser's folio number.
5. Code enforcement case number.
6. Type of code violation.

How to Deal with Local Code Enforcement Department Bureaucrats

There are many types of civil servants working at all levels and in every type of government bureaucracy. I've personally run into more than a few here in Tampa who might be more suited to solitary work than interacting with the people who pay their salaries. The way that I deal with these often uncooperative clerks or inspectors, some of whom work in code enforcement agencies, is to let them know right upfront in no uncertain terms that I am not about to put up with any of their crap. I am a straight-shooter, who doesn't try to bullspit my way through life. So when I encounter a public servant with a bad attitude, who gives me the run around, I go straight to the top of the organization and have a little chat with the head honcho. After I make my expectations of customer service absolutely crystal clear, I usually never experience any more rude behavior.

Two Types of Condemned Property Owners

When buying condemned properties, you're most likely to encounter the following two types of owners:

1. *Burned-out owners:* Generally people, who've finally grown tired of fighting a losing battle with their local code enforcement agency and have thrown in the towel. And now they just want the legal hassle with "city hall" to go away as soon as possible.

2. *Absentee owners or out-of-town owners:* Usually inherited the property or who don't have the time, money, or desire to make the repairs that are needed to correct the code violations and bring their property into compliance. In many cases, they want to unload the property in order to stop having to deal with the code enforcement board.

How to Contact the Owners of Condemned Properties

The most effective way that I've found, to contact the owners of condemned properties, is to send them a letter, like Form 8.1. As you can see from reading my letter, I don't beat around the bush. I keep it short, sweet, and right to the point. I tell property owners who I am, what I do, and how I can help them, without going on about what a swell guy I am and how I feel their pain during their hour of need.

To keep track of the condemned properties that you're pursuing, use a condemned property tracking worksheet, like Form 8.2.

FORM 8.1 Sample Letter to Condemned Property Owners

June 10, 2006

Leona P. Throckmorton
379 Crestview Avenue
Tampa, FL 33647

Dear Ms. Throckmorton,

My name is Thomas J. Lucier, and I specialize in buying properties that have been condemned for code violations by the City of Tampa.

I am writing to you today about the property that you own at 3108 Porter Lane that has been condemned by the City of Tampa for code violations.

If you're interested in selling your property, please call me at (813) 237-6267 or send me an e-mail message at tjlucier@tampabay.rr.com.

If we are able to agree on a sale price and terms for your property, I will be able to close on the purchase of your property within five business days or less, depending on your particular circumstances.

I promise not to waste your valuable time with games, gimmicks, or bullspit.

The sooner you contact me; the sooner I'll be able to help you get the City of Tampa off your back and stop the stress, aggravation, and legal hassle that you're going through.

Sincerely,

Thomas J. Lucier

Copyright Thomas J. Lucier, 2006. To customize this document, download it from www.thomaslucier .com/realestateforms.html. The document can then be opened, edited, and printed using Microsoft Word.

FORM 8.2 Sample Condemned Property Tracking Worksheet

Property's street address: _____

Property appraiser or assessor's folio or parcel number: _____

Property's tax assessed value: $_____

Owner's name: _____

Owner's mailing address: _____

Code enforcement case number: _____

Date property must be demolished and removed: _____

Date letter was mailed to property owner: _____

How to Verify a Condemned Property's Code Violations

The very first thing that you must do, before you ever meet with the owner of a condemned property, is to verify the property's code violations directly with your local code enforcement agency. For example, before I ever meet with the owner of a condemned property, I first go the Tampa Department of Code Enforcement and review the department's file on the property. Then I call the code enforcement supervisor, who's responsible for the area where the property is located to find out the bare minimum that needs to be done in order to bring the property into compliance. This way, I get the information straight from the horse's mouth, and I find out exactly what needs to be done to the property to bring it up to code. Once I have this information, I can come up with a rough cost estimate, so that there are no surprises later on down the road.

I Specialize in Single-Family Houses That Have Been Condemned for Demolition

Don't expect to find condemned houses in swanky neighborhoods. It has been my experience that most houses, which have been condemned for demolition, are located in older run-down neighborhoods, which are usually going through a transition, where local governments are helping to turn the neighborhood around. I focus on wooden single-family houses that have been condemned for demolition and are located on lots, which are hooked up to municipal water and sewer lines. Once I find a condemned house that meets my acquisition criteria, I use the city's condemnation order to negotiate a bargain basement purchase price with the owner. I like wooden houses because they can be can be easily and inexpensively demolished and removed from a lot. Plus, lots that already have utilities in place appeal to home builders, who don't want to pay costly impact fees. So once a house is demolished and the lot is cleared off, I market it to all of the home builders in Tampa, who specialize in building low-income housing.

I Also Buy Vacant Lots That Have Been Cited for Code Violations

In addition to buying single-family houses that have been condemned for demolition, I also buy vacant lots that have been cited for numerous code violations. These are lots that are large enough to build a single-family house on, but they're overgrown with vegetation and underbrush and littered with junk, trash, debris, rubble, discarded household furnishings, and appliances that have been dumped there illegally. And luckily for me, this is a real turnoff to most other investors, who are scared off by the thought of having to deal with the city to get the lot cleaned up. On the last lot that I bought, it took three large dump truck loads, to haul off all the junk and trash that had been dumped on the lot. But it was worth it, when I resold the lot a month later to a home builder for a $20,000 profit.

CHAPTER 9

How You Can Earn Tax-Free Income for the Rest of Your Life as a Serial Home Buyer

I am absolutely astonished whenever I meet a real estate investor or home owner who's unaware of the federal capital gains tax exclusion—which can be applied to the sale of a taxpayer's principal residence—that was granted to home owners under the Taxpayer Relief Act of 1997. As far as I am concerned, the home sale tax exclusion is the single best, wealth-building opportunity that's ever been made available to the average American. That's because under Section 121 of the Internal Revenue Code, a single home owner can exclude up to $250,000 from the sale of their principal residence from capital gains tax, and a married couple, filing a joint tax return, can exempt up to $500,000. The only requirement is that a home owner must have owned and occupied the home for a total of 24 out of 60 months prior to the sale. Best of all, home owners can use this home sale tax exclusion, every two years. This means that a serial home owner could live off of the proceeds from the sale of their principal residence every two years and legally never pay another penny in federal taxes. That's right. You read it correctly, and when I say no federal taxes, I mean the whole kit and caboodle: income tax, social security tax, and Medicare tax. If you live in Alaska, Florida, Nevada, South Dakota, Texas, Washington, or Wyoming—states that have no personal income tax—your tax obligation would be limited to sales and property taxes. New Hampshire and Tennessee tax only dividend and interest income. New Hampshire doesn't have a sales tax, so the only tax that would have to be paid is property taxes. Hopefully, by now, you can start to comprehend the wealth-building power that this perfectly legal tax shelter affords all home owners in America who know how to take full advantage of it. The capital gains tax exclusion on the sale of a principal residence is explained in Internal Revenue Service (IRS) Publication 523: Selling Your Home, and it can be downloaded from the following web site: www.irs.gov/pub/irs-pdf/p523.pdf.

Capital Gains Tax Exclusion Rules Available Online

The Taxpayer Relief Act of 1997 has been amended over the years by the following rules, which are available online:

Treasury Decision 9030: www.irs.gov/pub/irs-regs/td9030.pdf

Treasury Decision 9031: www.irs.gov/pub/irs-regs/td9031.pdf

Treasury Decision 9152: http://www.irs.gov/pub/irs-regs/td_9152.pdf

Why Being a Serial Home Buyer May Be the Ideal Real Estate Investment Strategy

To me, the capital gains tax exclusion, which was granted to taxpayers under the Taxpayer Relief Act of 1997, has made home ownership the safest and most profitable real estate investment opportunity available in America today. Think about it for a minute, the easiest and most inexpensive piece of property in America to finance, insure, maintain, and sell is an owner-occupied, single-family home. As a serial home buyer, you'll never wake up at night, in a cold sweat, worrying about tenants or vandals destroying your property or how you're going to come up with the loan payment for a vacant rental property. You alone will be in total control of your investment property—your home—24 hours a day, 7 days a week. To top it all off, as a serial home buyer, you'll have the opportunity to earn between $250,000 and $500,000 of tax-free income every two years, simply by selling your principal residence. In addition, thrifty home owners have the opportunity to amass a sizable savings account in a relatively short period of time. For example, if you were able to buy and sell a home every 2 years for a 10-year period, and you saved $50,000

from each sale, you would wind up with $250,000 in the bank ($50,000 ×
5 = $250,000). And $250,000 is a lot of dough by anyone's standards. I
challenge anyone reading this book to show me a real estate investment
strategy that has the safety and wealth-building potential of the serial
home buyer strategy.

Five Types of Properties That Qualify as a Principal Residence

The following five types of properties qualify as a principal residence for
tax purposes:

1. House.
2. Houseboat.
3. Mobile home.
4. Cooperative apartment.
5. Condominium.

Six Factors the IRS Considers When Determining a Home Owner's Principal Residence

When a taxpayer owns multiple homes, the IRS considers the following
six factors to determine which home is their principal residence for tax
purposes:

1. Location of the home owner's principal residence.
2. Location of the home owner's place of employment.
3. Mailing address used by the home owner for bills and correspondence.
4. Address listed on the home owner's federal and state tax returns, driver's license, automobile registration, and voter registration card.
5. Location of the home owner's bank.
6. Location of any recreational clubs or religious organizations that the
   home owner is a member of.

The Title to a Home Owner's Principal Residence Can Be Held in a Trust

The title to a principal residence can be held in a trust, provided that the trust was established by a home owner (known as the trustor or grantor) for their own benefit. The sale of a principal residence held in a trust is treated for capital gains tax purposes, as though it was made by the home owner.

Married Couples Can Earn Up to $500,000 Tax-Free Every Two Years

Married couples who file a joint income tax return can exclude up to $500,000 of capital gains tax from the sale of their principal residence provided they have:

1. Owned the home for two years.
2. Used the home as their principal residence for two years.
3. Not claimed the capital gains tax exclusion from the sale of another home within the past two years.

Please note that if either spouse doesn't meet all three of the requirements listed previously, the maximum exclusion that can be claimed by a married couple is the total of the maximum exclusions that each spouse would qualify for if they weren't married and the amounts were figured separately. For this purpose, each spouse is treated as owning the property, during the same period that either spouse owned the property.

Single and Joint Home Owners Can Earn $250,000 Tax-Free Every Two Years

A single home owner, or two people who own a home jointly, and file separate income tax returns can each exclude up to $250,000 of capital gains tax from the sale of their principal residence every two years, provided they have:

1. Owned the home for two years.
2. Used the home as their principal residence for two years.
3. Not claimed the capital gains tax exclusion from the sale of another home within the past two years.

How the Military Family Tax Relief Act of 2003 Effects Home Owners

Under the Military Family Tax Relief Act of 2003, home owners who are members of the Armed Forces or Foreign Service of the United States serving on qualified official extended duty for a period of more than 90 days, or indefinitely, and who are ordered to serve at a duty station, which is at least 50 miles from their principal residence, or to live in government quarters may elect to suspend, for up to 10 years of such duty time, the running of the five-year ownership-and-use period before the sale of their principal residence.

Home Owners Must Meet Ownership-and-Use Tests to Claim Maximum Exclusion

In order to claim the maximum capital gains tax exclusion, a home owner must meet the following ownership-and-use tests, during a five-year period from the date of sale:

1. Owned the home for two years during a five-year period.
2. Used the home as their principal residence for two years during a five-year period.

Please note that home owners don't have to live in a home for 24 continuous months in order to meet the use test. They just have to live in the home for a total of 24 months during a five-year period.

Partial Exclusion Is Available for Home Owners with "Unforeseen Circumstances"

The IRS will waive, on a case-by-case basis, the two-year use test and allow a home to qualify as a principal residence if the home owner owned and occupied the home for less than 24 months but had to sell their residence due to "unforeseen circumstances" such as:

1. Death.
2. Divorce or legal separation.
3. Ineligibility for unemployment compensation.
4. A change in employment that leaves the taxpayer unable to pay the mortgage or reasonable basic living expenses.
5. Multiple births resulting from the same pregnancy.
6. Damage to the residence resulting from a natural or manmade disaster, or an act of war or terrorism.
7. Condemnation, seizure, or other involuntary conversion of the property.

The amount of capital gains tax that can be excluded is based on how many months the home owner lived in their principal residence during a 24-month period. For example, if a single home owner lived in their home for 18 months, they could exempt 75 percent of the $250,000 maximum exclusion allowed, which would be $ 187,500 ($250,000 × .75 = $187,500).

There Is No Requirement to Report Tax Exempt Home Sales to the IRS

Under Section 121 of the Internal Revenue Code, there's no requirement for a home owner to report the sale of a principal residence that's excluded from capitals gains tax to the IRS. However, when a home owner's capital gain from the sale of their residence exceeds the $250,000 or $500,000 maximum exclusion, it must be reported on Schedule D of the home owner's federal income tax return.

Convert Rental Houses into Your Personal Residence

Another way that you can use the serial home buyer strategy is to buy rental houses and move into one every two years and convert it into your personal residence. This way, you can move from house to house every two years, without losing any time between sales. In the meantime, the rental houses will generate income, appreciate in value, and help shelter your ordinary income from federal income tax. However, you'll have to pay federal income tax on the recaptured depreciation that was deducted while the house was used as a rental property.

Use Real Estate Options to Keep Houses in the Pipeline for Future Purchase

In the very near future, my wife Barbara and I are going to start using the serial home buyer strategy. Before we sell our present home, I am first going to buy a one-year option to purchase an undervalued house at a fixed price. This way, I'll already have a house in the pipeline that I can purchase and move into right before I close on the sale of my present home. And the two-year ownership-and-use meter will start running for our new home the day after our present home is sold. This means that we won't be wasting any time between houses, which will allow us to sell and buy a principal residence every two years and take full advantage of the capital gains tax exclusion.

How Real Estate Options Work

A real estate option grants the party owning the option (the optionee) the exclusive, unrestricted, and irrevocable right to purchase the property under option from the party selling the option (the optionor) during the specified period of time for which the real estate option is in effect. A real estate option transaction consists of the following seven key elements:

1. *Optionee:* The name given to the party buying a real estate option. Once a real estate option is exercised, the optionee becomes the buyer.
2. *Optionor:* The name given to the party selling a real estate option. Once a real estate option is exercised, the optionor becomes the seller.

3. *Real estate option agreement:* Gives the optionee the exclusive, unrestricted, and irrevocable right and option to purchase the property under option, at a fixed purchase price, within a specified option period.

4. *Option consideration:* The amount of money paid by an optionee to buy a real estate option from an optionor.

5. *Option period:* The specific period of time stated in the real estate option agreement, during which the option is in effect.

6. *Exercise of option:* Occurs when the optionee notifies the optionor in writing that he or she is going to exercise his or her real estate option and purchase the property under option.

7. *Expiration of option:* A real estate option expires when an optionee fails to exercise his or her real estate option within the option period that's stated in the real estate option agreement.

You can learn everything you need to know about real estate options, by reading my book, *How to Make Money with Real Estate Options*, which can be purchased from my web site: www.thomaslucier.com.

Best to Buy Undervalued Homes with Upside Potential

If I were you, I would stay away from trophy-type homes in pristine condition. Instead, I would buy undervalued homes, with what's known in the business as "upside potential." Upside potential is just a fancy way of saying that a property has room for improvement, which can result in an increase in its resale value. At a minimum, I would buy a structurally sound three-bedroom, two-bathroom home, with an attached two-car garage and a fenced-in backyard, which is in need of paint, landscaping, new appliances, countertops, cabinet hardware, floor coverings, window treatments, bathroom fixtures, light fixtures, door hardware, or other cosmetic upgrades. These are the type of houses that are in, what I refer to as, a "used and bruised" condition, which can be inexpensively and quickly corrected, by giving a home a cosmetic facelift. And when you buy these types of homes, you'll have an opportunity to realize do-it-yourself appreciation from upgrading the home, market-wide appreciation from an overall increase in property values, and exclusion from paying $250,000 to $500,000 in capital gains tax.

However, if I were you, I would avoid buying homes that require costly and time-consuming repairs, which are hidden in walls, under floors, and in attics. In other words, don't buy homes in need of new wiring, plumbing, and heating and air conditioning ducts. They add zero to a home's curb appeal and very little to its overall resale value. That's because when someone buys a home, they expect that basic stuff—like a home's electrical, plumbing, and heating and air conditioning systems—to be in good working condition and they're not willing to pay extra for it.

The Serial Home Buyer Strategy Requires Planning, Organization, and Teamwork

The serial home buyer strategy that I've outlined in this chapter, requires planning, organization, and teamwork. Let's face it, packing up and moving every two years can be chaotic and extremely stressful if the move isn't well planned out and organized. It also takes planning and organization to make certain that each sale of your principal residence meets the IRS ownership-and-use tests and to find another home to buy, so you don't lose any time between homes sales. But most important, this strategy requires teamwork between married couples and joint owners, so that everyone pulls his or her fair share of the load. I am telling you this because there are few things in life that can be more stressful than packing up all of your worldly possessions and moving them to another home. The last thing that you need to deal with during a move is an uncooperative spouse or joint owner, who's dragging their feet and fighting you every inch of the way. So do yourself a huge favor and make certain that you and your spouse, or joint owner, are all on the same page before you decide that the serial home buyer strategy is right for you.

CHAPTER 10

How to Profit from Problem Properties That Scare Off Most Investors

As a real estate investor, I don't like competition. The way I see it, too many investors chasing the same type of property have a tendency to drive up prices and make it more difficult to find profitable deals, which in turn makes it that much harder for people, like me, to bring home the bacon and maintain a decent lifestyle. But luckily for real estate investors like me, opportunities are often disguised as problems, which, for whatever reasons, most investors are unwilling or unable to solve. And that's exactly why I seek out properties with problems that scare off most of my competitors, who, for the most part, are individual real estate investors like me. I do this by focusing on properties with correctable problems that appear, to most investors, to be much more complicated than they really are. This misperception of how difficult the problem is to solve usually intimidates most real estate investors. That's probably because, a lot of times, inexperienced investors have a tendency to come up with a solution that is much worse than the actual problem that they're trying to solve. I've found that most so-called traditional real estate investors are usually scared off by properties, which have:

1. Title problems that cloud a property's title and prevent the owner from having a clear and marketable title.
2. Structural problems resulting from wear and aging, or damage done by sinkholes and earthquakes that cause building foundations to crack and sink.
3. Stigma problems that affect properties, which have been the scene of various types of crimes or are located in close proximity to various

nuisances such as sewage treatments plants, hazardous waste materials, halfway houses for criminals, and group homes for sex offenders.

4. Property damage problems caused by man-made disasters such as wild fires and natural disasters like hurricanes, tornadoes, floods, and earthquakes.

I realize that some of you reading this may wonder why problem property owners don't correct the problem and turn around and sell the property themselves or list the property for sale through a real estate broker. But it has been my experience that most owners don't have the money, knowledge, time, or desire to solve their own problem property woes. The few owners who do attempt to sell their problem properties themselves usually do a pretty lousy job of marketing and end up with no takers. Plus, nowadays, most real estate brokers are very reluctant to list any type of problem property out of fear that the buyer will come back and sue them after the sale, and they'll somehow be found liable for wrongdoing.

Definition of a So-Called Problem Property

To me, a so-called problem property is any property that has problems that are a direct result of neglect, mistakes and oversights, man-made waste, government regulations, political decisions, legal decisions, criminal activity, and natural and man-made disasters.

The Most Important Advice in This Entire Chapter

If you don't get anything else from this chapter, please make certain that you at least get this: Not all property problems are correctable. That's why, in order to be a successful problem property investor, it's imperative that you know the difference between correctable and uncorrectable property problems. For example, almost all property title problems can be corrected by a knowledgeable real estate attorney or land title professional. But a building with a major flaw, which affects its structural integrity and can't be repaired, isn't the type of problem property that you would want to tackle. Case in point: When I was young and dumb, I almost made the financially fatal mistake of buying a small concrete block commercial building that had a badly sagging flat roof, which I initially thought would be a piece of cake to fix. But luckily, I had a friend who was a Florida licensed general contractor, and he told me to check the building's exterior walls for cracks and signs of movement, which could be caused by pressure from the sagging roof. Sure enough, on thorough inspection, I found numerous cracks in the walls and noticed that two of the side walls were actually starting to tilt toward the inside of the building. This meant that the whole roof would have to be removed in order to replace the cracked blocks and plumb all of the walls. At this point, I realized that it would probably be cheaper to demolish the building and rebuild it from scratch. So I did the smart thing and passed on buying the property.

Ninety-Nine Percent of Problem Solving Is Knowing Where to Look for Solutions

The old saying among problem property investors of "solve a problem, earn a profit" best describes this business. Over the past 26 years, I've learned how to quickly get to the root cause of a problem and then use good old-fashioned Yankee ingenuity to come up with a relatively fast and inexpensive way to solve it. As far as I am concerned, 99 percent of problem solving is in knowing where to look for solutions and which questions to ask. In other words, you must know where to look to find the information that contains solutions to your problem, and then you need to know the specific questions that must be answered to find the most efficient way to solve the problem. Today, thanks to the Internet, in almost all cases, the specialized knowledge that's needed to solve most property problems is available online and relatively easy to find. For example, when I first entertained the idea of possibly buying properties with indoor mold problems, I typed the term *indoor mold* into the Yahoo search engine and it came back with over 250,000 results for indoor mold. From my Internet search, I was able to gather all of the information that I needed from reliable sources in order to make an informed decision. Another time, I was doing research on a single-family house that had recently been home to more than 50 cats and reeked with the pungent smell of cat urine. Through a Google search, I was able to find out exactly how to permanently eliminate the odor of cat urine from the building.

The Most Efficient Ways to Find Problem Properties

The four most efficient ways that I've found to locate problem properties are:

1. Driving through residential neighborhoods and commercial and industrial areas.
2. Placing "property wanted" ads in newspapers.
3. Searching public records.
4. Keeping abreast of the local news.

How to Contact Problem Property Owners

Once I find, what looks to me, to be a problem property, I send the owner a letter, like Form 10.1, which tells them that I buy properties with certain types of problems and how to contact me, if they're interested in selling.

Properties with Clouded Titles

A property's title is clouded, when there's a claim or encumbrance recorded against it, which prevents the owner from having what is called a "clear and marketable title" to the property. The problem with having a clouded title is that title insurance companies will never issue a title insurance policy that insures against a cloud on a property's title. Instead, they will issue a title policy that lists the cloud as an exception to the policy, which means that the so-called exception clouding the title isn't covered by the policy. The most common types of problems that cloud a property's title are:

1. Failure of a previous owner to obtain and record a satisfaction of mortgage or deed of trust or lien at the time a loan or lien was paid off.
2. Missing heirs that must be located in order to sign the deed and transfer the title to the property.
3. Judgment liens recorded against the property's title and the lien holders can't be located in order to pay off the lien.
4. Multiple parties claiming ownership of a property by recording quit-claim deeds.

FORM 10.1 Sample Letter to Problem Property Owners

August 28, 2006

Mr. Walter D. Hodges
2450 Palmer Avenue
Tampa, FL 33629

Dear Mr. Hodges,

My name is Thomas J. Lucier, and I specialize in buying properties in the Tampa Bay Area that have problems with:

1. Clouded titles.

2. Hazardous waste.

3. Contamination.

4. Indoor mold.

5. Termite damage.

6. Structural defects.

7. Storm damage.

8. Stigmas.

If your property is currently experiencing this type of problem and you're interested in selling, please feel free to call me any time at (813) 237-6267 or e-mail me at tjlucier@tampabay.rr.com to discuss your situation.

If your property fits my needs and we are able to agree on a sale price and terms, I will be able to close on the purchase within five business days or less, depending on your particular circumstances.

I promise not to waste your valuable time with games, gimmicks, and bullspit.

I look forward to hearing from you soon and to helping you solve your property problems.

Sincerely,

Thomas J. Lucier

Copyright Thomas J. Lucier, 2006. To customize this document, download it from www.thomaslucier .com/realestateforms.html. The document can then be opened, edited, and printed using Microsoft Word.

5. Unsettled property boundary disputes involving flawed surveys.

6. A flawed foreclosure action that failed to properly extinguish all liens recorded against the property's title at the time of the foreclosure sale.

7. Mistakes in recorded documents, such as divorce decrees and wills, which didn't totally extinguish ownership rights.

8. Liens placed against a property's title for work, materials, or taxes that haven't been paid in full.

I use small classified ads, like the one below, which I run in newspapers to locate properties with title problems:

> I Buy Properties with Title Problems
> Call (813) 237-6267 Today

Once I find a property, the very first thing that I do is to hire an experienced professional title abstractor or researcher to do a title search at the public records library in the county where the property's title is recorded. Once I receive the property's title report, I send it to my real estate attorney who reviews it and gives me his opinion as to the cost and amount of time that it'll take to clear the cloud from the property's title. If it makes financial sense, I buy the property at a discounted price and have my attorney file a quiet title lawsuit in which all the parties claiming an interest in the property are named as defendants. At the same time, the required legal notices are published in the court's paper of record to give the public notice of the lawsuit. For example, in Florida, it can take anywhere from three to six months to complete a quiet title action. After all of the statutory procedures involved in a quiet title action have been completed, the judge hearing the case will make a decision based on the evidence presented by both parties. If the lawsuit is decided in the plaintiff's favor, the judge will order that a final judgment be issued that removes the cloud from the property's title.

Properties Damaged and Destroyed by Natural and Man-Made Disasters

After every man-made and natural disaster, there's always a segment of the population, especially in the areas that have been the hardest hit that throw in the towel and take their insurance money and run. Property owners who have been reimbursed by their insurer for their loss but, for whatever reason, have no desire to rebuild are the owners who are most likely to sell their damaged or destroyed property at a substantial discount. The investors that I know who specialize in these types of properties usually wait at least six months before they approach any property owners. They do this for three very good reasons: First, they don't want to be perceived by property owners as the usual vultures, who generally show up right after any type of disaster and try and buy property for a small fraction of its value. Second, they want to give property owners time to have their insurance claims settled and make a decision as to whether they're going to rebuild or pull up stakes and move on. And third, by the time they come around, the recovery is underway and it's pretty easy to identify the property owners who are most likely to sell them their property just by driving around the area. That's because any property that's not in the process of being rebuilt is an obvious candidate for purchase. Once they purchase a destroyed property, they have the lot cleared of all the remaining rubble and market the property to local home builders. Lots with existing utility hookups appeal to home builders because they are ready to build on, and they avoid having to pay impact fees to local government agencies.

Stigmatized Properties

In every real estate market nationwide, there are properties that have various types of stigmas attached to them, which negatively effect the public's overall perception of the property and subsequently its marketability and resale value. A stigmatized property is generally defined as: *A property that has been psychologically impacted by an event, which occurred or was suspected to have occurred on the property, such event being one that has no physical impact of any kind.* Most stigmatized properties are in flawless physical condition, but because of intangible or psychological stigmas, which are based on individual personal perceptions, they've become tainted, due to the fact that they were the site of murders, HIV-related deaths, rapes, suicides, robberies, kidnappings, child molestations, and accidental deaths or they're believed to be haunted by ghosts. Or a property can have what's known in the business as tangible or real stigmas, which are the result of a property being located in an area, which is:

1. Known for building defects.
2. Infested with gangs of criminals.
3. Next to a halfway house for soon-to-be-released criminals.
4. Bordering a group home for sex offenders.
5. Close to hazardous waste material.
6. Near a landfill, slaughterhouse, pig farm, sewage treatment plant, or other nuisance-type property.

Because of their history, stigmatized properties often scare away prospective buyers who are worried about decreases in property values and marketability. Today, many states have stigmatized property statutes that require property owners to disclose certain types of stigmas, which are part of a property's history. You can find stigmatized properties by reading police reports and by following the local news through reading newspapers and watching and listening to news broadcasts on television and radio.

Properties Damaged by Sinkholes

Sinkholes, which are common in Florida, develop when underground limestone is dissolved by acidic rainwater and forms cavities or hollow spaces, which eventually cause the overlying earth to collapse into them. When this happens, any building on or near a sinkhole begins to subside or settle, which usually causes damage to the building's foundation. What typically happens is that the owner of a sinkhole property receives a settlement from their insurance company, which is used to pay off any existing mortgage loans. Once the loans are paid off, the owner sells the property to an investor, who specializes in sinkhole properties. Investors find sinkhole properties by placing classified ads in newspapers, like the following sample copy, and by canvassing neighborhoods where sinkholes have developed in the past:

> I Buy Houses with Sinkhole Damage
> Call (813) 237-6267 Today

Sinkhole properties can be bought for 20 to 30 percent of their previous market value before the sinkhole was discovered. The two investors that I know who specialize in sinkhole properties hire a licensed geotechnical engineer, who analyzes a sinkhole property and then comes up with a plan to repair and stabilize it. Then they hire a properly licensed engineering company that specializes in repairing and stabilizing sinkhole properties. Sinkhole properties are stabilized by injecting cement grout slurry into the soil under the building and by the use of steel underpinnings that are attached to the property's foundation and the solid rock below the foundation. The investors that I know have the repairs supervised by the same engineer, who came up with the original repair plan. Once the job is completed, the engineer issues a detailed engineering report, which outlines all of the measures that were taken to repair and stabilize the building from further sinkhole damage. This is the equivalent of the property being given a clean bill of heath for insurance and financing purposes. I've been told by both investors, who are on the up-and-up that their engineering reports, which they show to prospective buyers, to document repairs made to the property, are great sales tools. They point out (and rightfully so) that a house that has been properly stabilized against further sinkhole damage is much safer than other houses, which haven't been affected by sinkhole damage but could be at any time in the future. Information on Florida sinkholes is available at the following web site: www.dep.state.fl.us/geology /geologictopics/sinkhole.htm.

Buildings Formerly Used as Methamphetamine Laboratories

Methamphetamine addiction is an ever-growing problem in many parts of the United States. According to the U.S. Drug Enforcement Administration (DEA), methamphetamine is an amphetamine, commonly referred to as speed, which can keep users up for days on end and is supposed to be much more addictive than crack cocaine. Building interiors become contaminated during the methamphetamine manufacturing process when chemicals are cooked, which produces vapors that are absorbed by walls, doors, windows and window coverings, ceilings, floor coverings and furniture, and appliances. Contamination also occurs when chemicals and other supplies are spilled inside the building and on the surrounding grounds. I know an investor in Lakeland, Florida, who specializes in buying properties in central Florida that have been used as laboratories to manufacture illegal methamphetamine. He gets his property leads from arrest reports that are posted online by local and county law enforcement agencies throughout central Florida. In most cases, these are rental properties, which belong to owners who don't have the money and expertise to clean up a building that has been contaminated by the chemicals used to manufacture methamphetamine. This guy is a real professional, who can turn a contaminated property around in 15 days or less. And just as soon as a property is cleaned up and certified as being fit for human habitation, he resells it. This guy claims to be averaging a deal a month with an average profit of $15,000 per property. The State of Colorado has published an extensive guide on how to clean up former methamphetamine laboratories, which can be downloaded from the following web site: www.cdphe.state.co.us/hm/methlab.pdf.

Properties with Correctable Structural Defects

In many cases, structural defects are the result of wear and aging, or damage caused by acts of nature, which have affected the structural integrity of a building. For example, in Tampa and Hillsborough County, there are a lot of older houses that have post and pier foundations, which were built on sandy soil that has settled over the years. This has resulted in a lot of houses that now have uneven and sloping floors. A post and pier foundation is made up of a series of wooden posts that support the perimeter and main beams that the floor joists rest on. The posts are set on individual concrete piers to keep the posts from sinking into the ground. I know of two investors in my county that specialize in properties with post and pier foundation problems. To locate properties with foundation problems, they place ads, like the following sample copy, in local newspapers:

> I Buy Houses with Foundation Problems
> Call (813) 237-6267 Today

Once they find a property with a foundation problem that can be fixed by jacking up the building and replacing the rotted posts and sunken piers, they buy it and hire a licensed contractor, who specializes in foundation repairs, to level the floors.

Properties with Indoor Mold Problems

Thanks to mold-chasing attorneys, who view indoor mold as the second coming of asbestos, and the mass media, which blows everything way out of proportion, the public perception surrounding indoor mold is such that even the suspicion that a building has just a smidgen of indoor mold is usually enough to strike fear into the hearts of most prospective buyers and stop them from pursuing the property. The fact of the matter is that probably every residential property in the United States contains a small amount of indoor mold, especially in bathrooms. But I have no qualms about buying a property with a moderate amount of indoor mold. I am not afraid of indoor mold because I understand what causes it to grow and how to quickly clean it up and stop it from reoccurring. Over the years, I've bought single-family houses and small rental properties in which all of the walls and ceilings in the bathrooms were pitch black with indoor mold. I find properties with mold problems, by placing small classified ads, like the following sample ad, in daily and weekly newspapers:

> I Buy Properties with Mold Problems
> Call (813) 237-6267 Today

The very first thing that I do after I buy a property with indoor mold contamination is to remove all of the moldy drywall and insulation and clean the mold from all the surfaces behind the walls and ceilings in accordance with established mold remediation procedures. Once the mold is cleaned up, I replace any studs or ceiling joist that are beyond cleaning, insulate the walls and ceilings, and then I hang drywall on the walls and ceilings. Georgia-Pacific makes a "mold-resistant drywall" called *Dens-Armor® Plus Interior Wallboard* that's sold at Home Depot and Lowe's home improvement centers. This drywall has a fiberglass surface instead of the paper facing that's on regular drywall where mold grows. To learn more about mold-resistant drywall, log onto the following web site: www .stopfeedingmold.com. You can get all of the nitty-gritty details about indoor mold by logging onto the following web site: www.epa.gov/iaq /molds/moldresources.html.

How You Can Make Money by Providing Residential Rental Housing to Underserved Tenants

Over the past six years, low interest rates, lax loan underwriting standards, and nothing-down loans have made more Americans home owners than at any previous time in our nation's history. This increase in home ownership has had an adverse effect on residential rental housing markets nationwide. That's because all of the large real estate investment trusts (REITS) and corporations that own most of the large apartment complexes nationwide are targeting their marketing toward the same group of tenants. As a result of a shrinking pool of tenants to draw from, they're lowering their tenant qualification standards, cutting monthly rental rates, and making numerous concessions in order to attract and retain tenants. However, right now, in most rental markets nationwide, there are three groups of tenants who are being underserved. That's because most landlords view these groups of tenants as being more of a problem to deal with, so they make no real effort to attract them. But when properly screened, people in these groups make excellent tenants, who aren't likely to pick up and move every year as most other tenants do. The three groups of underserved and overlooked tenants are:

1. Tenants with physical disabilities.
2. Tenants with pets.
3. Retired, low-income, single, or married tenants who are 55 years of age and older and receive government rental assistance.

Provide Rental Housing to Tenants with Physical Disabilities

The U.S. Census Bureau claims that one-fifth of all Americans, who are at least five-years of age, are disabled. According to the Census Bureau, the population of the United States is currently estimated to be 300 million people, which means that roughly 60 million people in America are mentally or physically disabled. To me, 60 million people, represent a pretty sizable pool of potential tenants who aren't being catered to by the mega-landlords of America. Let me put it to you this way, how many times have you seen ads in your local Sunday newspaper that read, "Physically Disabled Tenants Wanted?" I am willing to step out on a limb and say, "never." And this very obvious lack of competition is exactly why renting to physically disabled tenants makes financial sense. I recommend that you do what I've done and rent to tenants, who have physical disabilities that require the use of wheelchairs to get around, but still have the full use of their arms. This way, a standard bathroom can usually be modified for use by a disabled tenant by widening the door opening and installing a pocket door, lowering the vanity, removing the cabinet under the sink, and adding handrails and grab bars, which allow the tenant to use the toilet and bathtub or shower. In most cases, a rental property can be made accessible to disabled tenants who have full use of their arms but are confined to a wheelchair by:

1. Installing wheelchair ramps at the front- and rear-entry doors.
2. Widening all door openings to 36 inches.
3. Lowering light switches and thermostats.
4. Lowering kitchen cabinets, countertops, and sinks.
5. Installing handrails and grab bars in bathrooms.
6. Lowering bathroom vanities and sinks.
7. Removing the cabinets under kitchen and bathroom sinks.

The cost of making a rental property accessible to the disabled will depend on the type of property that's being modified and who's doing the work. For example, a single-family house will cost more than a multifamily rental unit. If you can't make the alterations yourself, you'll have to hire a contractor to do it for you, which could set you back several thousand dollars.

The good news is that most physically disabled tenants are covered by various types of government programs that offer financial assistance to cover the cost of making a rental unit accessible, which can be used to reimburse property owners. And the cost of making a rental unit accessible to disabled tenants can be written off for tax purposes as a capital improvement.

The Definition of Disabled

The Americans with Disabilities Act (ADA) defines an individual with a disability as: *A person, who has a physical or mental impairment that substantially limits one or more major life activities, has a record of such impairment, or is regarded as having such impairment.*

The Americans with Disabilities Act (ADA) Standards for Accessible Design

Although private landlords who own rental properties that don't receive government assistance aren't required to follow the Americans with Disabilities Act (ADA) Standards for Accessible Design, when making an existing rental property accessible to disabled tenants, I suggest that you use them as a guide. The ADA Standards for Accessible Design are available online at the following web site: www.usdoj.gov/crt/ada/reg3a .html#Anchor-17431.

Information on Accessible Housing for the Disabled Available Online

Information on accessibility for the disabled is available at the following web sites:

1. Access Board: www.access-board.gov
2. Accessible Housing Resource Center: www.abledata.com

3. Fair Housing Accessibility Guidelines: www.hud.gov/library /bookshelf09/fhefhag.cfm

4. The National Accessible Apartment Clearinghouse: www.forrent.com /naac

How to Find Physically Disabled Tenants

The best way that I know to find physically disabled tenants is to contact all of the government agencies and private organization in your area that are involved in providing services to the physically disabled, including:

1. City, county, state, and federal agencies that provide services to the disabled.
2. Physical rehabilitation centers.
3. Department of Veterans Affairs hospitals and outpatient centers.
4. Military hospitals.

Provide Rental Housing to Responsible Pet Owners

There are millions of tenants in America who are pet owners or who want to be pet owners. But because of liability concerns and other reasons, many landlords flatly refuse to rent to pet owners. A lack of rental housing that allows tenants to keep pets has put pet-friendly landlords in the driver's seat, when it comes to choosing which pets to allow and how much to charge tenants for the privilege of letting Rover live with them. I suggest that you limit your tenants' pets to nonaggressive breeds of dogs and cats and avoid renting to tenants, who have exotic pets such as boa constrictors and potbellied pigs. The key to being a profitable pet-friendly landlord is to only rent to tenants, who are responsible pet owners. And the only way to determine if a tenant is a responsible pet owner is to screen their pets by using a pet application like Form 11.1. Once I accept a tenant's pet, I require a refundable $300 pet deposit, and I charge them an additional $50 to $75 a month in rent for their pet. I use a pet agreement, like Form 11.2, which spells out exactly what the ten-

---

FORM 11.1 Sample Pet Application

Tenant's name: _____ Telephone number: _____

Type of pet: _____ Breed: _____ Sex: _____

Age: _____ Color: _____ Name: _____

Is the pet licensed? (   ) Yes (   ) No

If yes, please attach a photocopy of the license.

Is the pet housetrained? (   ) Yes (   ) No

Has the pet been spayed or neutered? (   ) Yes (   ) No

If yes, please attach a certificate of the spaying or neutering.

Is the pet current on all required vaccinations? (   ) Yes (   ) No

If yes, please attach copies of the pet's current vaccination certificates.

Has your pet ever bitten anyone? (   ) Yes (   ) No

If yes, please explain: _____

Name of the pet's veterinarian: _____ Telephone number: _____

Name of the pet's emergency caregiver: _____ Telephone number: _____

If the pet is accepted, tenant must provide proof of renter's insurance coverage at the time of signing the rental agreement. Tenants who have dogs must show proof of a renter's insurance policy that has dog bite liability coverage and that names the Landlord as an additional insured-and-loss payee in the policy.

_____   _____

Signature   Date

---

ant's responsibilities are, along with the consequences if any of the terms of the agreement are violated.

Where to Advertise Your Pet-Friendly Rental Property

The best places that I've found to advertise pet-friendly rental properties are veterinary offices, pet sitters, pet supply stores, grooming shops, boarding kennels, dog-training facilities, local chapters of the American

This Pet Agreement, known hereinafter as the Agreement, made on this first day of May 2006, between Roger P. Throckmorton, known hereinafter as the Landlord, and Sally B. Good, a single woman, known hereinafter as the Tenant. Landlord gives permission to the Tenant to keep one female Chihuahua dog, named Wiggles, known hereinafter as the Pet, at the rental premises located at unit 124, 7202 Brand Street, Tampa, Florida 33609, under the following terms and conditions:

1. Tenant agrees to pay a refundable pet deposit in the amount of $300. Landlord shall have the right to deduct the cost of repairing any damages or replacing any property damaged by the Pet.

2. Tenant agrees to pay additional rent in the amount of $75 per month for the Pet.

3. Tenant agrees to show the landlord verifiable proof that the Pet has no fleas and ticks and is properly licensed and has received all of the shots and vaccinations required by local ordinances for dogs prior to permission being granted by the Landlord to keep the Pet at the rental premises.

4. Tenant agrees to prevent the Pet from causing any disturbance, annoyance, or nuisance to other tenants, guests, or neighbors and to immediately remedy any legitimate complaints that are lodged against the Pet.

5. Tenant states that the Pet is housetrained and agrees to keep the Pet on a leash and under control and attended to at all times whenever outside of the rental premises.

6. Tenant agrees to keep the Pet and rental premises in a sanitary condition at all times and to remove the Pet's waste from the rental premises on a daily basis.

7. Tenant agrees to immediately pay upon demand, for any injuries, damages, losses, or any other expenses caused by the Pet. All damages to the rental premises, which are caused by the Pet, that exceed the $300 pet deposit, shall be paid by the Tenant at the same time the damages are repaired.

8. Tenant agrees to purchase a renter's insurance policy that provides dog bite liability coverage that names the Landlord as an additional insured-and-loss payee in the policy.

9. Tenant agrees to indemnify, hold harmless, and defend the Landlord against all liability and claims made by any person or entity for any injuries and damages caused by the Pet on the rental premises and grounds.

10. Tenant agrees that any breach of this Agreement, that isn't completely remedied by the Tenant, within twenty-four (24) hours, from receiving written notification from the Landlord, shall cause this Agreement to become null and void and the Pet must be removed from the rental premises, within twenty-four (24) hours.

Tenant hereby acknowledges that they have read this entire Agreement, understand it, agree to it, and have been given a copy of it.

IN WITNESS WHEREOF, Landlord and Tenant have signed this Agreement on the date aforesaid.

_____   _____
Landlord   Tenant
_____

Society for the Prevention of Cruelty to Animals, and the Humane Society. Here's a listing of web sites, where you can advertise your pet-friendly rental property online:

1. People with Pets: www.peoplewithpets.com
2. Pet Apartments: www.petapartments.net
3. Craigslist: www.craigslist.org/about/cities.html

Landlords Who Allow Tenants to Keep Pets Pay Higher Insurance Premiums

As I told you in Chapter 3, landlords who allow their tenants to keep pets pay higher casualty and liability insurance premiums because of the potential risks that pets pose in the eyes of insurers. The increase in insurance premiums can usually be easily offset by the additional $50 to $75 in monthly rent that landlords can charge tenants for allowing pets in their rental properties. For example, I owned a duplex and both units were rented to pet owners who each paid me $75 a month in extra rent for their pet dogs. My casualty and liability insurers ended up charging me an additional $225 annually, for insuring the dogs, but I was receiving an additional $1,800 in annual rental income ($75 × 2 = $150 × 12 = $1,800), which easily covered the $225 increase in insurance premiums.

Many Insurers Have Banned Certain Breeds of Dogs from Coverage

According to the Property Casualty Insurers Association of America, insurance companies nationwide pay out hundreds of millions of dollars a year to cover dog bite claims. As a result, many casualty and liability insurers have banned certain breeds and crossbreeds of dogs from coverage, which have a record of being overly aggressive and vicious. So before you start accepting tenants with dogs, first read your casualty and liability insurance policies to see if they exclude any breeds and crossbreeds of dogs from coverage. To reduce your insurance premium payments, do like I do and require your tenants, who have dogs, to purchase a renter's insurance policy that has dog bite liability coverage, which names you as an additional insured and loss payee in the policy. Here's a listing of some of the dogs that many insurers have refused to insure:

1. Pit bulldogs.
2. Akitas.
3. Wolf hybrids.
4. Rottweilers.
5. Chow Chows.
6. Presa Canarios.
7. Doberman pinschers.
8. German shepherds.
9. Siberian huskies.
10. Great Danes.
11. Airedales.
12. Alaskan malamutes.
13. Staffordshire bull terriers.

Provide Rental Housing to Tenants 55 Years of Age and Older

I specialize in buying residential rental properties, with two bedrooms and one bathroom (2/1), one bedroom and one bathroom (1/1), and efficiency size units. I rent the units out to married or single tenants, who are over the age of 55 and receiving government rental assistance payments. I've found that there are a lot of good people, who, for reasons beyond their control, end up broke in their "golden years," and they make excellent tenants. By renting to senior citizens over the age of 55, I can legally avoid having to rent to irresponsible parents with undisciplined children. But best of all, the tenants' monthly rental payments are electronically transferred from the local public housing authority (PHA) to my corporate bank account on the first day of every month, without fail. Thirteen months after I've purchased a property, I resell it as a turnkey operation to an armchair investor. I wait 13 months to take advantage of the long-term capital gains tax rate, which is applicable to property that has been owned for more than 12 months. This investment strategy is outlined in great detail in my book, *How to Find, Buy, and Turn Around Small Mismanaged Rental Properties for Maximum Profit*, which is for sale at my web site: www.thomaslucier.com.

The Housing for Older Persons Act of 1995

The Housing for Older Persons Act of 1995, commonly referred to as HOPA, covers residential rental properties in which 80 percent of the tenants are 55 years of age or older and exempts them from the Fair Housing Act's prohibitions against discrimination based on familial status. Section 807(b) (2) (C), of the Housing for Older Persons Act, states that rental housing: *"(C) intended and operated for occupancy by persons 55 years of age or older, and (i) at least 80 percent of the occupied units are occupied by at least one person who is 55 years of age or older; (ii) the housing facility or community publishes and adheres to policies and procedures that demonstrate the intent required under this subparagraph; and (iii) the housing facility or community complies with rules issued by the Secretary for verification of occupancy, which shall (I) provide for verification by reliable surveys and affidavits; and (II) include examples of the types of policies and procedures relevant to a determination of compliance with the requirement of clause (ii). Such surveys and affidavits shall be admissible in administrative and judicial proceedings for the purposes of such verification."* You can read The Housing for Older Persons Act of 1995 at the following web site: www.fairhousing.com/index.cfm?method=page.display&pageid=663.

How the HUD Section 8 Housing Choice Voucher Program Works

Under the HUD Section 8 Rental Voucher Program, the local PHA issues housing choice vouchers to income-qualified tenants to rent privately owned rental housing that meets the Section 8 health and safety standards. The housing authority pays a landlord a percentage of the monthly rental amount, which is based on the tenant's income, and the tenant pays the difference directly to the landlord each month. Information on the HUD Section 8 Housing Choice Voucher Program is available at the following web site: www.hud.gov/offices/pih/programs/hcv/index.cfm.

Some Public Housing Authorities Are Very Badly Mismanaged

I think that it's fair to say that anytime anyone does business with any government run agency, it's pretty much a crapshoot as to how things will turn out. And the PHAs in cities and counties, which administer the HUD Section 8 rental assistance program, are no different. How well a Section 8 rental housing program is run depends on the caliber of the people who are managing the local PHA. So it shouldn't come as any great surprise that some public housing authorities are plagued by mismanagement and, occasionally, corruption. For example, one of the former executive directors of Tampa Housing Authority was sent to federal prison on a list of felony convictions. I strongly recommend that you do a thorough background check of your local housing authority before you ever agree to participate, as a landlord, in any type of Section 8 rental housing program.

How to Successfully Manage Residential Tenants

Unfortunately, for residential landlords, tenants don't come complete with an operator's manual that tells landlords which buttons to push in order to program tenants to do exactly as they're told. That requires people-management skills, which are relatively easy to acquire. Contrary to what the so-called property management experts would want aspiring residential landlords to believe, you don't need 100 hours of dry, dull, boring property management courses, or 10 years of experience, in order to run a successful residential rental housing business. All that you really need, besides a heavy dose of good old-fashioned common sense, is the readily available knowledge that's required to:

1. Select the best qualified tenant applicants available.
2. Collect rental payments on the day they are due, or initiate eviction proceedings.
3. Maintain the property in an efficient, clean, safe, and cost-effective manner.
4. Administer accurate income, expense, tenant, property, and tax records.

I have three pieces of sage advice for all would-be residential landlords. First, read, study, and understand your state's residential landlord and tenant act, which should be available online or at your county's public law library. Second, visit my award-winning web site www.floridalandlord.com and bookmark it on your computer for future reference. Third, get your hands on a copy of my book, *The Florida Landlord's Manual,* which is available for purchase, at my web site www.thomaslucier.com and use it as your hands-on guide to running a profitable, hassle-free residential rental housing business. Ignore the "Florida" in the title, as 95 percent of the book's content is applicable to do-it-yourself residential landlords nationwide.

PART III

THE FUNDAMENTALS OF REAL ESTATE INVESTING

CHAPTER 12

What You Must Know about Your State's Statutes and Other Laws Pertaining to Real Estate Investing

As each year passes, the real estate investment business becomes more and more regulated. Lately, everyone from city councils to state legislatures to the Congress of the United States has gotten into the act and passed ordinances, statutes, and acts, which were supposedly enacted to protect the public from various types of so-called real estate predators. Ironically, most real estate related legislation is usually proposed by state Realtor associations, who claim to be acting in the public's best interest but, in reality, are trying to protect their members from real estate investors and other groups, who they somehow perceive as being competitors. Keep this in mind whenever you experience a moment of weakness and entertain thoughts of using the services of a real estate licensee. Regardless of how a rule, regulation, or statute comes about, once it's on the books, you want to make certain that you don't run afoul of the law and end up getting hauled before a judge and having the book thrown at you, which could result in a hefty monetary fine or jail time, or both. And this is exactly why you must always get your information straight from the local, state, and federal government agencies that are responsible for overseeing and enforcing the ordinances, rules, regulations, and statutes that pertain to running a real estate investment business in your state. A word of caution: Any information or advice, which you may have gleaned from reading real estate message boards should be disregarded as it's most likely incorrect or incomplete. The fact of the matter is that most of the real estate gobbledygook that's posted online is flat-out wrong and should never be relied on to make any type of decision. Quite frankly, I am appalled by the level of ignorance that's on display on most real estate message boards and blindly accepted as the gospel by the gullible, uninformed people who read it.

Ignorance of the Law Isn't an Acceptable Defense in a Court of Law

In order to avoid becoming cannon fodder for some slick, fast-talking government prosecutor, you must take the time and effort to become familiar with the numerous local, state, and federal ordinances, rules, regulations, and statutes that pertain to running a real estate investment business. If you ignore the sage advice that I am providing here and end up on the wrong side of the law, you can forget about using the "but your honor, I didn't know that it was against the law" defense in court. In every state in the union, the so-called "ignorance of the law" excuse, isn't an acceptable defense.

The Types of State Statutes That Real Estate Investors Need to Know About

The following is a listing of the types of statutes that pertain to regulating the real estate investment business in most states:

1. Residential and nonresidential landlord and tenant acts.
2. Real estate sales.
3. Title insurance.
4. Property forfeiture.
5. Construction liens.
6. Fictitious names.
7. Pest control.
8. Equity skimming.
9. Fair housing.
10. Vehicle towing.
11. Worthless checks.
12. Debt collection.

13. Public nuisances.
14. Discrimination.
15. Occupational licenses.
16. Code enforcement.
17. Building codes.
18. Business entities.
19. Contractor licensing.
20. Foreclosure.
21. Public records.
22. Recording documents.
23. Judgment liens.
24. Mortgages and deeds of trust loans.
25. Real estate options.
26. Installment sale contracts.
27. Income taxes.

Where to Find Your State's Civil Statutes Online

All state civil statutes are available online at the following web site: www.prairienet.org/~scruffy/f.htm.

What You Need to Know about "Practicing Real Estate" without a License

State real estate commissions are responsible for issuing and renewing real estate sales and brokerage licenses and for enforcing real estate sales rules, regulations, and statutes and disciplining licensees. Anytime an individual accepts compensation to act as a third party to facilitate any type of real estate transaction, such as the sale, purchase, appraisal, rental, exchange, or auctioning of real property, they must be properly licensed in the state where the transaction is taking place. For example, if an unlicensed person accepted compensation for acting as a middleman by bringing a buyer and seller together in a real estate transaction, this person would be practicing real estate without a license. In Florida, it's a third degree felony to practice real estate without a license.

State Real Estate Commissions Don't Regulate Individual Real Estate Investors

First things first: Contrary to what you may have been led to believe, state real estate commissions don't regulate private individual real estate investors. That's because real estate investors aren't required to be licensed by any state in the United States. A private individual real estate investor, who's acting as a principle on their own behalf and for their own account in principal to principal transactions in which there are no third parties involved, is engaged in nothing more than good old-fashioned American capitalism. I know of no case nationwide where a state real estate commission has successfully prosecuted a private individual investor for buying and selling real estate for their own account. The purchase and sale of real estate directly between a willing seller and a willing buyer is known as a transaction between principals, as there are no third parties such as real estate brokers involved. Private individuals, who are the principal parties in a real estate transaction, are in no way, shape, or form, brokering real estate deals.

Federal Statutes That Pertain to Running a Real Estate Investment Business

The following federal statutes pertain to running a real estate investment business:

1. Fair Housing Act.
2. Garn-St Germain Depository Institutions Act.
3. Fair Credit Reporting Act.
4. Americans with Disabilities Act.
5. Servicemembers Civil Relief Act.
6. Federal Eviction Regulation for HUD-Subsidized Housing.
7. Housing for Older Persons Act.
8. Civil Rights Act.
9. Civil Asset Forfeiture Reform Act.
10. Racketeer Influenced and Corrupt Practices Act.
11. Residential Lead Based Paint Hazard Reduction Act.

12. Federal Bankruptcy Code.
13. The Patriot Act.

The United States Code Available Online

The U.S. Code is available online at the following web site: http://uscode.house.gov.

The Federal Code of Regulations Available Online

The Federal Code of Regulations is available online at the following web site: www.gpoaccess.gov/cfr.

The Fair Housing Act

The Fair Housing Act prohibits discrimination in the sale or rental of residential housing based on a person's:

1. Race or color.
2. National origin.
3. Religion.
4. Sex.
5. Familial status.
6. Handicap.

Exemptions to the Fair Housing Act

The Fair Housing Act exempts:

1. The sale or rental of a single-family house by the owner, provided that the owner doesn't own or have any interest in more than three single-family houses at any one time, and that the house is sold or rented without the services of a real estate licensee or the facilities of any person in the business of selling or renting dwellings.
2. Owner-occupied dwellings, designed for occupancy, by no more than four families living separate of each other. This is known as the Mrs. Murphy's Exemption.

Fair Housing Act Information Is Available Online

Information on the Fair Housing Act is available online, at the following web sites:

Fair Housing Act: www.usdoj.gov/crt/housing/title8.htm

HUD Office of Fair Housing and Equal Opportunity: www.hud.gov /offices/fheo/index.cfm

HUD Fair Housing Booklet: www.hud.gov/offices/fheo/FHLaws /FairHousingJan2002.pdf

The Servicemembers Civil Relief Act

The Servicemembers Civil Relief Act covers all active duty members of the U.S. Armed Forces and allows members of the military to:

1. Terminate residential leases on receipt of orders.
2. Require that all interest rates on debts be capped at six percent.
3. Obtain a stay on legal proceedings.
4. Stop eviction proceedings, if the rent is below $2,400 per month.
5. Reopen legal cases involving default judgments.
6. Obtain temporary relief from making mortgage loan payments.
7. Terminate automobile leases on receipt of orders.

The Servicemembers Civil Relief Act is available online at the following web site: www.navy.mil/navydata/policy/hr100-scra.pdf.

The Residential Lead-Based Paint Hazard Reduction Act

The Residential Lead-Based Paint Hazard Reduction Act requires that all residential sale and rental agreements to sell and rent property built before 1978 must contain a disclosure statement, like Form 12.1, on the health hazards associated with lead-based paint in housing. The act also requires that sellers and landlords selling or renting property built before 1978 must provide their buyers and tenants with a copy of the EPA pamphlet entitled *Protect Your Family from Lead in Your Home*, which can be downloaded from the following web site: www.epa.gov/opptintr/lead /leadpdfe.pdf.

FORM 12.1   Sample Lead-Based Paint Hazards Disclosure Statement

---

Lead Warning Statement

Every purchaser of any interest in residential real property on which a residential dwelling was built prior to 1978 is notified that such property may present exposure to lead from lead-based paint that may place young children at risk of developing lead poisoning. Lead poisoning in young children may produce permanent neurological damage, including learning disabilities, reduced intelligence quotient, behavioral problems, and impaired memory. Lead poisoning also poses a particular risk to pregnant women. The seller of any interest in residential real property is required to provide the buyer with any information on lead-based paint hazards from risk assessments or inspections in the seller's possession and notify the buyer of any known lead-based paint hazards. A risk assessment or inspection for possible lead-based paint hazards is recommended prior to purchase.

Seller's Disclosure

(a) Presence of lead-based paint and/or lead-based paint hazards (check (i) or (ii) below):

   (i)   ____ Known lead-based paint and/or lead-based paint hazards are present in the housing (explain below).

   (ii) ____ Seller has no knowledge of lead-based paint and/or lead-based paint hazards in the housing.

(b) Records and reports available to the seller (check (i) or (ii) below):

   (i)   ____ Seller has provided the purchaser with all available records and reports pertaining to lead.

   (ii) ____ Seller has no reports or records pertaining to lead-based paint and/or lead-based paint hazards in the housing.

Purchaser's Acknowledgment (initial)

(c) ____ Purchaser has received copies of all information listed above.

(d) ____ Purchaser has received the pamphlet *Protect Your Family from Lead in Your Home.*

(e) ____ Purchaser has (check (i) or (ii) below):

   (i)   ____ Received a 10-day opportunity (or mutually agreed upon period) to conduct a risk assessment or inspection for the presence of lead-based paint and/or lead-based paint hazards; or

   (ii) ____ Waived the opportunity to conduct a risk assessment or inspection for the presence of lead-based paint and/or lead-based paint hazards.

Certification of Accuracy

The following parties have reviewed the information above and certify, to the best of their knowledge, that the information provided by the signatory is true and accurate.

_____   _____

Seller   Date

_____   _____

Buyer   Date

There's Nothing Illegal, Unethical, or Immoral about Flipping Property

The real estate investment strategy of property flipping has been around for hundreds of years. The term *property flipping* is generally defined within the real estate investment industry, as: *The process of buying a property and quickly reselling it for a profit.* But nowadays, thanks in large part to the print and electronic media, which has blown a relatively few cases of fraud involving illegal property flipping schemes way out of proportion, many uniformed members of the public erroneously believe that it's somehow illegal to flip a piece of property. There's absolutely nothing illegal, immoral, or unethical about making an honest profit from legitimately flipping a piece of property. It's called capitalism, which is the bedrock of America's free enterprise system, and I happen to be an unabashed capitalist and damn proud of it.

CHAPTER 13

Everything You Must Know about Real Estate Loans, Assumption Rules, Buying Subject to, and Loan Fraud

You can be a complete klutz when it comes to knowing which end of a hammer to hold and still be a successful real estate investor. But you're not going to make it in the real estate investment business, if you don't fully understand the nuts and bolts of exactly how mortgage and deed of trust loans work. I am telling you this because if you don't have a clue about the inner workings of real estate loans, you're never going to be able to figure out how to finance the purchase of a piece of property. If you don't know diddly-squat about financing real estate deals, you're dead in the water in this business. So if you're really serious about making money as a real estate investor, you must first take the time and effort to obtain a working knowledge of real estate loans, assumption rules, and buying subject to existing loans, along with knowing the legal consequences of committing loan fraud.

Two Types of Security Instruments Used to Secure Real Estate Loans

The two most common types of security instruments that are used to secure both residential and commercial real estate loans are:

1. *Mortgage:* When a real estate loan is secured by a mortgage, the lender (known as the mortgagee) makes a loan to the borrower (known as the

mortgagor) who signs a promissory note and mortgage, which is held by the mortgagee until the mortgagor pays the loan off.

2. *Deed of trust:* When a real estate loan is secured by a deed of trust, the lender (known as the beneficiary) makes a loan to the borrower (known as the trustor) who signs a promissory note and deed of trust, which is held in trust by the trustee, a neutral third party, until the loan is paid in full by the trustor.

Three Types of Residential Real Estate Loans

The three types of residential real estate loans or deeds of trust are:

1. *Conventional loan:* Is not guaranteed or insured by the U.S. government.
2. *FHA loan:* Is insured by the Federal Housing Administration (FHA).
3. *DVA loan:* Is guaranteed by the Department of Veterans Affairs (DVA).

Residential Mortgage and Deed of Trust Loan Documents Available Online

You can review copies of the conventional residential mortgage or deed of trust loan documents, which are used in your state at the following web sites:

Fannie Mae Loan Documents: www.efanniemae.com/sf/formsdocs /documents/secinstruments
Freddie Mac Loan Documents: www.freddiemac.com/uniform

The Difference between First, Second, and Third Mortgages and Deed of Trust Loans

The numerical designations that are given to real estate loans are used to distinguish their priority, or the sequence in which they were recorded against a property's title. For example, a first mortgage or deed of trust loan that was recorded on May 11, 2006, is superior to a second mortgage or deed of trust loan that was recorded on May 18, 2006. And that same second mortgage or deed of trust loan that was recorded on May 18, 2006, is superior to a third loan that was recorded on June 1, 2006.

Conforming versus Nonconforming Loans

The difference between conforming and nonconforming loans is as follows:

- *Conforming loan:* Meets all of the lending criteria established by the Federal National Mortgage Association, better known as Fannie Mae, and the Federal Home Loan Mortgage Corporation, also known as Freddie Mac, which dominate the secondary mortgage market where institutional lenders such as banks and mortgage companies sell their loans.
- *Nonconforming loan:* Doesn't meet the lending standards, which are required for a loan to be sold in the secondary mortgage market. Nonconforming loans are usually made by portfolio lenders who keep the loans instead of selling them.

How Recourse and Nonrecourse Loans Differ

The way in which recourse and nonrecourse loans differ from each other is as follows:

- *Recourse loan:* Hold a borrower personally liable for repayment of the principal and interest when a borrower defaults on their loan.
- *Nonrecourse loan:* Don't hold a borrower personally liable for repayment of the principal and interest when a borrower defaults on their loan. A lender's recourse is limited to the property securing the loan.

Loan Terminology Dictionary

The following web site has a loan terminology dictionary: www.bcpl.net /~ibcnet/terms.html.

The Difference between Assuming an Existing Loan and Buying Subject to an Existing Loan

When a buyer assumes an existing mortgage or deed of trust loan, they sign an assumption agreement with the lender, which makes them legally responsible for repayment of the loan. However, when a buyer takes title to a property subject to an existing mortgage or deed of trust loan all they're really doing is taking over the loan payments, without being personally liable for repayment of the loan and promissory note. The responsibility for repayment of any loan always lies with the last owner assuming the loan prior to its being taken subject to. For example, let's assume that you bought a single-family house subject to an existing FHA loan, which the previous owner had also bought subject to from the original borrower. And you sold the house and your buyer bought it subject to the same existing FHA loan, which was later foreclosed on. The original borrower would be on the hook for the loan because it was still in his or her name. They would be the party named by the lender as the borrower in a foreclosure action.

What You Need to Know about the Due-on-Sale Clause Contained in Loans

Virtually all residential loan documents that are used by institutional lenders include a so-called due-on-sale clause. In a nutshell, a due-on-sale clause is a provision in a loan that authorizes a lender to call a loan due and payable if a property securing a loan is sold or transferred without the lender's prior written consent. When a borrower sells or transfers a property's title without the lender's consent, it's a breach of the due-on-sale clause. But contrary to popular myth, no one is ever going to be arrested and carted off to the hoosegow for violating a loan's due-on-sale clause. When a lender discovers that a sale or transfer has taken place, the only thing it they can do is exercise its right to accelerate payments and demand that the unpaid loan balance is paid in full within 30 days. If the new owner fails to pay the loan off within the 30-day period, the lender can foreclose on the loan.

How the Code of Federal Regulations Defines the Due-on-Sale Clause

Section 591.2 (b) of Title 12 of the Code of Federal Regulations defines the due-on-sale clause as follows: *Due-on-sale clause means a contract provision which authorizes the lender, at its option, to declare immediately due and payable sums secured by the lender's security instrument upon a sale or transfer of all or any part of the real property securing the loan without the lender's prior written consent. For purposes of this definition, a sale or transfer means the conveyance of real property or any right, title or interest therein, whether legal or equitable, whether voluntary or, by outright sale, deed, installment sale contract, land contract, contract for deed, leasehold interest with a term greater than three years, lease-option contract or any other method of conveyance of real property interests.* Title 12 of the Code of Federal Regulations is available online at: www.fdic.gov/regulations/laws /rules/8000-8300.html.

Exclusions to the Due-on-Sale Clause Contained in Residential Loans

Under the Garn-St Germain Depository Institutions Act, a lender is prohibited from exercising its due-on-sale clause under the following nine circumstances when a borrower:

1. Creates a lien or other encumbrance subordinate to the lender's security instrument, which does not relate to a transfer of rights of occupancy in the property.
2. Creates a purchase money security interest for household appliances.
3. Transfers title by devise, descent, or operation of law on the death of a joint tenant or tenant by the entirety.
4. Grants a leasehold interest of three years or less not containing an option to purchase.
5. Transfers title to a relative resulting from the death of a borrower.
6. Transfers title where the spouse or children of the borrower become an owner of the property.

7. Transfers title resulting from a decree of dissolution of marriage, legal separation agreement, or from an incidental property settlement agreement by which the spouse of the borrower becomes an owner of the property.

8. Transfers title into an inter vivos trust in which the borrower is and remains a beneficiary and which does not relate to a transfer of rights of occupancy in the property.

9. Transfers title described by regulations prescribed by the Federal Home Loan Bank Board.

The Garn-St Germain Depository Institutions Act is available online at: www.phil.frb.org/src/Garn.html.

Loan Assumption Rule for Federal Housing Administration Insured Loans

Federal Housing Administration insured loans closed prior to December 14, 1989, can be assumed without qualification by paying an assumption fee, or taken subject to, without paying any assumption fee. FHA insured loans closed after December 15, 1989, can only be assumed by qualified owner-occupants and contain a due-on-sale clause, which bans investors from ever being able to assume them.

How You Can Legally Assume Federal Housing Administration Loans as an Owner-Occupant Investor

Nowadays, the only way that a real estate investor can legally assume an FHA mortgage or deed of trust loan is as an owner-occupant, who's purchasing the property to be used as their principal residence. The best part about assuming existing FHA loans as an owner-occupant is that there are no published restrictions in the *Department of Housing and Urban Development Handbook 4330.1 REV-5 Administration of Insured Home Mortgages* on how many times an individual can buy and resell properties that have FHA loans. Unlike the original borrower of an FHA loan, there's no published residency requirement, which requires the owner to stay in the property for a set period of time before it can be converted to a rental property. The only financial test that an owner-occupant buyer must pass in order to assume an FHA loan is a creditworthiness review. Please note that it's a federal crime, punishable by a monetary fine or imprisonment, or both, to falsely claim to the Department of Housing and Urban Development (HUD) and the lender funding the loan that you're buying a property to be used as your principal residence when, in fact, you're buying it as a nonowner-occupied (NOO) investment property. I know a former real estate investor in Orlando, Florida, who obtained an FHA loan under the false pretense that it was going to be used to finance the purchase of a single-family house, which was going to be her principal residence. Much to her surprise, three months later, an employee of the lender showed up on the front step of her supposed home to verify that she was living there. The tenant told the bank employee that he had been living in the house for the past three months. To make a long story short, the lender reported her to the Federal Bureau of Investigation (FBI) and she was charged with loan fraud. She ended up hiring a criminal defense attorney who was able to negotiate a deal with the U.S. Attorney's office in which she agreed to pay a $10,000 fine and serve two years of supervised probation. Ironically, at the time she bought the house, she had the credit and income to easily qualify for a nonowner-occupied loan. Instead, she lied on her loan application and committed loan fraud, which ended up costing her a ton of money and a ruined reputation.

Loan Assumption Rule for Department of Veterans Affairs Guaranteed Loans

Loans guaranteed by the DVA, which were closed prior to March 1, 1988, contain no due-on-sale clause and may be assumed by anyone without qualification by paying an assumption fee, or taken subject to, without paying an assumption fee. DVA guaranteed loans originated on or after March 1, 1988, contain a due-on-sale clause requiring prior approval by the DVA or its authorized agent before any DVA guaranteed loan can be assumed. All DVA mortgage or deed of trust loans contain the following statement, which is printed on the top of the first page of the loan document, in bold type: **THIS LOAN IS NOT ASSUMABLE WITHOUT THE APPROVAL OF THE DEPARTMENT OF VETERANS AFFAIRS OR ITS AUTHORIZED AGENT.**

How to Legally Get around the Due-on-Sale Clause Contained in DVA Loans

Installment sale contracts, allow investors to legally get around the due-on-sale clause that's contained in DVA loans. That's because Section 12 of DVA Circular 26-90-37 dated September 25, 1990, states: *Sale Agreements Not Subject to 38 U.S.C. 1814. When a borrower sells on an installment contract, contract for deed, or similar arrangement in which title is not transferred from the seller to the buyer, this is not considered a "disposition" of residential property securing a GI loan as stated in 38 U.S.C. 1814, and therefore does not require approval by VA or the loan holder prior to the execution of such an agreement. However, any borrower considering a sale in this manner should be cautioned that under such an arrangement he or she remains liable for repayment of the loan. Even if the agreement calls for the contract purchaser to make payments directly to the GI loan holder, the holder is not required by VA to change its records, and the contract seller is responsible for forwarding payment coupons and other information to the contract purchaser. Depending on the particular circumstances of a case, a holder may agree to change the account address to read in care of the contract purchaser, although the contract seller must promptly advise the holder of any change in his or her address.*

When a property is purchased on an installment sale or land contract, such as a contract for deed (CFD) or an agreement for deed (AFD), the owner retains an equitable interest in the property and has all of the rights of equitable ownership to include the right to deduct loan interest payments and property depreciation on his or her federal income tax returns. However, under a CFD or AFD, the title to the property isn't transferred to the new owner at the time of purchase. Instead, the property's title is transferred after the buyer has met all of the terms, which are spelled out in the land contract.

How to Protect Yourself When Buying Property on an Installment Sale Contract

First off, whenever you buy a property on an installment sale contract always require the owner to sign all of the title transfer documents—

warranty or grant deed—and place them in escrow with a reputable third party, such as title insurance or escrow company or a real estate attorney. This way, the owner you're buying the property from can't renege on your installment sale contact by refusing to transfer the property's title into your name. Once you have the money to satisfy the repayment terms of the installment sale contract, you can go to the third party holding the deed in escrow and give them a cashier's check made payable to the owner and get the signed deed in return, which you should have recorded in the public records on the same day that you make the final payment.

Second, whenever you buy a property under an installment sale agreement, you must require that all loan payments be made through a licensed loan servicing company instead of directly to the owner. The loan servicing company takes the money it receives from you to make loan payments directly to the lender whose holding the mortgage or deed of trust loan that's secured by the property under contract. This way, you have verifiable proof that the loan payment is being made to the lender, and it's not being pocketed by the owner. Here are the web sites of three loan-servicing companies that provide service nationwide:

1. U.S. Loan Servicing: www.usloanservicing.com
2. North American Loan Servicing: www.sellerloans.com
3. PLM Lender Services, Inc.: www.plmweb.com

How to Purchase a Property Subject to an Existing Loan

Whenever you purchase a property subject to an existing mortgage or deed of trust loan, you must insert a subject to clause, similar to the one that follows, in your purchase agreement: *Subject to that certain mortgage dated August 28, 1997, and executed by David D. Jones, as mortgagor, to Bank of Florida, as mortgagee, in the original amount of one-hundred and twenty-five thousand dollars, $125,000, which mortgage was duly recorded in the office of the Clerk of the Circuit court of Hillsborough County, State of Florida, in book 790346, on page 45905, of the public records of Hillsborough County, Florida.*

Taking Title to Property Subject to an Existing Loan Can Be Risky Business

As far as I'm concerned, buying property subject to an existing loan, without the prior approval of the lender, can be risky business. That's because there's a better than 50 percent chance that the lender will eventually discover the sale and call the loan and demand that the unpaid loan balance be paid in full within 30 days. The most common way that lenders discover subject to transactions is when they receive a hazard insurance policy that has the new owner's name as the insured, instead of the name of the borrower of record. If a lender decides to play hardball and call in a loan, and the new owner can't come up with the cash, or refinance the property to pay it off, the loan will be foreclosed on and the owner will be evicted. One method that you can use to try and gauge how aggressive a lender is about enforcing the due-on-sale clause contained in its loans is to send a matter-of-fact letter to the president of the lending institution stating that you plan on taking title to a property subject to its loan. I've done this twice, and I never received a response back from the lender either time. I went ahead and bought both properties subject to its existing loans and never heard a peep out of the lender during the three-month period that I owned each property.

If you're leery about the potential risk associated with taking title to a property subject to an existing loan, you can do what I usually do and ask the lender to modify the loan agreement so that you can formally assume the loan. It has been my experience that if you're creditworthy and have sufficient income and approach lenders in a professional manner, there's a better than 50-50 chance that the lender will approve your request and allow you to assume a nonassumable loan. The worst that can happen is that the lender will say no, but you'll never know unless you ask.

Don't Commit Fraud to Obtain a Loan

According to the FBI's Financial Institution Fraud unit, mortgage and deed of trust loan fraud is rampant nationwide. Loan fraud occurs when a loan applicant makes a material misstatement, misrepresentation, or omission on a loan application, which is used by a lender to fund, insure, or purchase a loan. For example, a borrower overstates their income to qualify for a loan, or they supply fraudulent documentation to support a loan request, or they submit a false loan application to a lender. Nowadays, federal law enforcement agencies are prosecuting real estate loan fraud cases in record numbers. Real estate fraudsters who get caught committing loan fraud can expect to receive a stiff monetary fine and some time in the pokey. So unless you have an uncontrollable craving to be nattily attired in khaki prison garb and live in a very small room with concrete walls and a steel door for an extended period of time, I wouldn't commit fraud in order to obtain a mortgage or deed of trust loan.

What You Need to Know about Equity Skimming

Equity skimming is one of the most common forms of loan fraud that's being committed today. It occurs when a property owner uses any part of the rents, assets, proceeds, income, or other funds derived from a property, which are pledged as security for a mortgage or deed of trust loan, as their personal funds without repaying the loan. In a typical equity skimming scam, a scam artist takes title subject to an existing mortgage or deed of trust loan and resells the property by using what's known as a wraparound mortgage, or all inclusive trust deed, and collects loan payments but never makes any payments on the underlying loan that was taken subject to. Or the fraudster rents the property out and collects rental payments for months on end without ever making a single loan payment to the lender. This charade goes on until the lender finally forecloses on the loan and evicts the unsuspecting new owner or tenant. In the meantime, the original borrower, whose name is still on the loan, now has a foreclosure listed in their consumer credit file. To add insult to injury, they could also be on the hook for a deficiency judgment, if the property was sold at a foreclosure sale for less than what was owed the lender.

The Federal Equity Skimming Statute

Whenever an equity skimming scam involves a mortgage or deed of trust loan, which is insured by the FHA or guaranteed by the DVA, it becomes a federal crime under Chapter 12, U.S. Code, Section 1709-2, which defines equity skimming as: *Whoever, with intent to defraud, willfully engages in a pattern or practice of (1) purchasing one-to four-family dwellings (including condominiums and cooperatives) which are subject to a loan in default at* *time of purchase or in default within one year subsequent to the purchase and the loan is secured by a mortgage or deed of trust insured or held by the Secretary of Housing and Urban Development or guaranteed by the Department of Veterans Affairs, or the loan is made by the Department of Veterans Affairs, (2) failing to make payments under the mortgage or deed of trust as the payments become due, regardless of whether the purchaser is obligated on the loan, and (3) applying or authorizing the application of rents from such dwellings for his own use, shall be fined not more than $250,000 or imprisoned not more than 5 years, or both. This section shall apply to a purchaser of such a dwelling, or a beneficial owner under any business organization or trust purchasing such dwelling, or to an officer, director, or agent of any such purchaser. Nothing in this section shall apply to the purchaser of only one such dwelling.*

CHAPTER 14

What You Must Know about the Real Estate Settlement Procedures Act, Closing Agents, Title Insurance, and Closing Costs When Buying and Selling Property

The closing or settlement is the final stage in a real estate transaction. It's where a property's title is transferred from the seller to the buyer. And it's, by far, the single most stressful part of being in the real estate investment business. In this chapter, you're going to get the lowdown on how to protect yourself, while navigating through the mazelike labyrinth of paperwork, rules, and regulations that make up the real estate closing process. This way, you'll have a working knowledge of exactly how real estate closings are supposed to work, and you won't be forced to blindly assume that the title or escrow agent or attorney who's handling your transaction actually knows what he or she is doing. By the time you're finished reading this chapter, you'll know all about:

- The Real Estate Settlement Procedures Act.
- How title insurance protects property owners.
- Why you should use a board-certified real estate attorney to act as your closing agent.
- How HUD-1 Settlement Statements are used to document closing costs.

Expect the Unexpected When Participating in a Real Estate Closing

However, just because you know what's supposed to take place at a real estate closing doesn't always mean that you're going to have smooth sailing. By their very nature, real estate closings are fraught with potential pitfalls that can derail a transaction at the very last minute. That's exactly why I've come to expect the unexpected when participating in real estate closings. For example, I once showed up at a closing to buy a six-unit apartment building that was owned by a New York limited liability company (LLC), which had six managing members. The one managing member who had signed our purchase agreement had shown me a notarized corporate resolution signed by the other five managing members that authorized him to sell the property and represent the LLC at the closing. But because of last minute concerns about a possible fraudulent transaction, the title insurance company that was underwriting my owner's title insurance policy balked at issuing me the policy until all six managing members of the LLC signed the warranty deed transferring the property's title to me. This delayed the closing by a week, while the warranty deed was sent to New York City by courier and signed by the five managing members of the LLC in the presence of a notary public and returned to my attorney in Tampa. And no matter how much you prepare, stuff like this happens all the time in this business.

What You Need to Know about the Real Estate Settlement Procedures Act

The Real Estate Settlement Procedures Act (RESPA) was enacted in 1974 to supposedly protect the public from being ripped off by the so-called real estate industry, which consists of title insurers, escrow companies, mortgage and deed of trust lenders, mortgage brokers, and real estate agents and attorneys who perform real estate settlements or closings. HUD is the government agency that is responsible for enforcing RESPA nationwide. According to HUD, the reason that RESPA was enacted into law was: *To help consumers become better shoppers for settlement services and to eliminate kickbacks and referral fees that unnecessarily increase the costs of certain settlement services.* However, in reality, RESPA hasn't been much of a deterrent in stopping predatory lenders, mortgage brokers, and closing agents from gouging the public. For this, I blame the career politicians who are members of the U.S. Congress, which has allowed lobbyists, who represent various professional trade associations to repeatedly block any meaningful reform of the RESPA from taking place. You can read the provisions of RESPA by logging onto: www.hud.gov/offices/hsg/sfh/res/respa_hm.cfm.

Most Closing Agents Routinely Overcharge Their Customers for Closing Costs

RESPA contains provisions that strictly prohibit closing agents from padding the fees, which are charged to buyers and sellers for services performed by third parties in real estate transactions. What typically happens is a closing agent uses third party vendors, who charge them a set fee for providing a service that is substantially below what they charge the participants in a real estate closing. Then they pocket the difference, which is usually 100 percent more than what they actually paid the vendor. In spite of RESPA, title and escrow companies and attorneys who act as closing agents in real estate transactions have pretty much been given carte blanche by the federal court system to charge buyers and sellers whatever they want in closing or settlement costs. That's because real estate service providers have filed lawsuits in federal courts nationwide that have prevented the provisions in RESPA that prohibit closing agents from marking up fees for no justifiable reason from being enforced nationwide. This attitude of laisser-faire on the part of some federal courts has resulted in the public being overcharged to the tune of tens of millions of dollars annually in bogus fees. As an example, closing agents are famous for marking up the cost of courier service fees, which they charge for transporting various types of documents that are used in real estate closings. I once had a well-known national title insurer try and extort a $120 courier fee out of me for having a letter size package delivered overnight from Orlando to Tampa, which came out to well over a dollar a mile. I flatout refused to pay it and very calmly explained to the office manager that I would file a lawsuit the very next morning against the company under Florida's Deceptive and Unfair Trade Practices Act for what's known as "unjust enrichment," which is a fancy legal term for price gouging. The manager relented and agreed to lower the courier fee to $25, which was still double what they had paid the courier service. I held my nose and let them close the deal. To this day, I wouldn't do business with them again, even if they offered their "services" for free. Here's a listing of the 10 types of fees that title and escrow companies and real estate attorneys are notorious for routinely overcharging buyers and sellers at real estate closings:

1. Closing or settlement fee.
2. Title search fee.
3. Title examination fee.
4. Courier fee.
5. Document preparation fee.
6. Processing fee.
7. Photocopying fee.
8. Notary fee.
9. Administration fee.
10. Escrow fee.

Closing Agents Have No Fiduciary Obligation to the Principal Parties in a Closing

It always amazes me how most people automatically assume that closing agents are somehow legally obligated to look out for the interests of the principal parties involved in a real estate closing. However, contrary to what the land title industry would want the real estate buying and selling public to believe, title and escrow agents are nothing more than disinterested or impartial third-party facilitators who have no fiduciary obligation, whatsoever, to the principal parties involved in a real estate closing. This means that when you're a principal in a real estate transaction in which a title or escrow agent or attorney is acting as the closing agent, there's no one but little old you looking out for your best interests. In other words, you're strictly on your own. The only parties that closing agents are obligated to look out for in a real estate closing are their employer and the title insurer underwriting the title insurance policies, which are issued at the closing. A closing agent's job is to:

1. Setup and coordinate the closing between all of the parties involved in a transaction.

2. Order and examine title reports.

3. Order payoff statements from lenders and lienholders.

4. Complete buyer's and seller's HUD-1 Settlement Statements.

5. Disburse funds paid at closings.

6. File documents to be recorded in the public record.

Title and escrow agents are legally prohibited from:

1. Providing legal, accounting, and financial advice.

2. Acting as a negotiator between the parties involved in a transaction.

3. Acting as a mediator between the parties involved in a transaction.

Hire a Board-Certified Real Estate Attorney to Close Your Transactions

I can tell you from my own personal experiences that most title and escrow companies aren't exactly what I would call "investor friendly." They're generally suspicious of any type of real estate transaction that involves more than a typical, run-of-the-mill, easy-to-close residential sale involving a buyer and seller and two real estate agents. It has been my experience that the average title or escrow agent doesn't have a very good grasp of how real estate transactions are structured. Like most people, they have a tendency to fear what they fail to understand. This fear factor, which most title and escrow companies seem to have today about doing business with real estate investors, fosters an atmosphere of mistrust that's not conducive to a good working relationship. That's exactly why I can't overemphasize how important it is to your overall success as a real estate investor that you hire an honest, competent, board-certified real estate attorney to act as your legal counsel and closing agent in all of your real estate transactions. This way, you'll have someone working for you who:

- Has a working knowledge of the real property statutory regulations and case law in your state.

- Is experienced in solving legal problems related to real estate transactions.

- Is affiliated with a reputable title insurance underwriter.

- Is licensed to sell title insurance in your state.

- Has a fiduciary obligation to act in your best interest.

Finding a Board-Certified Real Estate Attorney

The term *board certified* means that an attorney has passed the education and experience requirements established by their state's bar association to be certified as a specialist in a specific area of the law such as real estate. The best way that I know for you to find a qualified, board-certified real estate attorney in your area is to contact your local or state bar association's lawyer referral service. Once you have the names of board-certified real estate attorneys in your area, you'll need to do an online search of your state's bar association membership rolls to verify that the attorneys on your list are licensed to practice law in your state and to check if they've been disciplined or had their license revoked for misconduct. When you select a board-certified real estate attorney, stay away from the big name law firms in your town. Instead, focus on solo attorneys or attorneys who are in two- and three-person law firms. That's because large impersonal law firms have a well-earned reputation for being far more concerned about running up their clients legal bills than closing real estate transactions. Second, never allow an attorney to charge you by the hour to close a real estate transaction. Always insist on one set price for the closing but require an item-by-item breakdown for each charge. This way, your attorney will think twice about padding fees for services rendered by third-party vendors like couriers. The following four web sites provide online attorney locator services, which can be searched by both legal specialty and geographical location:

1. Martindale Hubbell Lawyer Locator: www.martindale.com/locator/home.html
2. Findlaw: www.findlaw.com/14firms
3. Lawyers: www.lawyers.com
4. Real Estate Lawyers: www.realestatelawyers.com

What You Need to Know about Title Insurance

Most recorded ownership, leasehold, and contractual interests, such as agreements for deed, contracts for deed, and other rights in real property, including real estate options, can be insured with title insurance. As a general rule, if an interest or right in real property is notarized and recorded in the public records of the county where the property's title is recorded, it can be insured with title insurance. There are two types of title insurance policies: (1) owners and (2) lenders. A standard owner's title insurance policy is written for the same amount as the purchase price of the property that's being covered. A standard lender's policy is written for the same amount as the loan that's being insured. Title insurers also issue endorsements to title policies, which provide additional coverage for specific situations or occurrences that aren't covered under a standard owner's or lender's title insurance policy.

How an Owner's Title Insurance Policy Protects Property Owners

When you purchase an owner's title insurance policy to insure a property's title, you pay a one-time insurance premium, and the policy remains in effect for as long as the property's title stays in your name. Typically, an owner's title insurance policy insures the policyholder against future losses or damages resulting from any valid claims that are made against the insured property's title. In other words, the title insurer will pay all legal fees for defending any valid claims made against the insured property's title as long as the policyholder retains an interest or right in the property. For example, the standard American Land Title Association (ALTA) owner's title insurance policy provides policyholders with coverage against title defects, which originated prior to the policy being issued. Common title defects covered in standard ALTA owner's title insurance policies include the following 14 items:

1. Errors, omissions, and insufficiencies in the abstract or title search.
2. Errors of judgment, negligence, and mistakes on the part of the title examiner.
3. Undisclosed errors and deficiencies in recorded documents, including the misfiling of recorded documents or improper indexing.
4. Forgeries within recorded documents.
5. Secret marriages or misrepresentations of marital status.
6. Unknown or undisclosed heirs.
7. False impersonation.
8. Instruments executed under expired or revoked powers of attorney.
9. Mental incompetence of the parties executing documents.
10. Confusion due to similar or identical names.
11. Lack of authority of the federal or state government to dispose of, or convey the insured property.

12. Children born after the execution of a will.

13. Discovery of a will of an apparent intestate.

14. Easements by prescription, which weren't disclosed by a land survey.

The very first thing that you must always do right after you sign a purchase agreement—which must include a clause that makes the sale contingent on the seller providing you with a clear and marketable title—is to have your closing agent order a title insurance commitment to determine if the title insurer will issue an owner's title insurance policy to insure the property's title at the time the closing takes place. An owner's title insurance policy commitment, sometimes referred to as a binder, is a temporary insurance contract that provides for the future issuance of a permanent owner's title insurance policy, after a warranty or grant deed has been signed by the seller and the property's title has been transferred to the new owner and recorded in the public records.

Always Obtain Title Insurance Coverage from a Reputable Underwriter

All title insurers aren't equal. A title insurance policy, like all types of insurance policies, is only as good as the company underwriting it. So when you buy any type of title insurance, always use the services of a board-certified real estate attorney or a title or escrow agent whose title insurance policies are underwritten by a reputable regional or national underwriter such as First American Title Insurance Company, Chicago Title & Trust Company, Lawyers Title Insurance Corporation, Old Republic Title Insurance Company, Fidelity National Title Insurance Company, or Stewart Title Insurance Company.

What You Need to Know about Title Insurance Rates

Title insurance premium rates vary from state to state. Some states, such as Florida, have what are called promulgated title insurance premium rates, which are set by the state insurance commissioner. Title insurance premium rates are based on a set dollar amount for each $1,000 worth of coverage. For example, in Florida, title insurance rates are $5.75 for each $1,000 of coverage from 0 to $100,000; $5 for each $1,000 of coverage from

$100,000 to $1,000,000; $2.50 per $1,000 of coverage from $1,000,000 to $5,000,000; $2.25 per $1,000 for coverage from $5,000,000 to $10,000,000; and $2 per $1,000 of coverage over $10,000,000. Whenever you're buying an existing property, always insist on buying an owner's title insurance policy at the reissue rate. The reissue rate is the discounted rate that title insurers charge policyholders when a property being sold or refinanced already has an existing owner's title insurance policy in place, which was issued usually within the past 3 to 10 years.

Title Insurance Premium Rate Calculator

The First American Title Insurance Company has a nationwide title insurance premium rate calculator at: www.titlefees.firstam.com/Titlefees.asp.

Title Insurance Underwriting Information

Title insurance underwriting information is available online at:

> Old Republic National Title Insurance Company: http://orlink .oldrepnatl.com/Underwriters/pages/Tablepercent20ofpercent20Contents.htm

> Chicago Title Insurance Company: www.ctic.com/operations.htm

> First American Title Insurance Company: www.firstam.com/faf /reference/uwtools.html

> Stewart Title Virtual Underwriter: www.vuwriter.com

HUD-1 Settlement Statements Document Real Estate Closing Costs

The Real Estate Settlement Procedures Act requires that HUD-1 Settlement Statements be used to document and account for all of the expenses that are associated with closing real estate transactions that involve federally insured or guaranteed mortgage or deed of trust loans. Nowadays, all closing agents use HUD-1 Settlement Statements to document buyer's and seller's closing costs and account for all of the funds that are disbursed in a real estate closing.

The HUD-1 Settlement Statement

You can complete a HUD-1 Settlement Statement online at my web site: www.thomaslucier.com/HUD1SettlementStatement.pdf. A detailed, line-by-line explanation of the HUD-1 Settlement Statement is available online at: www.hud.gov/offices/hsg/sfh/res/sc3secta.cfm.

Closing Costs Are Generally Divided between Buyers and Sellers

Although closing costs are a negotiable item in a real estate transaction in most parts of the country, closing costs are usually divided between buyers and sellers according to what's "customary and traditional" for a particular area. For example, in Florida, the buyer usually pays all of the closing costs that are associated with taking title to the property, while the seller pays all closing costs that are associated with delivering a marketable title to the property.

Double-Check All Closing, Loan, and Title Transfer Documents

It has been my observation that most participants in a real estate closing automatically assume that all of the information that's contained in closing, loan, and property title transfer documents is 100 percent accurate and up to date. Needless to say, this is very seldom the case. In fact, I've never been involved in a real estate closing in which I didn't find at least one glaring mistake that should have been spotted long before I found it. That's why I always have my attorney send me all of the closing documents, including a copy of my HUD-1 Settlement Statement, in an e-mail attachment on the day prior to the scheduled closing date. This way, I can go over everything with a fine-tooth comb and double-check for any mistakes, which were made in:

- Calculations.
- Transposing numbers and letters.
- Spelling and typing.

Prorate Property Taxes Using the 365-Day Method

I always have my attorney use the 365-day method to prorate property taxes. For example, if the annual property tax bill for a property is $2,200 and the seller owned the property for 270 days, the seller's prorated portion of the tax would be $1,627.40 ($2,200 divided by 365 days equals $6.027 per day multiplied by 270 days equals $1,627.40). However, if the property taxes for the current year can't be ascertained, stipulate in the closing statement that any tax proration based on an estimate shall be readjusted on receipt of the tax bill.

Read All Utility Meters on the Day before the Closing

Whenever I am buying any property, I always have all of the utility meters read on the day before the scheduled closing by the utility companies that are providing utility services to the property. I do this for two very important reasons: First, this notifies the utility service providers that the property is under new ownership. Second, it prevents the utility companies from trying to bill me for utility services that were provided to the previous owner.

Take a Walk around the Property on the Day of the Closing

On the day of the closing, I conduct a final walk around to double-check for any last-minute changes that may have occurred to the property that could have an adverse effect on its value. I normally stop by a property on my way to the closing and take a last minute look-see to make sure everything is okay before I sign the closing documents and take possession of the property.

Always Protect Your Personal Privacy during a Real Estate Closing

You'd have to be living off the grid in East Snowshoe, Utah, to not know that identity theft is the fastest growing crime in America today. Identity theft occurs when a criminal steals a person's social security account number, bank account number, credit card number, or driver license number in order to perpetrate fraud. The best way that I know to avoid becoming the victim of an identity thief is to keep your personal information under lock and key at all times. This means that you don't give out your full social security account number (SSAN) to anyone, for any purpose, and that includes real estate closing agents. If asked to do so, tell the closing agent that because of rampant identity theft you're willing to provide the last four digits of your SSAN but that's all. If you're buying property through a business entity, such as a limited liability company or Subchapter S corporation, use the federal employer identification number (FEIN), which was issued to the business by the IRS.

Use a Checklist at the Closing

The best way that I've found to keep all of my paperwork straight during a real estate closing is to use a closing checklist like From 14.1. As a result, I don't overlook anything that could come back to haunt me later on, after the seller has packed up and left town.

FORM 14.1 Sample Closing Checklist

1. Review the title insurance policy.

2. Review the survey of the property.

3. Verify the property's legal description.

4. Verify the property's zoning designation.

5. Check with government agencies for building, fire, safety, and health code violations.

6. Review the hazard insurance policy.

7. Review the termite inspection report.

8. Verify the property's tax payment status.

9. Compute the mortgage or deed of trust interest proration.

10. Compute the real property tax proration.

11. Check with government agencies for environmental hazard citations.

12. Review the bill of sale for personal property.

13. Review the deed.

14. Review the promissory note.

15. Review the mortgage or deed of trust.

16. Review the loan assumption documents.

17. Review the HUD-1 Settlement Statement.

18. Verify that a certificate of occupancy is in effect for the property.

PART IV

NINE-STEP PROCESS FOR BUYING AND SELLING REAL ESTATE

CHAPTER 15

How to Find Owners Who Are Willing to Sell Their Property below Market Value

My number one rule as a real estate investor is to never, ever pay full market value for a piece of property, and my number two rule is to never, ever forget my number one rule. As I told you earlier in this book, savvy real estate investors almost always make the lion's share of their profit upfront—on the day they close on the purchase of a property. They're able to do this by buying property at a discounted or wholesale price instead of paying full retail, which gives them a built-in profit right from the get-go. As a matter of fact, I've never met anyone, who claimed they got rich in real estate by buying property at full or fair market value. As far as I am concerned, your chances of striking it rich in real estate today by buying properties at full market value are slim and none. The term *market value* refers to a property's full or fair market value, which is based on comparable sales or income data for similar properties that have sold within the same area. Granted, real estate investing is generally a get-rich-slow type of business venture, but buying any type of property at full price in the hopes that market wide appreciation will increase its value some time in the unforeseeable future isn't an investment strategy that's conducive to achieving financial independence. The key to you accumulating wealth as a real estate investor is in finding owners who are willing to sell you their property at a price that is at least 20 percent below market value. The only way that I know to go about finding owners who are willing to sell their property at a wholesale price is to mount an ongoing search to seek them out. For example, I work alone and have no hourly employees at my beck and call. I've had to learn how to search for owners, by using methods that don't require my physical presence in order to be effective, and keep my name in front them. This way, when they decide to throw in the towel, they can call me for help. I keep my name and telephone number and e-mail address in front of property owners by:

- Mailing letters to property owners.
- Paying finder's fees to bird dogs who tell me about properties that I buy.
- Placing classified "property wanted" ads in daily newspapers.
- Using a "property wanted" web page and e-mail.

I want to warn you right now that finding owners who are willing to sell their property below market value isn't for weak-willed people, who give up and quit at the first obstacle they encounter. To be successful at this, you must not only be a good detective, you must also have a detailed property search plan, a willingness to work hard, dogged determination, persistence, timing, and a certain element of luck.

Always Keep a Consistent Message throughout Your Advertisements

The secret to successfully marketing your service to distressed or motivated property owners is to repeat the same message throughout all of your advertising materials. You want to consistently stress the benefits of doing business with you over and over again, until they become synonymous with your name. From my years of experience, I've found that the following five benefits resonate with most property owners:

1. No games, gimmicks, or bullspit.
2. Immediate debt relief.
3. No costly repairs.
4. No sales commissions.
5. Fast closings.

You'll notice that near the end of all of my sample letters to property owners, I've included the following sentence: *I promise not to waste your valuable time with games, gimmicks, and bullspit.* From what I've been told by property owners who've responded to my letters over the years, this one sentence alone has prompted more calls than anything else in my letters. Fact is, Americans, are fed up with the hyperbolic bullspit that most advertisements are comprised of today. As a result, most property owners find my direct writing style to be a refreshing respite from the usual malarkey that fills their mailboxes.

Establish Your Own Property Acquisition Criteria Prior to Searching for Owners

The very first thing that you must do prior to starting your search for property owners is to establish your own acquisition criteria or standards for the type of property that you're searching to buy. This way, you'll be able to form a mental picture in your mind of exactly what you're looking for and you'll have a basis of comparison, which you can use to identify properties that come closest to meeting your property acquisition criteria. Your acquisition criteria must include a physical description of the property that you're seeking, along with the financial conditions under which you're willing to purchase the property. For example, I specialize in buying vintage 1970s and 1980s Class "B" and "C" single-story, side-by-side, separate-metered residential rental properties that are made of concrete block construction and have:

1. One or two bedrooms and efficiency size units.
2. A sale price that's below the replacement cost of the property.
3. An owner who's willing to finance up to 90 percent of the purchase price at the same market rate and terms that institutional lenders are charging.
4. Potential to increase the monthly rental income and resale value.

Look for Owners with Problems, Situations, and Circumstances They Can't Handle

After you've established your property acquisition criteria, you must focus all of your efforts on finding owners who are experiencing various types of problems, situations, and circumstances that they can't handle and are unable to straighten out on their own. By problems, situations, and circumstances, I am referring to any type of personal, family, financial, or business hardship—such as foreclosure, divorce, sickness, death, arrest, incarceration, litigation, and business breakups—which can eventually force owners to sell their property. I hone in on this particular group of owners because they provide the most opportunities for me to buy their property at wholesale prices. It's a fact of life that, in our capitalistic society, one person's problems, situations, and circumstances can be another person's source of opportunity. I realize that some readers, who've led a sheltered life may be repulsed by the very thought of profiting from another person's misfortune, but I make no apologies. I offer property owners in distress a valuable service, which for whatever reason, most real estate investors are unwilling or unable to provide. I put my hard-earned capital at risk to come up with workable solutions to complex problems, which help property owners out of very bad situations and circumstances that are usually of their own making. I am paid handsomely for helping them, and you will be too, provided you follow the advice and step-by-step instructions contained in this book.

Insight into Why Owners Are Willing to Sell Their Property below Market Value

I realize that some of the people reading this chapter may have a hard time understanding why any owner, in their right mind, would ever agree to sell their property at a price that is 20 percent below market value. That's probably because they've never heard of what's known in the real estate investment lexicon as a "don't wanter." The term *don't wanter* refers to a property owner who, for whatever reason, no longer wants to own a piece of property. When a property owner reaches the point of being a serious don't wanter, they'll usually agree to just about anything in order to unload the property and get on with their life. For example, I once bought a duplex in South Tampa from an Air Force pilot for 75 percent of the property's fair market value. The pilot had been transferred from MacDill Air Force Base in Tampa to an air force base in the United Kingdom. The property management company that he had hired to manage his property had totally dropped the ball, and both units had been vacant for two months when he came to Tampa on a 10-day leave to try and straighten the mess out. Five days into his leave, the pilot had an epiphany of sorts and realized that he was in over his head and decided right then and there that he no longer wanted to be the proud owner of a vacant duplex rental property. He immediately placed a classified ad in the *Tampa Tribune,* which I read at 5 A.M. on the following morning. By lunchtime that very same day, I had delivered a signed purchase agreement to buy the duplex for 25 percent below its fair market value to my attorney. Two days later, I was the owner of a duplex and the pilot was relieved to be rid of his albatross and on his way back to merry old England.

Where to Find the Names of All of the Property Owners in Your County

You can find the names of every single property owner in your county at your county's property appraiser or property assessor's office. They maintain property tax rolls, which list every parcel of land in a county. Each parcel of land is assigned a separate tax identification number, which is known as a property assessor's parcel number (APN) or a property appraiser's folio number. Nowadays, the property records of most counties are online and available to anyone with a personal computer and an Internet connection. In Chapter 16, you'll get step-by-step instructions on exactly how to search property records.

Obtain the Names of Property Owners with Problems

As I've told you, I specialize in buying small mismanaged rental properties from landlords, who don't have the temperament or management know-how that's needed to successfully run a residential rental housing business. One of the ways that I find mismanaged rental properties is by searching the Hillsborough County Civil court records online for landlords who have filed eviction lawsuits against their tenants. The eviction lawsuits list the name of the landlord (the plaintiff) and the name of the tenant (the defendant) and include the tenant's address, which is the street address of the rental property and the landlord's mailing address. I go through the eviction lawsuits and select properties that appear to be owned by individuals and are located in zip codes that are in stable areas. Next, I go online to the Hillsborough County Property Appraiser's web site and look up the addresses of the rental properties that I've chosen and check each property's:

- Zoning designation.
- Number of units.
- Latest sale price.
- Latest sale date.
- Tax-assessed value.

Once I've compiled a listing of landlords, who have filed eviction lawsuits within the past 30 days and own 2- to 12-unit rental properties, I send each owner a letter like Form 15.1 on page 190.

Use Direct Mail to Contact Property Owners

I use direct mail because I can contact property owners directly, without having to go through third parties such as real estate agents. When properly used, direct mail can be a quick, efficient, and relatively cost-effective way to keep your name and contact information in front of a select group of property owners. I use Microsoft Word software, which can merge names and addresses with letters and envelopes. All I have to do is to sit down at my computer and point and click my mouse a couple of times, and my printer will crank out my standard letter to property owners that I sign, fold, and insert into window envelopes with first-class postage stamps affixed to them. I use window envelopes because they eliminate the need to address envelopes and thus save time and money.

Mail Letters to the Owners of Residential Rental Properties Every 90 Days

I mail letters to selected owners of small—2- to 10-unit—residential rental properties in my county every 90 days. I use 90 days as a mailing benchmark because I've found that problems can occur, and situations and circumstances can change during three months, which can force an owner to have to sell their property. Experience has shown me that by mailing out letters every 90 days, I have a better chance of being at the right place, at the right time, when an owner decides it's time to sell their property. To find potential property in my targeted areas, I order customized property data on CD-ROM from the Hillsborough County Property Appraiser's Office. The property data is broken down by Florida Department of Revenue (DOR) land use or zoning codes and costs $60 per code designation. I purchase a CD-ROM containing property data for all of the parcels in Hillsborough County that are designated DOR land use codes 08, duplexes, and 0803, multifamily properties with less than 10 units. The CD-ROM contains the following information on each parcel:

- Parcel's street address.
- Owner's mailing address.
- Parcel's tax assessed value.

I don't employ the shotgun method and mail out letters willy-nilly to every property owner who is listed on the CD-ROM. Instead, I go through the listing of properties and cull the addresses that fall within the zip codes where I've chosen to buy property. These are zip codes that are located in so-called blue collar areas, which are stable and have below average crime rates and above average rental rates. Every 90 days, I purchase a new CD-ROM and update my mailing list. I send each owner a letter, like Form 15.1, which is to the point and asks owners to sell me their property.

You'll notice that in my letter, I repeatedly make references to my desire to purchase their property. I do this to emphasize throughout my short letter that I am standing by, and that I am ready to offer the landlord a way out of what's probably a very bad situation. All they have to do to end their misery is to pickup the telephone and call me, or go to their computer and send me an e-mail message.

Use Bird Dogs to Find Properties That Aren't Advertised as "For Sale"

A bird dog is a person who comes into frequent contact with property owners within a specific neighborhood or area and is in a position to learn

---
FORM 15.1 Sample Letter to Small Residential Rental Property Owners
---

June 6, 2006

Ms. Velma Moore
218 Booker Lane
Tampa, FL 33647

Dear Ms. Moore,

My name is Thomas J. Lucier, and I specialize in buying small (two to twelve unit) residential rental properties, in as-is condition, in Hillsborough County.

If you're interested in selling your property, please call me anytime at (813) 237-6267, or e-mail me at tjlucier@tampabay.rr.com, to discuss the sale of your property.

And if we're able to agree on a sale price and terms, I'll be able to close on the purchase of your property within 10 business days or less, depending on your particular circumstances.

I promise you that I won't waste your valuable time with games, gimmicks, or bullspit!

I look forward to hearing from you soon and to speaking with you about selling your property.

Sincerely,

Thomas J. Lucier

Copyright Thomas J. Lucier, 2006. To customize this document, download it from www.thomaslucier .com/realestateforms.html. The document can then be opened, edited, and printed using Microsoft Word.

---

about unadvertised properties that are never formally advertised. In other words, a property's availability is only made known by word of mouth, which means that the general public never knows about them. In most cases, a relative, friend, or neighbor may be the only person who knows about a property owner's willingness or need to sell. The best way that I know to find bird dogs to join your spy network of paid informants is to tell everyone that you come into frequent contact with that you're in the market to buy real estate, and that you're willing to pay your bird dogs a finder's fee when you buy a property that they've told you about. For example, my standard finder's fee is $500 cash, payable on the same day that

I close on the purchase of a property that one of my bird dogs told me about. To me, the best part about using bird dogs and paying finder's fees is that I only have to pay them when I buy a property. In the meantime, I have the benefit of a lot of people looking for properties for me, without the cost of having employees on a payroll. Here's a listing of the type of people, who make the best bird dogs:

- Mail carriers.
- Trash collectors.
- Door-to-door salespeople.
- Delivery truck drivers.
- Cable installers.
- Repairmen.
- Taxicab drivers.
- Utility meter readers.

Use the Internet to Advertise Your Finder's Fee

To get an idea about how to advertise your finder's fee online, log onto my real estate investment company's web page at www.homeequitiescorp.com /cashreward.html and see how I advertise my $500 cash reward to people who provide me with information that results in the purchase of a dirty, neglected, run-down, 2- to 12-unit residential rental property in the Tampa Bay Area.

Use Classified "Property Wanted" Ads to Find Owners

When properly written and placed under the correct heading, classified "property wanted" ads can be an effective way to find unadvertised properties, which belong to owners who don't have the time, desire, or money to market their properties themselves. Or they don't want to go through the hassle of listing their property with a real estate broker. Nowadays, most newspapers have a four-line minimum for classified ads. Each line is right around 26 characters long. So when you write your classified ad, you want to get right to the point. I suggest that you do like I do and place a two-line ad using letters that are two lines high in boldface type. The top line will be the headline and the bottom line will be the contact line. For example, if you wanted to run a property wanted ad for vacant properties, you would write, "Vacant Properties Wanted" as your headline and "Call (123) 555-6969 Today" as your contact line. While you're at it, don't be afraid to experiment with your property wanted ad by running it on various days of the week to find out which days pull the best response in your area. For example, in Tampa, when I run one of my property wanted ads, it's usually only in the Sunday edition of the *Tampa Tribune*. I've found that I get just about the same response whether I run the same ad for 30 consecutive days or just on Sundays. Ultimately, the response rate for a property wanted ad will pretty much depend on the following three factors:

1. How well the ad is written.
2. The classified heading under which it's placed.
3. The size of the newspaper's circulation.

To ensure you get the best possible response from your classified property wanted ad, place it in the classified real estate section of your daily newspaper under various headings such as:

- Investment property wanted.
- Income property wanted.
- Commercial property wanted.
- Property wanted.
- Real estate wanted.

Direct Property Owners to Your Web Page

Another option you can use in your ongoing search for owners who are willing to sell their property below market value is to build a property wanted web site and include its address in your classified wanted ads. This way, you can direct owners to visit your web site to provide you with information about their property. To see an example of a property wanted web page, log onto my company's web site at www.homeequities-corp.com /propertywanted.html and click on the "submit a property" button to check out my property submission web page, where owners can tell me about their property by filling out the submission form. When you choose a property wanted domain or a web site name, select a moniker that incorporates your geographical location. For example, if you were searching for property owners in Lodi, California, you would be smart to register the domain name www.lodipropertywanted.com.

Have a Property Wanted Domain Forwarded to Your Web Site

If you already have a web site, for an annual fee of around $50, you can have your property wanted domain, or web site name forwarded to a specific web page on your web site. Uniform resource locator (URL) forwarding lets you link your property wanted domain directly to a property wanted web page on your existing web site. This way, you avoid the cost of building a separate web site for your property wanted domain. For example, my company Home Equities Corp owns the domain name www.rentalpropertywanted.com, which has URL forwarding to the property wanted web page at www.homeequitiescorp .com/propertywanted.html. Whenever the domain name www .rentalpropertywanted.com is typed into a computer's browser window, the URL is automatically forwarded to the Home Equities Corp web site, which is the destination domain.

Always Place a Property Wanted Ad at the End of All of Your E-Mail Messages

We live in a society that is becoming more and more dependent on electronic messaging or e-mails with each passing day. From what I've seen, very few real estate investors use e-mail to search for property owners. At the very least, all real estate investors should run a tagline or signature at the end of all their personal and business e-mail messages, which advertises the type of properties they're interested in buying. For example, I alternate between running the following two signature ads at the end of all my e-mail messages:

> **Wanted: small—two to twelve-unit—residential rental properties, in as-is condition, in Hillsborough County, Florida.** Please send me an e-mail message at tjlucier@homeequitiescorp.com, if you own or know of a small residential rental property, in Hillsborough County, which fits this description.

> **I buy vacant commercial and industrial property in the Tampa Bay Area.** Please send me an e-mail message at tjlucier@ tampabay.rr.com, if you own or know of a vacant commercial or industrial property in the Tampa Bay Area.

Keep Track of When You Make Contact with Property Owners

The best method that I've found to keep track of the times you make contact with owners is to use a property tracking worksheet, like Form 15.2. I've created a file in Microsoft Word, which uses the same format as this worksheet to store information on the times I make contact with owners.

Determine Owners Level of Motivation during Your Initial Phone Conversation

Most real estate investors waste their valuable time chasing owners who aren't really serious about selling their property. In other words, they have no reason or motivation for wanting to sell their property today. That's exactly why, during your initial telephone conversation with owners calling

FORM 15.2 Sample Property Tracking Worksheet

Property street address: _____

Property appraiser or assessor's folio or parcel number: _____

Tax assessed value: $_____   Date of last assessment: _____

Owner's name: _____   Telephone number: _____

Owner's address: _____

First date owner contacted: _____   Method of contact: _____

Second date owner contacted: _____   Method of contact: _____

Comments: _____

Property street address: _____

Property appraiser or assessor's folio or parcel number: _____

Tax assessed value: $_____   Date of last assessment: _____

Owner's name: _____   Telephone number: _____

Owner's address: _____

First date owner contacted: _____   Method of contact: _____

Second date owner contacted: _____   Method of contact: _____

Comments: _____

Property street address: _____

Property appraiser or assessor's folio or parcel number: _____

Tax assessed value: $_____   Date of last assessment: _____

Owner's name: _____   Telephone number: _____

Owner's address: _____

First date owner contacted: _____   Method of contact: _____

Second date owner contacted: _____   Method of contact: _____

Comments: _____

about your various ads, you must determine how motivated they are to sell their property today. I've found that the more motivated an owner is to sell, the more willing they are to sell their property below market value. The best way that I know to determine a property owner's level of motivation is to ask pointed questions, which are designed to weed out unmotivated owners from those who are ready, able, and willing to sell their property today at a wholesale price that is at least 20 percent below market value. Always keep in mind that your sole objective during your initial telephone conversation with every property owner is to try and gauge how badly they want to sell their property. I have my cellular telephone number prominently displayed in all of my advertisements. This way, I am able to personally answer all incoming calls from early morning until late at night. Keep in mind that when you're screening telephone calls for motivated sellers, how you open a phone conversation is just as important as how you end it. For example, I always answer my phone by saying, "Tom Lucier speaking, how may I help you?" I purposefully answer telephone calls with a question to get the owner to start off the conversation and keep him or her talking. I do this because I know that I am not going to learn anything about the owner's problems, situations, and circumstances if I am constantly running my mouth and monopolizing the conversation. As far as I am concerned, there's a very good reason we humans are equipped with one mouth and two ears: All the better to listen with. I never employ rapid-fire interrogation tactics that make owners feel like they're being grilled by a gung ho member of the FBI's Counterterrorism Unit. Instead, I casually weave the following six questions into the course of my telephone conversations with property owners:

Question 1: Why are you selling your property?

Question 2: What's the asking price for your property?

Question 3: What's your asking price based on?

Question 4: Are you willing to sell your property on flexible terms?

Question 5: If we're able to agree on a sale price and terms, will you be able to close on the sale of your property within the next 10 days?

Question 6: Can we meet at the property this evening to discuss the sale in detail?

I ask Question 1 to gain insight into what's motivating the owner to sell the property. I pose Question 2 to see whether the owner has a realistic expectation as to what the property will sell for in its current condition. The answer I get from Question 3 lets me know if the owner has done his or her homework and has given any real thought to what the property is worth. Question 4 is an open-ended question to determine if the owner is receptive to discussing the various ways in which I can structure a transaction to buy the property. As I begin to slowly wind down the telephone conversation, I ask Questions 5 and 6 to see if the owner is truly a so-called motivated seller who's ready, willing, and able to get down to serious negotiations today. If the owner is hesitant and wants to think things over before committing to a meeting, I politely tell him or her to please keep me in mind and to give me a call when they finally do decide to sell the property. By not reacting in a negative way—throwing a hissy fit—to the owner's rejection of my offer to meet, I keep the door open for possible future dealings between us.

Don't Waste Your Money on So-Called Bandit Signs

To me, those ubiquitous bandit or snipe signs that usually have some variation of "I'll Buy Your House Today," which litter public right-of-ways and are nailed onto utility poles and attached to road signs, are a waste of money. They're illegal in most areas nationwide to boot. For example, the problem with snipe signs on public right-of-ways has gotten so bad in Tampa that the city has mounted a campaign to remove the tacky signs and fine the people who put them up. I consider bandit signs to be a waste of money because they're a form of so-called shotgun advertising, which is too broad based and very seldom works well. In addition, the signs are primarily aimed at passing motorists who often never notice them, especially if they're driving by at a fairly high rate of speed. Even if a motorist or passenger did notice a bandit sign, while stopped at a street intersection and was interested in calling the telephone number on the sign, he or she most likely wouldn't have access to a pen or pencil or piece of paper on which to write the number.

CHAPTER 16

How to Perform Preliminary Due Diligence When Buying Property

Before you ever plunk down your hard-earned money to buy any type of property, you must first perform preliminary due diligence in order to learn as much as possible about the property and its owner. I perform my preliminary due diligence by researching various types of public records to investigate a property and its owner. I do this to evaluate a property's profit potential and to determine if it's worth pursuing. The only way that I've found to obtain reliable, up-to-date information about a property and its owner is to go directly to the various sources of public record information. Nowadays, anyone with a computer and Internet connection can tap into the vast amount of real estate related public record information that's readily available from a myriad of web sites, which contain information on a property's:

- Ownership.
- Liens.
- Sales history.
- Tax-assessed value.
- Environmental hazards.
- Crime rate.
- Demographic information.

To me, the Internet is the single best property research tool available to individual real estate investors today. If your county's property records are available online, you can quickly find out who owns a property, when it was purchased, how much it sold for, and its tax-assessed value. For example, I can log onto the Hillsborough County Property Appraiser's web site and, armed only with a property's street address, I can almost instantly obtain the current owner's name, post office mailing address, sale price, dates for the latest and prior sales, and the tax-assessed value of the property, broken down by land and improvements. I can also get a site map plotting the improvements on the property, along with the tax account or folio number assigned to the property. Once I have the property's tax folio number, I log onto the Hillsborough County Tax Collector's web site to obtain property tax information about the property to include any tax exemptions claimed, special tax-district assessments, and tax payment status. After I've completed my online research, I call the customer service departments at the property appraiser's and tax collector's offices to verify the accuracy of the information that's posted online.

Search the Public Records for Property Information

Although the functions of city and county government agencies vary from state to state, the following four government agencies are where most of the public records pertaining to real property are maintained:

1. County recorder or prothonotary's office.
2. Clerk of the circuit, superior, or county court's office.
3. Clerk of the United States Court's office.
4. Municipal clerk's office.

Obtain Property Information from Government Agencies

As part of your preliminary due diligence, check the property's street address against the records maintained by the following five government agencies:

1. *Zoning department:* Don't just automatically assume that the zoning designations shown on property records are up to date. Always verify zoning designations with your city or county's zoning department. For example, when I need to verify a zoning designation in Tampa, all I have to do is call the city zoning department and give them the property's tax folio number, which they look up on their computerized zoning maps, and they tell me the property's current zoning designation.

2. *Code enforcement department:* In most areas, when properties are ordered vacated because of building, safety, or health code violations,
   brightly colored—dark red or orange—placards are conspicuously
   posted on the property. However, some property owners will try to
   conceal the fact that their property has been cited for code violations—commonly referred to as being red-tagged. They do this by illegally removing code violation placards from their buildings. This is
   why you need to check with your local code enforcement department
   to verify that a property's certificate of occupancy hasn't been revoked because of code violations.

3. *Property tax collector's office:* Check with your city or county property
   tax collector's office to verify the property's tax payment status and
   to check if there are any tax liens recorded against it.

4. *City and county clerk's offices:* Check with your city or county clerk's office to see if there are any liens recorded against a property for nonpayment of municipal services such as water, sewage, solid waste, or gas.

5. *City, county, and state environmental protection agencies:* Check with
   your city, county, and state environmental protection agencies to see
   if the property has been cited for having any type of environmentally
   hazardous waste on it.

How Parcels of Land Are Identified for Tax Purposes

Most counties are divided into map or plat books. Each plat book is given
a separate number, and each parcel of land is given a separate tax identification number, an assessor's parcel number (APN), or an appraiser's
folio number, by the county property assessor or appraiser. These folio or
assessor's parcel numbers are used to compile annual property tax assessments and to list each parcel owner's name, post office mailing address,
and the assessed value of both the parcel of land and any improvements
that are made on the parcel.

Where to Search Property Records Online

As I told you in Chapter 15, the names of virtually every property owner in
your county are available at your county property appraiser or assessor's

office. The following web sites list the county property appraiser and assessor offices, which have their property records available online:

Public Record Finder: www.publicrecordfinder.com/property.html

Search Systems: www.searchsystems.net

Tax Assessor Database: www.pulawski.com

Public Records Online: www.netronline.com/public_records.htm

Public Records United States: www.factfind.com/public.htm

In so-called nondisclosure states, only the principals and any real estate licensees involved in a real estate transaction know the sale price. The sale price of real estate transactions aren't publicly disclosed in the following six nondisclosure states:

1. Indiana.
2. Kansas.
3. Mississippi.
4. New Mexico.
5. Utah.
6. Wyoming.

If you live in a nondisclosure state, you'll have to get sales data from a private company that maintains real property ownership records for your county or from real estate licensees, who have access to the local multiple listing service records. The following is a listing of web sites of two companies that maintain real property ownership record databases:

1. First American Real Estate Solutions: www.firstamres.com/jsp/index.jsp
2. DataQuick: www.dataquick.com

When Property Records Aren't Available Online

If your county's property records aren't yet available online, contact your property appraiser's or assessor's customer service department to see if they provide property record information over the telephone. In most counties, you can call your property appraiser's or assessor's customer service department and give them a property's street address, and they'll be able to tell you the parcel or folio number, the owner's name and post office mailing address (if it's different than the property's address), when and how much the property last sold for, and the property's current tax-assessed value. This way, you won't have to go traipsing down to your property appraiser's or assessor's office every time you want to look up information on a property. However, if you're unable to obtain information over the telephone, you'll have to visit your county's property appraiser's or assessor's office to look up property records, which are stored on microfiche or microfilm.

Two Types of Property Liens

Property liens are legal claims placed against a debtor's or lienee's real property by creditors or lienors such as lenders, creditors, and government agencies to secure the repayment of a debt. The two types of real property liens are:

1. *Voluntary liens:* Voluntary or consensual liens, such as mortgage or deed of trust loans, are placed against the title to real property with the owner's approval.

2. *Involuntary liens:* Involuntary or nonconsensual liens, such as federal and state income tax liens, property tax liens, judgment and mechanic's liens, are placed against the title to real property as a result of legal action by a creditor, lender, or government agency.

A Lien's Priority Is Determined by the Date It Was Recorded and the Type of Lien

A lien's priority or seniority over other liens placed against a property's title is determined by the date or chronological order in which it was recorded in the public record and the type of lien. For example, a mortgage or deed of trust lien that was recorded on April 25, 2006, would have priority over another mortgage or deed of trust lien that was recorded on April 28, 2006, against the same property, because it would be in a first or senior position over the next lien recorded. In most states, property and special assessment tax liens, including liens placed against real property for unpaid governmental services, have priority over previously recorded mortgage or deed of trust liens. However, judgment liens, mechanic's liens, and even IRS tax liens don't have seniority over previously recorded mortgage or deed of trust liens and are considered subordinate or junior liens.

Types of Liens to Check for When Searching Property Titles

The following is a listing and brief description of the 16 most common types of liens that must be checked when searching a property's title:

1. *Real property tax lien:* Placed against properties by local taxing authorities—city and county tax collectors—when property owners fail to pay their property taxes.

2. *Federal tax lien:* Statutory liens that the IRS places against the titles of real property belonging to taxpayers who fail to pay their federal income tax.

3. *Federal judgment lien:* Placed against the titles of real property, belonging to debtors who are in default on federally guaranteed loans, such as Small Business Administration and student guaranteed loans.

4. *Mechanic's lien:* Statutory liens that allow mechanics, contractors, material men, architects, surveyors, and engineers who have furnished work or materials for the improvement of real property to file a lien against the debtor's real property on which they are working.

5. *Judgment lien:* Result from lawsuits awarding monetary damages. Once recorded, a lien is placed against both the real and personal property of the debtor until the judgment is paid.

6. *Mortgage or deed of trust lien:* A voluntary lien created when real property is pledged as security for the repayment of a debt.

7. *State inheritance tax lien:* Most states have an inheritance tax, which is levied against the estates of deceased persons. The amount of inheritance tax owed becomes a lien against the estate.

8. *Corporate franchise tax lien.* States having a corporate franchise tax will tax corporations for the right to do business within the state. When a corporation fails to pay its franchise tax, the state files a lien against any real property, within the state, which belongs to the corporation.

9. *Bail bond lien:* Created when real property is pledged as a bail bond in order to allow a person arrested on criminal charges to be released on bail pending trial.

10. *Code enforcement lien:* Placed against a property's title by a local code enforcement board when a property owner has been fined for failing to correct code enforcement citations and fails to pay the fine.

11. *Municipal lien:* Placed against a property's title by local government agencies when a property owner fails to pay for municipal services such as water, sewage, and trash removal.

12. *Welfare lien:* Placed against a property's title by state and federal government agencies when a property owner receives welfare payments to which they're not legally entitled.

13. *Public defender lien:* Placed against a property's title by federal, state, and local governments when a property owner fails to pay for a court appointed public defender.

14. *Marital support lien:* Placed against a property's title by federal and state governments when a property owner fails to pay court ordered marital support payments.

15. *Child support lien:* Placed against a property's title by federal and state governments when a property owner fails to make court ordered child support payments.

16. *Home owners' association lien:* Placed against a property's title by a home owners' association when a member fails to pay his or her home owner's dues, as required by the deed to the property.

Some county recorders are slow to index or place recorded documents into the public records, which can result in a recently recorded lien not being discovered during a search of the public records. Because of the time lag between when a document is recorded and when it's actually indexed in your county's public records, you must always check the *lis pendens* index at the clerk of the circuit, superior, or county court or recorder's office for notices of any pending lawsuits, which may be filed against the property's title.

Common Types of Property Title Searches

The two most common types of property title searches are:

1. *Current owner title search:* Sometimes referred to as a title or property report, this is a search of the public records from the date the property's title was transferred to the current owner to the present.
2. *Full title search:* Involves an in-depth search of the property's chain of title from the date the current owner took title back to a maximum of 60 years.

Hire an Experienced Title Professional to Search Property Titles

Researching property title records can sometimes be very tricky, even for title professionals who are extremely knowledgeable and have years of experience. To me, any investor who bases buying decisions on the results of a do-it-yourself title search isn't playing with a full deck. I am telling you this because a recorded mechanic's lien, federal tax lien, or judgment lien that, for whatever reason, wasn't discovered during a title search can come back to haunt an investor at a later date, usually when they're in the process of trying to refinance or sell the property. For example, I know an investor in St. Petersburg, Florida, who's a legal secretary. When she was starting out, she thought that she knew it all when it came to searching property titles, but she really didn't know diddly-squat on how to search a property's title. She overlooked a $12,000 judgment lien, which was filed against a property owner by an auto insurer for unpaid medical bills, stemming from an automobile accident for which the owner had been cited. Because she bought the property on an agreement for deed and made the mistake of closing the deal on the seller's kitchen table, without purchasing an owner's title insurance policy, she didn't discover her blunder until three years later when she applied for a loan and the lender ordered a title report, which showed the previously unknown $12,000 judgment lien. This is exactly why you must always hire an experienced title abstractor or researcher to search property titles for you. Most title and escrow companies and real estate attorneys provide title search services to the public. To find an experienced title abstractor in your county, log onto: www.abstractersonline.com.

When to Perform Preliminary Due Diligence

Perform preliminary due diligence just as soon as you've made an appointment to meet with a motivated owner who responded to one of your property wanted ads. This way, you'll have information about the property and its owner, which you can use during your meeting to compare what the owner tells you against what's on the public records. This will enable you to know if you're dealing with a straight shooter or someone who has a problem telling the truth.

What to Search for When Performing Preliminary Due Diligence

Once you've made an appointment to meet with a property owner, you need to search the following nine public records:

1. *Property records search:* Check your county property appraiser or assessor's property records for ownership, sale, and tax-assessment information.
2. *Property tax records search:* Check your county tax collector's property tax records for tax payment information.
3. *Property owner name search:* Check online to see if the owner is in anyway involved in any type of ongoing civil or criminal court proceedings.
4. *Comparable sales search:* Check your county's property records for recent sales of comparable properties during the past six months.
5. *Neighborhood crime search:* Check the crime risk rating for the property's address with local law enforcement agencies.
6. *Flood zone map search:* Check the property's address on federal flood maps to determine if it's located in a flood zone.
7. *Hazardous waste search:* Check the property's address for environmental hazards with local, state, and federal environmental protection agencies.

8. *Demographic data search:* Check demographic data for the property's address with local, state, and federal agencies.
9. *Code violation search:* Check the property's address for code violations with your local code enforcement department.

I can complete a preliminary due diligence search of a property and its owner in less than an hour. I have all of the pertinent public records web sites bookmarked on my computer. My computer has a high-speed connection to the Internet, which allows me to quickly access records online. The only telephone call that I have to make is to the Tampa Department of Code Enforcement to check a property for code enforcement citations.

Do an Online Search of a Property Owner's Name

Whenever I am performing preliminary due diligence on a piece of property, I want to know as much about a property owner's physical, emotional, legal, mental, and financial condition as I do about the physical and financial condition of the property under consideration for purchase. I do the equivalent of a strip search on property owners to find out if there are any outside factors, such as bankruptcy, divorce, death, arrest, criminal charges, or imprisonment, which could influence a property owner's decision-making process. Nowadays, as part of my standard preliminary due diligence procedure, I log onto www.google.com and enter the property owner's name into the browser window and wait to see what pops up on my computer screen.

How to Locate Hard to Find Property Owners

When you come across a vacant property that belongs to an owner who no longer resides at the post office mailing address listed on the local property appraiser's or assessor's property records, check the following 12 records in the county and state of the property owner's last known address:

1. County voter registration records.
2. City and county public library patron records.
3. City and county business license records.

4. City and county jail inmate records.
5. State fishing and hunting license records.
6. State professional license records.
7. State department of motor vehicles.
8. State bar association membership records.
9. State vital statistics records.
10. State prison inmate records.
11. Federal prison inmate records.
12. Social Security Administration's Death Index.

Where to Search for People Online

The following web sites provide people locator and street address information online:

Internet Address Finder: www.iaf.net

Pretrieve: www.pretrieve.com

Switchboard: www.switchboard.com

Skipease: www.skipease.com

Social Security Administration Death Index: www.ancestry.com /search/rectype/vital/ssdi/main.htm

Street Address Information: www.melissadata.com/lookups/index.htm

Reverse Telephone Directory: www.reversephonedirectory.com

Critical Factors Investors Must Consider When Selecting Areas in Which to Invest

Whether you realize it or not, whenever you buy any type of property you're also buying the area in which it's located. No matter how much money you plow into fixing up a piece of property, it'll most likely turn out to be a colossal waste of time and money if the property is located in a substandard area, which has serious flaws that can't be overcome by individual real estate investors operating on their own. That's why, when you're selecting areas to invest in, you must use an area selection checklist, like Form 16.1, to consider the critical factors, which have a direct impact on an area's desirability.

FORM 16.1 Sample Area Selection Checklist

1. Does the area have potential for economic growth? (   ) Yes (   ) No

2. Are properties being maintained? (   ) Yes (   ) No

3. Is there adequate storm water drainage? (   ) Yes (   ) No

4. Is the public perception of the area bad? (   ) Yes (   ) No

5. Are building, safety, health, and fire codes being enforced? (   ) Yes (   ) No

6. Are zoning regulations being enforced? (   ) Yes (   ) No

7. Is the crime rate above average? (   ) Yes (   ) No

8. Are public nuisances present? (   ) Yes (   ) No

9. Is the area easily accessible from surrounding highways? (   ) Yes (   ) No

10. Are municipal services available? (   ) Yes (   ) No

Copyright Thomas J. Lucier, 2006. To customize this document, download it from www.thomaslucier
.com/realestateforms.html. The document can then be opened, edited, and printed using Microsoft Word.

Demographic Information Available Online

The following is a listing of online sources of demographic information:

FFIEC Geocoding System: www.ffiec.gov/geocode/default.htm

U.S. Census Bureau FactFinder: www.factfinder.census.gov/servlet
/BasicFactsServlet

U.S. Census Bureau QuickFacts: http://quickfacts.census.gov/qfd

U.S. Census Bureau zip code statistics: www.census.gov/epcd/www
/zipstats.html

CHAPTER 17

How to Conduct a Thorough Pre-Buy Property Inspection So You Know What You're Buying

Now more than ever before, investors must be on the lookout for unscrupulous owners who'll go to extraordinary lengths to try and bamboozle an unsuspecting investor into buying a lemon of a property. Because of these types of shady owners, I can't overemphasize just how important it is to have a property inspected before you close on the purchase. I am telling you this because after a property's title has been transferred into your name, it's almost always too late to do anything meaningful about any hidden surprises, which you may discover after the sale is finalized. That's why, whenever possible, I do my pre-buy inspection before I make an offer to buy the property. This way, I can use any needed repairs that I uncover during my property inspection to negotiate a lower purchase price. I fully realize that the timing of when to have a property inspected can pose a catch-22 for most real estate investors who don't have the construction knowledge and experience to perform their own inspections. Investors face the dilemma of either paying for an inspection on a piece of property before they've signed a purchase agreement to buy it, or signing a purchase agreement for a fixed price before they've had an opportunity to inspect the property they've agreed to buy. Granted, you may be able to include a clause in your purchase agreement, which makes the sale contingent on the property passing an inspection that you pay for. But if a property inspection reveals a slew of needed repairs, your options are somewhat limited. You can do three things:

1. Negotiate a reduction in the purchase price.
2. Buy the property for the agreed on price and eat the repair costs.
3. Exercise your inspection contingency clause and void the purchase agreement.

However, in so-called hot real estate markets, where there are many more buyers than sellers, it may be hard to find an owner who'll allow you to include any type of contingency clause in your purchase agreement. Without an inspection contingency clause, you wouldn't be able to get out of a purchase agreement because the property failed an inspection. The best advice that I can give you is to evaluate each property and base your decision about when you have it inspected on the property's age and physical condition. In other words, if a property is old and decrepit looking, I suggest that you have it inspected prior to signing a purchase agreement. On the other hand, if a property is relatively new and well maintained, I advise you to sign a purchase agreement, which makes the sale contingent on the property passing an inspection within five business days from the date the agreement was signed by you and the owner. But under no circumstances, do I recommend that you ever buy any property without first having it inspected for the following 11 things:

1. Structural roof damage.
2. Sinking and cracking foundations.
3. Mold contamination.
4. Electrical, fire, and safety hazards.
5. Structural dry rot damage.
6. Water and moisture intrusion.
7. Collapsed water and sewer lines.
8. Signs of termite infestation.
9. Missing roofing material, gutters, and downspouts.
10. Rotting wood.
11. Stripped mechanical systems and missing electrical wiring.

Be Aware of Any Nonpermitted Work That's Been Done to a Property

You need to be aware that some owners make improvements and additions to their property without obtaining building permits from their local building department. This is referred to as nonpermitted work, which means that it hasn't been inspected and approved by the local building department to ensure that it was done in compliance with the building code. Tearing down and rebuilding nonpermitted work to meet the building code can be a costly and time-consuming process. The two most common telltale signs of nonpermitted work are shoddy workmanship and substandard building materials, which make the botched job stick out like a sore thumb. As an example, I once inspected a single-family house in Tampa that had a second-story room addition attached to the rear of the house, above a concrete patio, which was supported by four, four-inch posts. Just as soon as I laid my eyes on this monstrosity, I knew that I was looking at an illegal room addition. I asked the owner about it and he swore up and down to me that he had pulled all of the necessary permits and that all of the work had been inspected and approved by building inspectors from the City of Tampa. But when I asked to see the building permit, he told me that it had been lost. So I called the City of Tampa Building Department to verify his claim, and, just as I had suspected, it had no record of a room addition ever being built at the property's address.

Check for Indoor Mold When Inspecting a Property

Nowadays, thanks to exaggerated media reports about various types of illnesses that are supposedly caused by indoor mold and the fear of mold-related lawsuits, the American public has pretty much developed a phobia about indoor mold. This irrational fear of indoor mold is exactly why you must always check for it when inspecting any type of property. Indoor mold grows in the parts of buildings that are damp, poorly ventilated, and receive little or no natural sunlight. Indoor mold is pretty easy to spot. It has a dark green or black color and a very strong musty odor. The most common place indoor mold is found, in residential properties, is in bathrooms. In fact, there probably isn't a bathroom in America that doesn't have a small amount of undetected indoor mold. As I told you in Chapter

10, I buy properties that have a moderate amount of indoor mold, and I recommend you do the same provided that you have the mold contamination checked by a mold-remediation specialist.

The following web site has information on indoor mold: www.epa.gov/iaq/molds/moldresources.html.

EPA Guide on How to Prevent and Clean Up Indoor Mold Growth

The Environmental Protection Agency (EPA) has published an excellent guide on how to prevent and clean up indoor mold entitled *A Brief Guide to Mold, Moisture, and Your Home,* which is available online at: www.epa.gov/iaq/molds/moldguide.html.

Inspect Properties for Environmental Contamination

Properties that have been used to house businesses, such as gas stations, dry cleaners, automobile repair shops, and other types of businesses that use petroleum products, cleaning solvents, and hazardous chemicals may be contaminated with environmentally hazardous materials, which could adversely affect the property's value. If you suspect that a property has any type of environmental contamination, use phase one environmental audit checklist in Form 17.1 to conduct your own inspection.

Information about Environmentally Hazardous Waste Sites Available Online

The following web sites have information about environmentally hazardous waste sites nationwide:

EPA superfund hazardous waste site search: www.epa.gov/superfund /sites/query/basic.htm

Environmental hazards zip code search: www.scorecard.org

EPA Enviromapper zip code search: www.epa.gov/cgi-bin/enviro /em/empact/getZipCode.cgi?appl=empact&info=zipcode

FORM 17.1 Sample Phase One Environmental Audit Checklist

1. Examine the property's chain of ownership for the past 50 years.

2. Interview the current and available past owners of the property to determine if any present or past uses of the property would have an adverse affect on the environment.

3. Review available past city cross-reference street directories to determine how the property was previously used.

4. Review available topographic maps of the property.

5. Review available historical aerial photographs of the property.

6. Review available geological reports affecting the property.

7. Research local, state, and federal government files for records of environmental problems affecting the property.

8. Research local, state, and federal government files for records of environmental problems affecting adjacent properties.

9. Conduct an on-site inspection of the property for obvious signs of past or present environmental problems such as odors, soil staining, stress vegetation, or evidence of dumping or burial.

10. Determine the existence and condition of above-ground storage tanks.

11. Determine the existence and condition of underground storage tanks.

Copyright Thomas J. Lucier, 2006. To customize this document, download it from www.thomaslucier .com/realestateforms.html. The document can then be opened, edited, and printed using Microsoft Word.

Housing Built before 1978 May Pose Potential Lead-Based Paint Hazards

As I told you in Chapter 12, the Residential Lead-Based Paint Hazard Reduction Act requires that all sale agreements to sell residential property built before 1978 contain a Seller's Lead-Based Paint Disclosure Statement, which discloses whether the property has been inspected for lead-based paint hazards and if lead-based paint hazards have been found on the property. The abatement process to remove lead-based paint from a building is tedious, extremely expensive, and usually not financially feasible. Often there's a stigma attached to residential properties that have been known to contain lead-based paint that's nearly impossible to overcome because prospective tenants are fearful that all the paint wasn't removed from the property.

Lead-Based Paint Hazard Information Available Online

The following is a listing of web sites that have information on the hazards of lead-based paint:

> EPA National Lead Information Center: www.epa.gov/lead/nlic.htm
>
> Lead-Based Paint Disclosure Fact Sheet: www.epa.gov/opptintr/lead/fs-discl.pdf
>
> HUD Lead-Based Paint Abatement Guidelines: www.lead-info.com/abatementguidelinesexamp.html
>
> EPA Lead information Pamphlet: www.epa.gov/lead/leadpdfe.pdf

Conduct a Property Inspection

I have over 30 years of hands-on experience inspecting various types of residential and commercial properties. When I conduct a property inspection, I come prepared with my clipboard and inspection checklists, searchlight, high-powered binoculars, handheld voice recorder, digital camera, and ice pick. I use the binoculars to inspect the roof, chimney, fascia, and soffit. The ice pick is used to check wood for dry rot and termite damage. I use the handheld voice recorder to record detailed descriptions of needed repairs. And the digital camera is used to take pictures of needed repairs, which are e-mailed to contractors to obtain repair cost estimates. The main thing that I am looking for during a property inspection is any type of structural damage, which would be costly and time consuming to repair. In addition, I also check out the area where the property is located between the hours of 10 P.M. to 12 A.M. I do this to check for excessive noise, drag racing in the streets, gang activity, and any other public nuisances, which could adversely affect the property's resale value. I also drive through an area after a heavy rainfall to check for drainage and flooding problems.

Locate a Competent Building Inspector

Unless you're a seasoned construction professional, who has the knowledge and experience that is needed to conduct a thorough property inspection, I highly recommend you hire a licensed professional building or home inspector to do your property inspections. However, you need to know that because most states don't have any licensing requirements, the building inspection profession has more than its fair share of phonies, fakes, frauds, and scam artists. The best advice that I can give you is to use an inspector who's licensed by your state or is a member of the American Society of Home Inspectors (ASHI), which has very strict membership requirements. To find ASHI members, who are located in your area, log onto: www.ashi.org.

Use My Inspection Checklists to Conduct Your Pre-Buy Property Inspections

The following 12 pages (Forms 17.2 through 17.13) contain my pre-buy property inspection checklists, which contain a repair cost column, where a rough cost estimate of each needed repair that's uncovered during the inspection can be included.

FORM 17.2 Sample Exterior Property Checklist

Street address _____

Item	Good	Fair	Bad	Repair Cost
Roof				
Foundation				
Siding				
Windows				
Doors				
Carport				
Garage				
Paint				
Screens				
Soffit and fascia				
Chimney				
Steps				
Other				

FORM 17.3 Sample Grounds Inspection Checklist

Street address _____

Item	Good	Fair	Bad	Repair Cost
Lawn				
Plants and shrubs				
Trees				
Driveway				
Sidewalks				
Pot holes				
Sink holes				
Drainage				
Streets				
Outside lighting				
Other				

FORM 17.4 Sample Attic Inspection Checklist

Street address _____

Item	Good	Fair	Bad	Repair Cost
Ventilation				
Insulation				
Floor				
Lighting				
Roof rafters				
Ceiling joists				
Wiring				
Air ducts				
Termite damage				
Mold				
Other				

FORM 17.5   Sample Garage and Carport Inspection Checklist

Street address _____

Item	Good	Fair	Bad	Repair Cost
Walls				
Floor				
Ceiling				
Doors				
Windows				
Lighting				
Heat				
Air conditioning				
Paint				
Roof				
Soffit and fascia				
Mold				
Other				

FORM 17.6   Sample Electrical Inspection Checklist

Street address _____

Item	Good	Fair	Bad	Repair Cost
Riser				
Service panel				
Capacity				
Circuit breakers				
Electrical outlets				
Lighting				
Wiring				
Electrical meter				
Other				

FORM 17.7 Sample Plumbing Inspection Checklist

Street address _____

Item	Good	Fair	Bad	Repair Cost
Water supply				
Hot water heater				
Toilets				
Sinks				
Tub				
Shower				
Septic system				
Water pipes				
Drains and sewer lines				
Water pressure				
Plumbing fixtures				
Water supply lines				
Well				
Mold				
Other				

FORM 17.8 Sample Heating and Air Conditioning Inspection Checklist

Street address _____

Item	Good	Fair	Bad	Repair Cost
Natural gas				
Central heat and air				
Oil furnace				
Window and wall units				
Solar panels				
Vents				
Condenser unit				
Heat pump				
Mold				
Other				

FORM 17.9   Sample Kitchen Inspection Checklist

Street address _____

Item	Good	Fair	Bad	Repair Cost
Floor				
Walls				
Ceiling				
Doors				
Windows				
Lighting				
Electrical outlets				
Sink				
Plumbing				
Cabinets				
Countertops				
Refrigerator				
Oven				
Ceramic tile				
Paint				
Mold				
Other				

FORM 17.10   Sample Bathroom Inspection Checklist

Street address _____

Item	Good	Fair	Bad	Repair Cost
Floor				
Walls				
Ceiling				
Doors				
Windows				
Lighting				
Electrical outlets				
Shower				
Toilets				
Tub				
Ceramic tile				
Sink and vanity				
Ventilation				
Linen closet				
Mirrors				
Paint				
Mold				
Other				

FORM 17.11 Sample Dining Room Inspection Checklist

Street address _____

Item	Good	Fair	Bad	Repair Cost
Floor				
Walls				
Ceiling				
Doors				
Windows				
Lighting				
Electrical outlets				
Paint				
Carpet				
Mold				
Other				

FORM 17.12 Sample Living Room Inspection Checklist

Street address _____

Item	Good	Fair	Bad	Repair Cost
Floor				
Walls				
Ceiling				
Doors				
Windows				
Lighting				
Electrical outlets				
Paint				
Carpet				
Mold				
Other				

FORM 17.13   Sample Bedroom Inspection Checklist

Street address _____

Item	Good	Fair	Bad	Repair Cost
Floor				
Walls				
Ceiling				
Windows				
Doors				
Lighting				
Electrical outlets				
Closets				
Carpet				
Paint				
Mold				
Other				

How to Accurately Estimate a Property's Market Value So You Don't Pay More Than What It's Worth

When you're in the market to buy a new or used car, you can go online and log onto the *Kelley Blue Book* web site and look up a car's value, and based on the year of manufacture, make, model, and mileage, you can get a pretty accurate estimate of its market value. The closest thing that real estate investors have to a *Kelley Blue Book* is property records that are maintained by county property assessors or appraisers. But property records by themselves aren't of any value to investors who don't know how to use them. That's why in this chapter, you're going to learn all of the nitty-gritty details that you need to know in order to use property records to accurately estimate a property's market value. Typically, most real estate investors overestimate a property's market value and underestimate its repair and holding costs. As a result, they often make the financially fatal mistake of overpaying for their first, and usually last, investment property. Knowing how to accurately estimate a property's market value is the single most important aspect of the entire buying process. Your success as a real estate investor will be tied directly to how well you're able to estimate property values. Nowadays, thanks to the Internet, investors who are located in counties where property records are available online can get an accurate estimate of a property's market value within a short period of time. For example, in my county, I can log onto the Hillsborough County Property Appraiser's web site and click on the "sales search" tab, which takes visitors to the sales search web page and, from there, I can search my county's property records for comparable sales information by:

- Section, township, and range.
- Property use code.
- Sale dates.
- Sale prices.
- Market area.
- Neighborhood.
- Subdivision.
- Land use code.
- Year built.

Real Estate Markets Are Highly Inefficient

There are so many opportunities to profit from real estate because real estate markets are highly inefficient. That's because, unlike the stock and bond markets where the prices for stocks and bonds are set and nonnegotiable, there's no set price for any single type of property nationwide. This allows knowledgeable real estate investors, who know how to accurately estimate property values, to negotiate below market purchase prices.

How Inept Real Estate Investors Skew Property Values

The old Wall Street expression *price is what you pay for something, value is what you get in return* is very apropos to the real estate investment business today, where clueless investors routinely buy overvalued properties. Most competent business owners welcome incompetent competitors with open arms, as it makes them look better and drives more business their way. However, the real estate investment business is the only business that I know of where incompetent competitors can have an adverse affect on the entire profession. That's because inept real estate investors who don't have a clue about how to estimate a property's market value can wreak havoc in a real estate market by overpaying for property, which artificially raises property values and causes prices to be inflated. This ends up cutting into the profit margins of seasoned professional investors, like me, who know what they're doing.

How Market Value Is Defined

The Appraisal Foundation's *Uniform Standards of Professional Appraisal Practice* defines market value as: *the most probable price a property should bring in a competitive and open market under all conditions requisite to a fair sale, the buyer and seller each acting prudently and knowledgeably, and assuming the sale price isn't affected by undue stimulus.* This definition assumes that the following five conditions are met:

1. The buyer and seller are motivated.
2. Each party is well informed and acting in his or her own best interest.
3. A reasonable amount of time is allowed for the property to be exposed on the open market.
4. Payment is made in cash in U.S. dollars or in comparable financial arrangements.
5. The price represents the normal consideration of the property sold and is unaffected by special or creative financing or sales concessions, granted by anyone associated with the sale.

The Difference between Tax-Assessed Value and Appraised Value

The difference between a property's tax-assessed value and its appraised value is as follows:

- *Tax-assessed value:* The value established by the local taxing authority for a parcel of land and the improvements placed on the land for property tax purposes. For example, in Florida, owner-occupied single-family houses are generally assessed at around 70 percent of their fair market value by county property appraisers.

- *Appraised value:* The value estimate given to a property by a licensed property appraiser, using accepted appraisal methods, for the type of property being appraised. For example, the accepted appraisal method to accurately estimate the fair market value for an owner-occupied single-family house is the comparison sales method, where a property's value is based on the recent sale of comparable properties within the same area.

Don't Confuse As-Is Value with As-Repaired Value

All too often, investors mistakenly confuse a property's as-is value with its as-repaired value. As-is value is the value of a property in its present physical condition. As-repaired value refers to the value of a property after it has been repaired and put in a marketable resale condition. One of the worst financial blunders that any investor can make is to pay market value for a property in dire need of repair and end up spending what they thought was going to be their profit on repair costs. That's why, when you're calculating an estimate of a property's market value, you must deduct the amount that it's going to cost to spruce up the property in order to maximize its curb appeal and resale value. You can calculate a rough estimate of the total fix-up cost of a property by using the list of needed repairs, which were uncovered during your pre-buy property inspection. Once you have your total cost estimate, do as I do and add a 10-percent cushion to cover any repairs that you may have underestimated.

Everything You Need to Know about Property Appraisal Reports

To avoid being snookered by dishonest property owners, who use bogus appraisal reports to help substantiate the asking price for their property, you must know what to look for when reading a residential or commercial property appraisal report. A sham appraisal report isn't that difficult to spot, when you know what to look for. The best way to check the validity of an appraisal report is to use an appraisal report checklist like Form 18.1.

FORM 18.1   Sample Property Appraisal Report Checklist

1. Is the purpose for the appraisal accurately stated in the appraisal?

2. Is there a certificate of value included with the appraisal?

3. Does the appraisal include a summary of conclusions?

4. Does the appraisal analysis identify significant trends?

5. Does the appraisal focus on the factors affecting the property's value?

6. Does the appraisal describe the economic base?

7. Does the appraisal describe the property's neighborhood?

8. Does the appraisal describe neighborhood trends?

9. Does the appraisal contain errors in mathematical computations?

10. Does the appraisal contain errors in land, area, and building sizes?

11. Does the appraisal include an adequate history of the property?

12. Do the photographs contained in the appraisal adequately show the property?

13. Is the appraisal written in a clear, concise, complete, consistent, and factual manner?

14. Does the appraisal outline both the negative and positive features of the property?

15. Does the appraisal contain inconsistencies between the market comparison, income and replacement cost methods, remaining economic life, and depreciation?

16. Were recent comparable sales used in the appraisal?

17. Was special financing used in any comparable sales?

18. Were more than three comparable sales used in the appraisal?

19. Were comparable property sale locations similar to the subject property being appraised?

20. Was all comparable sales data fully analyzed and adjusted?

21. Is the subject property compatible with other properties in the area?

22. Are comparable sales locations being put to their best use?

23. Was the market data used to calculate the capitalization rate selected from similar properties within the same market area?

24. Were vacancy and rent collection losses and operating expenses included in calculating the capitalization rate?

25. Does the current market data support the capitalization rate?

Property Appraisal Information Available Online

Property appraisal information is available online at the following web sites:

Appraisal Foundation: www.appraisalfoundation.org

Appraisal Institute: www.appraisalinstitute.org

American Society of Appraisers: www.appraisers.org

Three Methods That Appraisers Use to Estimate Property Values

Property appraisers use the following three methods to estimate property values:

1. *Comparison sales method:* Bases a property's value on the recent sale prices of properties that are located within the same area and that are comparable in size, quality, and amenities.

2. *Income method:* Used to estimate the value of an income producing property, based on the amount of net income that the property produces.

3. *Replacement cost method:* Based on what it would cost to replace a building using similar building materials and construction methods.

The Comparison Sales Method

The comparison sales method is based on the recent sale prices of at least three properties within the same area that are comparable in size, amenities, and features. To get an accurate estimate of a property's value when using the comparison sales method, you must check each comparable property's:

- Sale date.
- Sale price.
- Sale terms.
- Age and condition.

- Quality of construction.
- Design, amenities, and architectural style.
- Amount of livable square feet.
- Lot size, shape, and landscaping.

When using the comparison sales method to estimate a property's value, you'll also need to make adjustments to the sale price of comparable properties that have been sold at unrealistically low prices or on overly favorable financial terms, which aren't available to the general public. For example, sales conducted between parents and their children, or among relatives and friends, may have been priced below the property's fair market value. Comparable sales data for single-family houses is available online at the following web sites:

DataQuick: www.dataquick.com

HomeGain: www.homegain.com

REAL-COMP: www.real-comp.com

HomeRadar: www.homeradar.com

Domania Home Price Check: www.domania.com

The Income Method

The income method is used to estimate the value of income-producing property, based on the amount of net income that the property generates. Under the income method, value is calculated by using the following:

- Capitalization rate.
- Gross rent multiplier.

The Oregon Department of Revenue has an excellent publication entitled *The Income Approach to Value* that's a self-study course for property assessors and appraisers, which has in-depth explanations of capitalization rates and gross rent multipliers and can be downloaded from the following web site: www.oregon.gov/DOR/PTD/docs/303-458-3.pdf.

What You Need to Know about Capitalization Rates

A property's capitalization rate (cap rate) is calculated by dividing its annual net operating income by the owner's asking price for the property. Net operating income (NOI) refers to a property's gross income minus operating expenses, excluding interest payments and property depreciation for tax purposes. For example, a property with an annual NOI of $36,000 and an asking price of $360,000, would have a cap rate of 10 percent ($36,000 divided by $360,000 equals 10). There's an inverse relationship between cap rates and asking prices. The higher the cap rate, the lower the asking price, and the lower the cap rate, the higher the asking price. As a general rule of thumb, I stay away from properties with single digit cap rates. Although it's next to impossible to verify the income and expense data that's used to calculate cap rates, they can be a fairly accurate indicator of a property's value, provided that the market data was derived from comparable properties, which are similar in location, size, age, and condition. However, one major drawback about using cap rates is that they don't take future expenses, such as the cost of repairs that have been deferred, into account. When needed repairs and other expenses aren't factored into value estimates, they can skew a property's market value. Depending on the volume of sales of residential rental properties in your market, you should be able to get reliable cap rate data from local:

- Property assessors or appraisers.
- Apartment owners' associations.
- Commercial mortgage lenders.
- Commercial property appraisers.

It's generally next to impossible to find reliable cap rates to estimate the market value of small—two- to four-unit—rental properties That's because there usually aren't that many sales of small rental properties taking place in most markets. So instead of using unreliable cap rates, I suggest that you use a gross rent multiplier and comparable sales data to estimate the value of small rental properties.

Use Gross Rent Multipliers to Estimate an Income Property's Value

A gross rent multiplier (GRM) is similar to a capitalization rate except it uses a property's gross rental income, instead of its NOI, to estimate income property values. And like a cap rate, a GRM is only as accurate as the market data that's used to calculate it. To be valid, the multiplier must be based on the sales of comparable properties that are located in the same area and similar in age, size, and condition. A property's GRM is calculated by dividing the asking price of a property, by either the monthly or annual gross rental income. For example, if the asking price for a property is $200,000 and its monthly gross rental income is $2,500, the GRM would be 80 ($200,000 divided by $2,500 equals 80). As a general rule, properties with low GRMs usually have a higher net income. I won't buy a small rental property with a GRM above 80, unless it's mismanaged and has rental rates that are substantially below the market rate. One drawback of using a property's monthly gross income to calculate its GRM is that it doesn't take vacancy and credit losses into account. Instead, it's based on the assumption that the property has a 100 percent occupancy rate. That's why, when I calculate a GRM, I use the property's annual effective gross rent, which is the actual amount of rent that was collected during the past 12 months and includes vacancy and credit losses.

Sources of Property Valuation and Analysis Software Programs

Property valuation and analysis software programs are available at the following web sites:

> Real estate investment analysis software: www.invest-2win.com /index.html
>
> Z-Law real estate software catalog: www.z-law.com
>
> Real Data real estate software: www.realdata.com
>
> Marshall & Swift: www.marshallswift.com

Comparable Property Sale and Income Data Available Online

Comparable sale and income data for all types of residential and commercial properties are available online for free, or for a relatively small fee, at the following web sites:

CoStar Exchange: www.costar.com

Loopnet: www.loopnet.com

National Real Estate Index: www.realestateindex.com

IDM Corporation: www.idmdata-now.com

DataQuick: www.dataquick.com

Real Estate Information Source: www.reis.com

Owners May Fudge the Numbers on Income and Expense Statements

One surefire defense against being victimized by property owners who cook their books by fudging the numbers on their property's income and expense statements is to do like I do and take a see-it-to-believe-it attitude. The way that I get the true numbers for an income-producing property is by requiring that the owner provide me with verifiable documentation to support the numbers that they're claiming on their income and expense statements. This way, I can reconcile everything that's listed on a property's monthly income and expense statement, like Form 18.2, against what's shown on:

- Schedule E, Supplemental Income and Loss, of the owner's latest federal income tax return.
- The property's latest annual tax assessment income and expense statement on file at the county property assessor or appraiser's office.
- All of the rental agreements for the past year.
- Water, sewage, solid waste, gas, and electric receipts for the past year.
- Repair and capital improvement receipts for the past year.

Reconcile the Rent Roll against the Rental Rates Listed in Rental Agreements

From what I've seen over the years, most rental property owners have a tendency to exaggerate or overstate their property's rental income. The only foolproof method to avoid being bamboozled by a dishonest owner is to reconcile the rental rates that are listed on the rent roll against the rental rates that are stated in the rental agreements. A rent roll typically

FORM 18.2 Sample Monthly Income and Expense Statement

1. Gross monthly rental income: $_____

2. Total monthly income: $_____

3. Less vacancy allowance and credit losses: $_____

4. Gross monthly operating income: $_____

5. Property taxes (divide annual amount by 12): $_____

6. License fees (divide annual amount by 12): $_____

7. Property management fee: $_____

8. Employee wages and benefits: $_____

9. Natural gas: $_____

10. Electricity: $_____

11. Trash removal: $_____

12. Water and sewer: $_____

13. Telephone: $_____

14. Internet: $_____

15. Advertising: $_____

16. Building maintenance and repairs: $_____

17. Lawn care and landscaping: $_____

18. Swimming pool maintenance and repair: $_____

19. Parking, walkway, and driveway maintenance: $_____

20. Insurance premiums (divide annual amount by 12): $_____

21. Maintenance and office supplies: $_____

22. Automobile expenses: $_____

23. Net monthly operating income: $_____

lists the names of all the tenants, their monthly rental rate, and the period of their tenancy. For example, I once had an owner who claimed on the rent roll that the annual gross rental income for a six-unit rental property was $46,800 (6 units multiplied by $650 times 12 months equals $46,800). However, this didn't jibe with the contract rental rates that were listed in the rental agreements, which showed that only four units were actually rented for $650 a month, while the other two units were rented for $600.

The Replacement Cost Method

The replacement cost method is based on the cost of replacing the improvements on a piece of property minus the cost of the land. Replacement costs are calculated on a per-square-foot basis, by dividing the total number of square feet in a building by the per-square-foot construction cost. For example, a 2,000 square foot building that cost $275,000 to build would have a replacement cost of $137.50 per square foot ($275,000 divided by 2000 equals $137.50). You can usually get a free building replacement cost estimate by calling a local independent insurance broker who represents insurers that specialize in providing property and casualty insurance coverage for residential and commercial buildings. Replacement costs are calculated by using a replacement cost formula, which is based on the property's geographical location and its:

- Street address.
- Age.
- Type of construction.
- Number of stories.
- Type of roof.
- Current use.
- Heating and cooling system.
- Square footage.

Construction Replacement Cost Calculators Available Online

Construction replacement cost calculators are available online at the following web sites:

Construction cost calculator: www.get-a-quote.net

Construction material calculators: www.constructionworkcenter.com
/calculators.html

Building cost calculator: www.rsmeans.com/calculator/index.asp

Accurately Estimate the Market Value of a Residential Rental Property

To accurately estimate the market value of a residential rental property follow the 10 steps listed here:

Step 1: Verify the property's income and expenses and calculate its annual NOI.

Step 2: Search your county's property records for recent sales of small rental properties that are comparable in size and located within one mile of the property.

Step 3: Calculate the property's cap rate by dividing its NOI by its estimated value, which was derived from recent sales of comparable properties.

Step 4: Estimate the property's value by multiplying its NOI by the cap rate.

Step 5: Calculate the property's GRM by dividing its estimated value by its monthly gross rental income.

Step 6: Estimate the property's value by multiplying its monthly gross rental income by the GRM.

Step 7: Compare the property's three value estimates to each other, add them together, and divide the total by three. This will give you the property's median estimated value.

Step 8: To calculate the property's estimated market value, deduct the property's repair costs from its median estimated value.

Step 9: Call an insurance broker for a cost estimate to replace the property, using the same building materials and method of construction.

Step 10: Compare the property's estimated market value minus the cost of the land to the property's replacement cost estimate. Your estimated market value should be below the property's replacement cost.

CHAPTER 19

How to Prepare Purchase and Sale Agreements So Your Position Is Protected during the Transaction

The two main reasons you should never use any of those generic real estate purchase and sale agreements that are available for purchase on the Internet and at office supply stores is because they're too vague and are not state specific. The problem with standard boilerplate purchase and sale agreements is that they're poorly written and fail to fully protect the rights and interests of buyers and sellers during a real estate transaction. Most novices to this business, who are ignorant of the fact that real estate contract law varies from state to state, wrongly assume that it's hunky-dory to use these run-of-the-mill agreements to document a real estate transaction in their state. A real estate purchase agreement that passes muster in Georgia would probably be deemed unconscionable in California. This is exactly why you must always use well-written purchase and sale agreements, which conform to your state's real estate sales statute and fully protect your position as a buyer or seller and clearly spell out all of the provisions of the agreement in plain English, without the usual legal gobbledygook.

Avoid Using the Same Agreements That Real Estate Licensees Use in Your State

A lot of investors use the same purchase and sale agreements that are used by real estate licensees in their state to document the purchase and sale of property. As far as I am concerned, this is a big no-no. I am telling you this because virtually all of the real estate agreements used by real estate licensees are written to protect the licensees' sales commissions and to shield them against lawsuits from sellers, who have listed their property through real estate brokers. They provide absolutely zero protection to buyers. In other words, the purchase and sale agreements used by real estate licensees are heavily stacked against buyers. They're also way too long and laden with unnecessary legal gibberish, which makes them confusing and not the least bit user-friendly.

Require All Real Estate Agreements Be in English

Unfortunately, in some parts of the United States, there are areas where people are unable to read, write, and speak English. Often, non-English speakers will want to use real estate documents that are written in their native language. To me, this is an invitation to all kinds of unforeseen problems. And today, there are already more than enough potential legal booby traps and landmines that real estate investors must guard against, without the added burden of having to worry about being sued because of language mistranslations in a real estate agreement. So regardless of whether English is your native language, you should require that all real estate agreements be written in English.

Use Separate Purchase and Sale Agreements to Document Transactions

Some real estate investors use the same purchase and sale agreement to buy and sell property. However, I recommend that you use separate purchase and sale agreements. This way, your position as a buyer is protected in the purchase agreement, while your position as a seller is protected in the sales agreement. For example, in my real estate purchase agreement, I include a provision, which gives me the right to assign the agreement to a third party. But in my real estate sales agreement, the buyer is prohibited from assigning the agreement. I've done this so that my buyer can't assign our agreement to a third party, who may not be able to obtain a loan to finance the purchase of my property, which would leave me stranded without a qualified buyer and right back at square one.

Have Your Agreements Drawn up by a Board-Certified Real Estate Attorney

In Chapter 14, I told you to use the services of a board-certified real estate attorney to close your transactions. In this chapter, I am telling you to use the same attorney to write or draw up your purchase and sale agreements. I realize that the services of a competent real estate attorney don't come cheap, but after your attorney has drawn up separate purchase and sale agreements and copied them onto a floppy disk or CD-ROM, you can use them as a template or master copy. Doing this will eliminate the need to hire your attorney to prepare a new agreement, every time you buy or sell a property, which will save you a considerable amount of money in the long run.

Key Provisions That Must Be Included in Your Purchase Agreements

I very highly recommend that you include the following 14 key provisions in each one of your purchase agreements:

1. *Parties to the agreement:* Designate all parties to the purchase agreement as buyer and seller to include their legal status as to whether they are a single individual, husband and wife, or a business entity such as a corporation or limited liability company.

2. *Earnest money deposit:* State that if the buyer fails to perform this agreement within the time specified, the full amount of earnest money deposit made by the buyer shall be forfeited as liquidated damages and such forfeiture shall jeopardize the seller's right to sue for specific performance.

3. *Legal description of property:* Use the exact same legal description that's written on the recorded deed of the property in the purchase agreement.

4. *Purchase price:* State the firm purchase price of the property.

5. *Terms of purchase:* Specify exactly how the purchase of the property is going to be financed.

6. *Marketable title:* Specify that the seller must provide the buyer with a clear and marketable title to the property at the time of the closing.

7. *Assignment of the purchase agreement:* Include a clause that gives the buyer the right to assign or sell the purchase agreement to a third party without the seller's consent.

8. *Default by buyer:* Specify that the earnest money paid is the sole and exclusive remedy in the event that the buyer fails to close on the purchase of the property.

9. *Default by seller:* State that the buyer shall have the right of specific performance in the event the seller defaults on the agreement by refusing to sell the property.

10. *Eminent domain:* Specify that the buyer shall be entitled to a full refund of the earnest money deposit paid, plus any accrued interest, in the event the property is condemned by eminent domain prior to the scheduled closing date.

11. *Buyer's right of entry:* State that the buyer, or the buyer's assigns, has the right, on giving the owner 24 hours notice, to enter the property and inspect, repair, market, and show it to third parties prior to the scheduled closing date.

12. *Risk of loss:* Specify that the buyer is entitled to a full refund of the earnest money deposit paid, plus accrued interest in the event the property is damaged or destroyed by fire, storm, or earthquake prior to the scheduled closing date.

13. *Right to examine records:* State that the buyer has the right to examine all of the financial and tax records associated with the property prior to the scheduled closing date.

14. *Seller must vacate property:* Require that the seller completely vacate the property and grounds prior to the scheduled closing date.

I have included the sample real estate purchase agreement in Form 19.1 for informational and instructional purposes only. For specific information on how to properly document the purchase and sale of real estate in your

---

FORM 19.1 Sample Real Estate Purchase Agreement

This Agreement is made this ninth day of July 2006 between Roger P. Throckmorton, a single man, known hereinafter as the Buyer and Charles M. Troutman, a single man, known hereinafter as the Seller. Seller agrees to convey, transfer, assign, sell, and deliver to Buyer or assigns, all of Seller's rights, title, and interest in and to the following property known as: 45735 Hillsborough Avenue, Tampa, Florida 33603, and legally described as: Lots 47, 48, and 49 of Carters subdivision according to map or plat thereof as recorded in plat book 69, page 89, of the public record of Hillsborough County, Florida, which Seller agrees to sell to Buyer and Buyer or assigns agrees to buy from Seller.

Purchase Price.. $335,000.00

Method of Payment:

Earnest money deposit paid in the amount of $1,000.00

Buyer to assume that first mortgage loan with an approximate principal
balance of $295,000.00

and dated August 28, 1997, and executed by Charles M. Troutman, as mortgagor, to Bank of America, as mortgagee, in the original amount of three-hundred and five thousand dollars ($305,000), which mortgage was duly recorded in the office of the Clerk of the Circuit Court of Hillsborough County, State of Florida, in book 790346, on page 45905, of the public records of Hillsborough County, Florida.

Balance to close the transaction payable in U.S. currency by cashier's check drawn on a local bank, subject to prorations or adjustments $39,000.00

Any net differences between the approximate balance of the existing encumbrance shown above and the actual balance at closing, to include all unpaid loan payments, accrued interest, late charges, legal fees, taxes, liens, judgments, assessments, and fines shall be adjusted to the purchase price at closing. All proration computations shall be made as of the previous day before the closing date, using the three hundred sixty-five-day (365) method. The following items are to be prorated:

1. Real estate taxes for the year of the closing. If the taxes for the current year can't be ascertained, any tax proration based on an estimate shall be readjusted on receipt of the tax bill on condition that a statement to that effect is in the closing statement.

2. All statutory liens and assessments recorded against the property, as of the closing date, shall be paid by the Seller.

3. All water, sewage, electricity, natural gas, and other similar utility charges.

4. Rents due from tenants of the property, as set forth on the rent roll. Seller shall be entitled to receive rent payments for the period up to the day before the closing. Buyer shall be

entitled to receive all rent payments from and including the day of the closing. All rents shall be prorated on the basis of rents actually received.

Seller shall furnish to Buyer copies of all rental agreements, and an estoppel letter from each tenant specifying the nature and time of occupancy, amount of rent, and advance rent and security deposits paid. At the closing, Seller shall deliver the following to the Buyer:

1.   Possession of the property, subject to those rental agreements set forth on the rent roll. Delivery of possession of the property shall not be subject to the rights of any other person or entity.

2.   Bill of sale for all personal property.

3.   Assignment of all tenant rental agreements.

4.   All tenant security deposits.

5.   A valid certificate of occupancy issued by the appropriate government agency.

6.   All blueprints, surveys, and keys to the property.

7.   Rent roll listing all tenants residing at the property.

8.   All insurance policies and mortgage documents being assumed by the Buyer.

Buyer may assign or otherwise transfer any of Buyers rights, title, and interest in and to this Purchase Agreement to a third party without the Seller's consent.

Buyer or the Buyer's assigns, shall have the right, upon giving the owner twenty-four (24) hours notice, to enter the property and inspect, repair, market, and show said property to third parties, prior to the scheduled closing date.

The earnest money paid shall be the sole and exclusive remedy in the event that the Buyer fails to close on the purchase of the property.

Buyer shall be entitled to a full refund of the earnest money deposit paid, plus any accrued interest, in the event the property is condemned by eminent domain prior to the scheduled closing date.

Buyer shall be entitled to a full refund of the earnest money deposit paid, plus accrued interest, in the event the property is damaged or destroyed by fire or storm, prior to the scheduled closing date.

Buyer shall have the right of specific performance in the event the Seller defaults on the agreement, by refusing to sell the property.

Seller shall provide the Buyer with a clear and marketable title to the property at the closing.

Title to the property shall be conveyed from Seller to Buyer by warranty deed at the closing.

Buyer and Seller authorize Mr. John B. Good, Attorney at Law, to act as Escrow Agent to receive, deposit, and hold funds and other items in escrow, subject to clearance, and to disburse them on proper authorization and in accordance with the terms of this Real Estate Purchase Agreement.

IN WITNESS WHEREOF, Seller has set his hand the date aforesaid.

Charles M. Troutman
Seller

Roger P. Throckmorton
Buyer

Robert B. Big
Witness

Sally M. Little
Witness

state, please follow my advice and consult with a board-certified real estate attorney who's licensed to practice law in your state.

Make Certain That Your Agreements Are Properly Witnessed

You can have the world's greatest purchase and sale agreements, but if the signatures of both the buyer and seller aren't properly witnessed, the agreement may end up being good for wrapping garbage or lining birdcages. You must check your state's real estate sales statute to determine how many witnesses are required on real estate agreements. In Florida, two witnesses are required to attest the signatures on real estate agreements. I am telling you this because agreements that aren't properly witnessed may not be enforceable in a court of law. For example, owners who get cold feet and try to get out of a purchase agreement they've signed with you will go over your agreement with a fine-tooth comb in search for a way to weasel out of it. And an agreement, which wasn't properly witnessed, could give the owner the out that he or she is looking for if it rendered your agreement unenforceable.

Have the Owner Complete and Sign a Property Disclosure Statement

At the same time you and the owner sign your purchase agreement, you must have the owner complete and sign a property disclosure statement that is approved for use in your state. At a minimum, the disclosure statement should ask the following 10 questions:

Question 1: Are there any hazardous substances at, on, under, or about the property? The term *hazardous substances* shall mean and include those elements or compounds, which are contained in the list of hazardous substances and toxic pollutants adopted by the EPA, or under any hazardous substance laws.

Question 2: Have any documents ever been filed in the public records that adversely affect the title to the property?

Question 3: Are there any liens against the property for unpaid bills owed to architects, surveyors, engineers, mechanics, laborers, or material men?

Question 4: Are there any actions, proceedings, judgments, bankruptcies, liens, or executions recorded among the public records, or pending in the courts, which would affect the title to the property?

Question 5: Are there any unpaid taxes or claims of lien, or other matters that could constitute a lien or encumbrance against the property, or any of the improvements on it?

Question 6: Have any improvements been placed on the property in violation of applicable building codes and zoning regulations?

Question 7: Are there ongoing legal disputes concerning the location of the boundary lines of the property?

Question 8: Is any person or entity other than the owner presently entitled to the right to possession, or is in possession of the property?

Question 9: Has the title or ownership of the property ever been disputed in a court of law?

Question 10: Are there any unrecorded mortgages or deed of trust loans or promissory notes for which the property has been pledged as collateral?

Key Provisions That Must Be Included in Your Sale Agreements

In order to fully protect your position as seller, you must include the following four key provisions in your real estate sale agreements:

1. This agreement shall not be assigned to a third party.
2. This agreement shall not be recorded in the public records.
3. In the event the buyer fails to perform as agreed, seller shall have the right to file a specific performance lawsuit for damages.
4. This sale is made as-is and the seller makes no expressed or implied warranties as to the property's condition and is under no obligation to make any repairs to the property at anytime.

CHAPTER 20

How to Negotiate So You Get the Best Possible Deal for Yourself

To me, real estate negotiations are about two things and two things only: price and terms. And that's why your objective during negotiations should always be to obtain a purchase or sale price and terms that will give you the best possible deal. By "best possible deal," I mean a price and terms that an investor can realistically expect a seller or buyer to agree to and which will allow them to earn what they consider to be a reasonable profit from the property. For example, when I am negotiating to buy a small mismanaged residential rental property, the best possible deal that I can realistically expect to receive is a purchase price that's 20 percent below market value and owner financing, which includes a six month moratorium or delay before I am required to begin repaying the loan. How to obtain a short-term moratorium on repaying a seller-financed loan is covered in Chapter 21. In this business, knowing how to negotiate the best possible deal when buying and selling property is second only in importance to knowing how to accurately estimate a property's market value. The price and terms that you're able to negotiate depend entirely on how good a negotiator you are. If you're a shrewd negotiator, you can usually buy a property below market value and resell it for your full asking price. If you're a lousy negotiator, the odds are that you'll end up overpaying for a property and reselling it for a substantial loss. On the other hand, you must also have the good sense and self-discipline to walk away from properties that can't be bought at a price and terms that make financial sense to you. In this chapter, you're going to learn the nuts and bolts of how to obtain the best possible deal when buying and selling property.

Knowing the Other Party's True Needs Is the Key to Getting the Best Possible Deal

The key to getting the best possible deal during negotiations is to determine the other party's true needs and then meet them in a way that's financially feasible to you. An important part of your job as a negotiator is to be able to distinguish between a want and a need. To me, a want is what someone wishes for, while a need is what they'll accept to fulfill their wish. For example, you may want a brand spanking new Lexus, but if you can't get it, you'll settle for a Nissan, instead of being forced to rely on public transportation to get around town. If you're a good listener, you can usually pickup on clues about what the other party really needs versus what they claim they want.

For example, I once bought a duplex from a guy who had mentioned something during our initial telephone conversation about wanting to sell the property so that he could take an Alaskan cruise. He started off negotiations by telling me that he was flexible on the price but that he had to have $10,000 as a down payment. I quickly put our earlier telephone conversation and the $10,000 down payment together and realized that what he truly needed, in his mind at least, was an Alaskan cruise, not $10,000. I told him that I needed a day to think it over. So I went back to my office and looked up prices for Alaskan cruises on the Internet. The next day, I came back with a counteroffer in which I agreed to buy him a seven-day Alaskan cruise of his choice on Princess Cruise Lines, pay his round trip airfare from Tampa to Seattle on Southwest Airlines, and give him $1,000 in cash as the down payment. He accepted my offer on the spot and I ended up shelling out less than $4,000 to buy the duplex. Another time, an owner wanted a $20,000 down payment, but, based on what I was able to glean from our discussions, I had a hunch that $10,000 would probably satisfy her immediate need for cash. So I told her that I couldn't give her $20,000 right now, but I could give her $10,000 on the day the deal closed and pay her the remaining balance of $10,000 over the next 18 months at $555.55 per month. As an added incentive to get her to accept my proposal, I offered to close on the purchase of the property within the next 10 business days. Two days later, she agreed to my terms and we closed the deal a week later.

It's Your Job as a Negotiator to Get the Best Possible Deal for Yourself

Your sole job during negotiations is to get the other party to agree to a price and terms that gives you the best possible deal. But I must warn you that this isn't going to happen unless you're willing to follow the advice that I gave you in Chapter 16 and perform preliminary due diligence in order to learn as much as possible about the property and seller or buyer, before you sit down at the negotiating table. That's because, contrary to what you may have been told elsewhere, it isn't the job of the party that you're negotiating with to tell you what they want. Rather, it's your job as a negotiator to find out the price and terms that they're willing to accept. I can tell you that you're not going to get the best possible deal for yourself, if you're lazy and try to cut corners by asking the other party really lame questions such as:

- What's the least amount that you'll take for your property?
- Is this your best offer?
- Are your price and terms negotiable?

Negotiate with the Other Party instead of against Them

Whenever I hear the catchphrase "win-win negotiations" (which by the way is a misnomer), I always wince. The term *win-win* implies that both parties received everything that they bargained for. And quite frankly that's virtually impossible to achieve during any type of negotiation. Successful negotiations require both parties to be willing to compromise, give and take, and split the difference to meet the other party in the middle. Negotiations aren't a winner-takes-all proposition, or a game of one-up-manship, where each party tries to outdo the other. If you want to get beyond first base during negotiations, you must negotiate with the other party and not against them. In other words, you should focus on expediting the negotiation process instead of impeding it, by being part of the problem instead of the solution.

Don't Negotiate with People Who Aren't Motivated to Do Business with You

I've never been able to understand why investors waste their valuable time trying to negotiate with sellers and buyers who really aren't serious about doing business with them in the first place. As a matter of policy, I never enter into negotiations with property owners or prospective buyers who aren't motivated to do business with me. And as I told you in Chapter 15, it's a colossal waste of time, money, and energy to try and buy property below market value from owners who have no compelling reason to sell you their property at a discounted price. Plus, you have absolutely no leverage, whatsoever, with which you can bargain when you're negotiating with an owner or buyer who has no motivation to close the deal. In Chapter 23, you'll learn how to screen out the tire kickers from the serious buyers who are ready, willing, and financially able to pay your asking price.

Try to Establish Rapport with the Party with Whom You're Negotiating

You don't need to be buddy-buddy with the party that you're negotiating with in order to get the best possible deal for yourself. But you do want to try and build rapport by finding something that you both have in common. For example, when I go to someone's home, office, or business, I always look for something on their automobile, walls, table, or desk that tells me something about the person's background, such as a military discharge, college degree, professional license, or membership certificates, which I can use as an ice breaker to engage in a friendly conversation.

You Never Get a Second Chance to Make a Good First Impression during Negotiations

When you're involved in negotiations you never get a second chance to make a good first impression. How you're perceived by the party that you're negotiating with can have a direct impact on whether you're able to negotiate the best possible deal for yourself. That's why, as a negotiator, you want to project the image of a polished professional, but without coming across as some slick-talking wheeler-dealer who missed their true calling selling used cars. By polished professional, I mean an individual who's sincere, personable, confident, knowledgeable, well spoken, well mannered, well dressed, well groomed, and in control of his or her emotions. The point that I am making here is that if you want to be taken seriously, you must look and act like a professional who knows what they're doing.

Have Realistic Expectations about the Price and Terms That You Can Negotiate

In order to be a successful real estate negotiator, you must have realistic expectations about the price and terms that you'll be able to negotiate with the other party. For example, if you enter into negotiations with the expectation that you can get an owner to sell a $250,000 property for $100,000 below market value, there's an excellent chance that you're going to come away from the negotiating table empty-handed. That's because it's unrealistic to expect the owner of a property with a market value of $250,000 to shave $100,000 off the asking price. However, under the right circumstances, it would be realistic to expect the owner of a one million dollar property to lower their asking price by 10 percent or $100,000. The point that I am making here is to be reasonable when negotiating price and terms with sellers and buyers. Fact is, the quickest way that I know for an investor to bring negotiations to a screeching halt is to begin by making unreasonable demands to which no sane person would ever agree. I know that I'll break off negotiations in a New York minute with anyone who starts off by making outlandish demands, which are beyond the realm of reason.

Don't Try to Think for the Party with Whom You're Negotiating

A lot of investors fall into the trap of trying to think for the party with whom they're negotiating. They automatically assume that just because they wouldn't accept a price or terms, the party that they're negotiating with wouldn't either. It's this type of a mind-set that stops investors from making what they consider to be so-called lowball offers. Needless to say, this type of thinking isn't conducive to negotiating bargain-basement prices on buyer-friendly terms. There's an old expression that professional negotiators often use, which says, *You'll never pay less than your initial offer.* In other words, once you make an offer to purchase a piece of property, the only way that the price can go from that point forward is up. You'll never know what price and terms an owner will accept, unless you make an offer. The worst that can happen is that your offer gets rejected or the owner makes a counteroffer.

How to Get a Feel for the Mind-Set of the Person with Whom You're Negotiating

The very first thing that I want to know about the person who's sitting across the negotiating table from me is his or her mind-set or how they think. So when I am negotiating to buy, I always start off by asking an owner to tell me about their property. I do this to get a reality check to see if I am dealing with a reasonable, rational adult or someone who still believes in the Tooth Fairy and lives in fantasyland. For example, if a property is in a rundown condition and in dire need of repairs and the owner comes back with a line about how it just needs a little tender loving care to put it back into tip-top shape, I immediately know that I am probably not dealing with a reality-based adult. Once I get a feel for how an owner perceives their property, I ask him or her what they think the property is worth today. I pose this question to see if an owner has done their own market research and has a realistic asking price in mind. When they tell me their price, I ask them how they came up with that figure. If an owner's asking price is based on market data, I continue the conversation. If they come up with a price that's based on nothing more than wishful thinking, I write a lowball offer on the back of my business card and tell them to call me, if they want to talk about it at a later date.

Always Insist That Negotiations Be Conducted between the Principal Parties

My first rule of negotiating is that all negotiations must be conducted between the principal parties in the transaction. In other words, I don't allow third parties or surrogates to come between me and the seller or buyer during negotiations. They can have a small army of advisors at their beck and call, but the seller or buyer must be sitting across the table from me during negotiations. I require principals to be present for all negotiations for two very important reasons. First, I flat-out refuse to negotiate through intermediaries, who don't have the authority to say yes or no to my proposal. When married couples and partners show up to negotiate without their spouse or partner, they're promptly told that the only way that I'll continue negotiations is if I can sit down face-to-face with everyone at the same time. This way, I don't get stuck in a situation where the person that I am trying to negotiate with has to run everything by another person—a higher authority—before a decision can be reached. By having both parties present during negotiations, the possibility that an incompetent go-between, who wasn't paying close attention to what was said during our discussion, could garble or misrepresent my offer is totally eliminated.

Know the Price and Terms You're Willing to Accept before Negotiations Begin

The last thing that you must do before you ever sit down at the negotiating table is to determine the price and terms that you're willing to accept in order to close the deal. For example, before I ever sit down at the negotiating table, I already know:

- The maximum amount that I am willing to pay for a property.
- The minimum amount that I am willing to sell a property for.
- The terms of the purchase that I am willing to accept.
- The terms of the sale that I am willing to accept.

Sixteen Rules to Follow to Negotiate the Best Possible Deal for Yourself

Here are 16 rules that you should follow to negotiate the best possible deal for yourself:

Rule 1: Establish a negotiating time line.

Rule 2: Make a checklist of the terms to be negotiated.

Rule 3: Prepare answers to possible objections that may be raised during negotiations.

Rule 4: Maintain a professional and dispassionate demeanor.

Rule 5: Use a negotiating strategy that fits your personality.

Rule 6: Base your decisions on verifiable facts and figures and not on emotions.

Rule 7: Don't alienate the other party by rude behavior or hardball negotiating tactics.

Rule 8: Never underestimate the party that you're negotiating with.

Rule 9: Spend more time listening than speaking.

Rule 10: Assume nothing, verify everything, and be prepared for anything.

Rule 11: Use mouthwash and deodorant to protect against bad breath and smelly body odors, which could bring negotiations to a standstill.

Rule 12: Determine the other party's negotiating timetable and use it to your advantage.

Rule 13: Use the property's physical and financial condition and the owner's personal circumstances to negotiate the best possible deal for yourself.

Rule 14: Take the path of least resistance and agree to mundane negotiating points, which don't affect the price or terms.

Rule 15: Know when it's time to stop talking.

Rule 16: Make a counteroffer within 24 hours of your offer being rejected.

Where to Hold Negotiations

I always want my initial meeting with the buyer or seller to be held at the property that's under consideration for purchase. This way, I get to kill two birds with one stone: I meet them face-to-face and we have an opportunity do a cursory walk-through of the property together. However, I like to conduct the actual negotiations at a neutral site of the seller or buyer's choosing, such as a diner or family restaurant. I do this because I've found that most people don't feel comfortable going to a stranger's home or office to negotiate a real estate deal. By letting the other party choose the place where he or she wants to negotiate, I've shown that I am a flexible person, who doesn't want to run the whole show. This initial show of goodwill on my part, which doesn't cost me anything, has come in handy during negotiations. For example, on more than one occasion during negotiations, I've been in situations where I've used my gesture of goodwill as my ace in the hole to persuade the other party to meet me halfway on a sticking point that was keeping us from moving forward.

How to Finance Your Real Estate Deals Even When You Don't Have a High Income, Huge Bank Account, and Perfect Credit Score

Contrary to what many uninformed members of the financial press would want you to believe, you don't need a six-figure income with a lifetime employment contract, a humongous bank account, and an 850 FICO score in order to be a successful real estate investor. The term *FICO*, refers to the popular consumer credit scoring model that was developed by the Fair Isaac Corporation. FICO scores range from a low of 300 to a high of 850. In fact, it has been my experience that most beginning real estate investors—more than 51 percent—don't fall into the well-heeled financial bracket that I've just described. And I have a strong suspicion that most of the people who get involved in real estate investing earn much less than a six-figure annual income. Please don't misconstrue what I am telling you here to mean that you don't need money and credit to be a successful real estate investor, because you most certainly do. However, if you're reading this book and you still believe in the fairytales that are constantly being told on those cheesy real estate infomercials that run on cable TV, about how anyone with a pulse can become a real estate millionaire lickety-split, even if they're unemployed, flat broke, and have really rotten credit, you definitely need a reality check. The fact of the matter is that 99 percent of all legitimate real estate investment strategies require cash and credit to implement. The actual amount of start-up capital and credit that you'll need to get your real estate investment business off the ground, pretty much depends on where you live and in which segment of your local market you decide to invest. In most cases, it's reasonable to expect that you'll need to be able to make at least a five percent down payment and pass the minimum financial tests for income and creditworthiness that are required to qualify for most types of mortgage or deed of trust loans. But that shouldn't be a problem for most people, as it has never been easier to borrow money for real estate than it is today. Nowadays, mortgage and deed of trust lenders have a smorgasbord of loan programs for just about every conceivable type of financial situation under the sun, including:

1. Low and no documentation loans for borrowers who don't like the intrusive loan approval process.
2. Fixed and adjustable rate equity loans and lines of credit for home owners.
3. Interest only and adjustable rate loans for cash-strapped borrowers.
4. Hard money equity loans for property owners.

Understand That Cash Is Always King in the Real Estate Investment Business

I would be remiss if I didn't start this chapter off by telling you that cash is always king in the real estate investment business. The old expression "money talks and bullspit walks" that has been commonly used in business circles for decades to describe the buying power of cash is especially true today in our credit-based economy, where even meals at fast-food restaurants are now regularly charged on credit cards. The fact of the matter is that the average American has become addicted to the various forms of easily obtainable credit that were once only available to a select few. Today, it's not uncommon for people to charge almost all of the basic necessities of life on various types of credit cards. This buy now and pay later mentality, which has permeated American society is most prevalent in the real estate industry, where virtually 95 percent of all transactions are financed using various types of mortgage and deed of trust loans. Don't get me wrong, I believe in using leverage whenever it makes financial sense. However, I don't like the fact that a lender holds all the cards in a leveraged real estate transaction and can quash a deal at anytime simply by refusing to approve a loan. One of the keys to being successful in this business is to maintain control of a real estate transaction from start to finish. That's exactly what happens when you're a cash buyer. You get to call all of the shots without some uptight banker in a cheap suit looking over your shoulder. As a cash buyer, you'll be able to buy all types of properties at prices that are substantially below market value. That's because nothing maximizes a real estate investor's buying power the way cash does, especially when the property or owner is in a distressed situation that requires a fast sale. Believe me, having the financial capability to close on a property purchase on 24 hours notice will automatically eliminate 95 percent of the competition in any real estate market nationwide.

Why Real Estate Investors Must Maintain Excellent Credit Scores

Whether you like it or not, credit scoring is here to stay. If you aspire to be a successful real estate investor, you must do everything humanly possible to maintain an excellent credit score. An excellent credit score is like having money in the bank and is one of the main building blocks to lasting financial wealth. Creditors generally consider anyone with a FICO credit score of 720 and above to be an excellent credit risk. Lenders use borrowers' credit scores to determine interest rates on mortgage and deed of trust loans. They do this by grading loans as A, B, C, or D paper, based on the borrower's credit score. Borrowers' numerical credit scores are assigned loan letter grades ranging from A+ to E. For example, borrowers with credit scores of 670 and above qualify for low-interest prime loans; while borrowers with credit scores below 620, qualify for so-called subprime loans, which have higher interest rates and more expensive closing costs. The following credit score and corresponding loan grade guidelines may vary from lender to lender:

Borrower's Credit Score	Grade of Loan
670+	A+ to A
650	A–
620	B+ to B–
580	C+ to C–
550	D+ to D–
520–	E

FICO Credit Scoring Information Available Online

The Fair Isaac Corporation, which developed the popular consumer credit scoring model named FICO, has published a booklet entitled *Understanding Your Credit Score,* which gives a detailed explanation of exactly how the credit scoring process works. The booklet can be downloaded from the following web site: www.myfico.com/Downloads/Files/myFICO_uycs percent20booklet.pdf.

Obtain Copies of Your Credit Reports from Credit Reporting Agencies

To obtain copies of your consumer credit files, you can contact the three main credit reporting agencies at the following web site addresses and toll-free telephone numbers:

1. Equifax: www.equifax.com (800) 685-1111.
2. Experian: www.experian.com (888) 322-5583.
3. Trans Union: www.transunion.com (800) 916-8800.

Consumer Credit Information Available Online

The following web sites offer information and advice on consumer credit:

Credit Info Center: www.creditinfocenter.com

Credit Net: www.creditnet.com

Credit Boards: www.creditboards.com

Four Types of Lenders That Make Real Estate Loans

Residential and commercial mortgage and deed of trust loans are generally made by the following four types of lenders:

1. *Institutional lenders:* Banks, mortgage companies, and credit unions that make conventional and government-backed residential loans that are sold in the secondary mortgage market to Fannie Mae and Freddie Mac.

2. *Portfolio lenders:* Usually small community banks and finance companies that originate loans for their own portfolio and not for resale in the secondary mortgage market. Because portfolio loans aren't sold in the secondary market to Fannie Mae or Freddie Mac, lenders have much more flexibility about the loan terms that they can offer borrowers and the physical condition of the property securing their loans.

3. *Private lenders:* Usually high net worth individuals, such as attorneys, accountants, medical doctors, and business owners, who make mostly first mortgage or deed of trust loans on residential and commercial property.

4. *Hard Money lenders:* Make true equity loans that are based solely on the amount of equity that a borrower has in the property being pledged as collateral for the loan. Hard money lenders make loans on properties that don't conform to standard loan underwriting guidelines. And they're generally considered to be "lenders of last resort" because they usually charge exorbitant loan fees and sky-high interest rates.

Factors That Lenders Consider When Deciding to Approve a Loan

When deciding whether to approve a loan, institutional, portfolio, and private lenders consider the following three factors:

1. *Character:* The borrower's credit history based on consumer credit reports.

2. *Capacity:* The borrower's ability to repay the loan based on income.

3. *Collateral:* The property pledged as collateral to secure repayment of the loan.

Why You Shouldn't Obtain Real Estate Loans through Mortgage Brokers

I've held a Florida mortgage broker license since 1995. I spent the time, effort, and money to obtain a mortgage broker license in order to get a better understanding of exactly how the residential and commercial lending process works. However, based on my experiences and observations of the mortgage brokerage industry over the past 26 years, I very strongly recommend that you avoid obtaining loans through mortgage brokers. I am telling you this because in my professional opinion, most—more than 51 percent—mortgage brokers are dishonest, unethical, and grossly incompetent. Luckily today, anyone with a personal computer and Internet connection can gain instant access to literally hundreds of lenders and a cornucopia of loan programs. To me, this is reason enough for anyone not to pay a mortgage broker to find a lender.

How the Loan Approval Process Works with Institutional Lenders

Depending on the lender, the loan approval process can be a slow and time-consuming process, which can drag on for 30 days or longer. The institutional loan approval process is comprised of the following six steps:

Step 1: Borrower contacts institutional lender for the purpose of obtaining a mortgage or deed of trust loan.

Step 2: Lender receives permission from the borrower to obtain copies of his or her consumer credit files to ascertain the borrower's creditworthiness.

Step 3: Borrower completes a loan application and provides lender with the necessary supporting loan documentation.

Step 4: Lender calculates the loan amount and interest rate it's willing to lend, based on the borrower's creditworthiness, annual income, and the property's age, location, and condition.

Step 5: Lender approves the loan and provides the borrower with a loan commitment letter that states the loan amount, interest rate, and terms.

Step 6: Lender provides the borrower with the funds necessary to close on the purchase of the property.

Lenders May Charge Exorbitant Junk Fees to Close a Loan

Lenders are notorious for charging borrowers exorbitant loan fees, which are known in the real estate industry as junk fees, to close mortgage or deed of trust loans. Loan fees are supposed to cover legitimate costs associated with preparing a mortgage or deed of trust loan package. However, in most cases, borrowers are charged so-called junk fees for services that were never rendered, or to pay for duplicate services that aren't needed. I flat-out refuse to do business with any lender who tries to pad its bottom line by charging me any type of junk fee. Here's a listing of the eight most common junk fees that lenders routinely charge unsuspecting borrowers:

1. Loan application fee is what lenders charge borrowers for the privilege of completing a loan application.
2. Loan document preparation fee is to pay lenders for preparing all of the documentation that makes up a loan package.
3. Loan document review fee is charged to have a loan package reviewed after the closing takes place.
4. Loan funding fee is what lenders charge for making the loan.
5. Loan processing fee is what lenders charge borrowers to process the paperwork that's necessary to originate a loan.
6. Loan underwriting fee is to pay the lender for completing a mortgage or deed of trust loan document and promissory note.
7. Property tax service fee is charged for sending a property tax payment to the local taxing authority.
8. Loan warehousing fee is what lenders charge borrowers for holding a loan until it's sold in the secondary mortgage market to either Fannie Mae or Freddie Mac.

Always Obtain a Good Faith Estimate of Loan Costs from Lenders

The Real Estate Settlement Procedures Act requires that lenders provide borrowers with a good faith estimate, which is supposed to include an itemized list all of the costs associated with obtaining a loan. The best way to ferret out junk fees is to do what I do and obtain a good faith estimate from lenders before you ever go through the time and effort of filling out a loan application. I require lenders to give me a written good faith estimate right upfront as part of their loan quote. This way, I can challenge a lender's junk fees right on the spot and then leave if they refuse to drastically cut or waive the fee altogether. For example, I recently had one of the largest banks in America try and charge me a $200 loan application fee along with a $500 loan processing fee to obtain a loan to refinance the mortgage on my personal residence. I sent the president of the bank a very starchy letter, requesting that the bogus fees be waived. Lo and behold, the following week I received a warm and fuzzy telephone call from the branch manager where I applied for the loan telling me that the loan fees had been waived.

What You Need to Know about Loan-to-Value Ratios

Lenders use loan-to-value ratios to determine the maximum amount that they're willing to lend against a piece of property. The loan-to-value (LTV) ratio is the difference—expressed as a percentage—between the amount of the mortgage or deed of trust loan and the appraised value of the property securing the loan. For example, a LTV of 70 percent on a property appraised at $100,000, means that the maximum amount that can be borrowed is $70,000.

How Balloon Loans Work

Balloon mortgage or deed of trust loans are short-term—3, 5, 7, or 10 years—fixed-rate loans that have fixed monthly payments, which are usually based on a 30-year amortization schedule, with a lump sum or balloon payment due once the loan matures. They're called balloon loans because they can blow up just like a balloon if they're not paid off. As far as I am concerned, the main advantage of using balloon loans is that they allow real estate investors to obtain short-term seller-financed loans from property owners, who are reluctant to make long-term loans. The obvious disadvantage of balloon loans is that they must be paid in full or refinanced once the term of the loan expires. Over the years, I've used seller-financed 10-year balloon mortgage loans to finance the purchase of small residential and commercial properties. In fact, I had two sellers, who grew so accustomed to receiving monthly loan payments that they offered to modify the terms of my balloon loans and extend them for 20 years. Once they agreed to make their loans fully assumable by qualified borrowers, I accepted their offers and resold the properties a short time later.

Information on Residential Loan Programs Available Online

Nowadays, lenders have a wide variety of loan programs that are geared toward people with all types of financial situations, including borrowers with little cash on hand and a less-than triple-A credit rating. You can find loan information on all of the various types of residential loan programs that are available nationwide from the following web sites:

> Fannie Mae: www.fanniemae.com/homebuyers/homepath/index.jhtml ?p=Homepath
>
> Freddie Mac: www.freddiemac.com/sell/factsheets/frm.htm
>
> FHA: www.hud.gov/fha/loans.cfm
>
> DVA: www.homeloans.va.gov/veteran.htm

Freddie Mac and Fannie Mae Limit Investors to 10 Loans at One Time

The Federal National Mortgage Association (Fannie Mae) and the Federal Home Loan Mortgage Corporation (Freddie Mac) are congressionally chartered corporations or government sponsored enterprises that buy existing mortgage and deed of trust loans from lenders who originate loans in the primary mortgage market. The loans are then pooled and resold as mortgage-backed securities to investors on the open market. Fannie Mae and Freddie Mac resell loans in what is known as the secondary mortgage market. In order to be sold on the secondary market, a mortgage or deed of trust loan must conform to these two organizations' loan underwriting standards. Fannie Mae and Freddie Mac each limit the number of outstanding loans that a borrower can have as an individual or joint owner at one time to 10. The 10-loan limit applies to one- to four-unit residential properties. This means that a borrower could have his or her personal residence and nine investment properties financed with either Freddie Mac or Fannie Mae conventional mortgage or deed of trust loans.

Low Documentation and No Documentation Loans

To me, most real estate loan applications are overly intrusive and require far too much supporting documentation that has little or no bearing on a borrower's ability to repay the loan. But luckily for people like me, who have a high credit score and don't want to disclose their annual income and assets on loan applications, there are various types of loans that don't require borrowers to divulge their income and assets. These type of no documentation and low documentation loans are also available to people who can't provide verifiable proof of their income. However, watch out for lenders who misrepresent their loans in advertisements as being true no or low documentation type loans. I once had a lender ask me to sign a blank copy of IRS form 4506-T, Request for Transcript of Tax Return, as part of the loan application process for what was supposed to be a no income and no asset verification loan. I promptly told the lender, in no uncertain terms, just what he could do with his loan application. I dumped this nosy lender because I didn't want him snooping around my federal tax returns after I had closed on the loan. Filling out a copy of IRS form 4506-T would have defeated the whole purpose of using a no documentation loan in the first place. The only downside to no or low documentation loans is that the interest rate is usually one or two interest points above the going rate for full documentation loans. But I am willing to pay a little more in interest payments for a nonintrusive loan that lenders can process in a couple of days. The two most popular types of no and low documentation loans are:

1. No income and no asset verification loans
2. No income verification loans

No Income and No Asset Verification Loans

So-called no income and no asset verification loans (NINA), or no documentation loans, allow borrowers to obtain a mortgage or deed of trust loan without going through the rigmarole of having their income and assets verified by the lender. When making NINA type loans, lenders base their approval on the credit history of the borrower and the appraised value of the property being financed.

No Income Verification Loans

No income verification loans (NIV), or stated income loans, allow borrowers to obtain loans without having to go through the hassle of providing proof of their income with stubs from payroll checks, W-2, 1099, and 4506-T IRS forms and federal tax returns. The only documentation that lenders generally require for stated income loans is a copy of a business license or certificate of incorporation, or a letter from the borrower's accountant or tax preparer, simply stating that the borrower is self-employed. Borrowers who are employees must provide a letter from their employer stating that they're an employee.

Home Equity Loans

If you own your home and have a sufficient amount of equity, I recommend that you use a fixed-rate home equity loan to finance the down payment on investment properties. However, I would avoid using any type of variable-rate home equity line of credit. I am telling you this because the term *variable-rate* is just another way of saying "adjustable-rate." As you'll learn in this chapter, any type of adjustable-rate loan can be risky. In addition, most types of home equity lines of credit come with strings attached. For instance, borrowers are usually required to write checks in a certain dollar amount when making withdrawals from their home equity credit lines. I don't believe that investors should use all of the equity in their personal residence to fund their real estate investment business. In fact, I think that it's downright imprudent for anyone to use more than 70 percent of the available equity that he or she has in their home at any one time. Call me old school if you want, but, as far as I am concerned, it's financially reckless to suck all of the equity out of your home for any purpose. It's also entirely unnecessary given today's lax lending climate where just about anyone with a pulse can qualify for some sort of real estate loan. I recommend that you read the Federal Reserve Board's brochure entitled *What You Should Know about Home Equity Lines of Credit* that's available at: www.federalreserve.gov/pubs/equity/equity_english.htm.

Interest-Only and Adjustable-Rate Loans

Today, borrowers have gone gaga over interest-only and adjustable-rate mortgage and deed of trust loans. Interest-only (IO) loans usually allow borrowers to delay making payments on the principal loan balance for a fixed term of three to seven years. The problem with interest-only loans is that once the interest-only payment period expires, the principal often increases the size of the loan payment beyond the borrower's ability to repay it. Adjustable-rate (ARM) loans have an initial fixed-rate period, generally ranging from three to five years, during which the interest rate doesn't change. However, once the fixed-rate period expires, the loan's interest rate is adjusted every 3, 5, 7, or 10 years to a predetermined market index such as the 11th District Cost of Funds Index (COFI) or the London Interbank Offered Rate (LIBOR). As far as I am concerned, ARM loans are a financial crapshoot in which the borrower is at the mercy of the market. Needless to say, IO and ARM loans have the potential to be ticking financial time bombs. This is especially true for borrowers, who have interest-only ARM loans in which the commencement of principal loan payments happen to coincide with an upward adjustment in the loan's interest rate. This double whammy often causes a jump in loan payments that many borrowers simply can't handle. Usually, this results in the lender foreclosing on the loan.

Use a Second Mortgage to Pull Tax-Free Money out of Property That You Own

If you have sufficient equity in an investment property that you own, I recommend that you use a second mortgage or deed of trust loan to pull money out of the property. The best part about taking cash out of a property this way is that the loan proceeds aren't taxable, and you can write off most of the costs associated with obtaining the loan, along with all of the interest that you pay during the life of the loan. The amount of money that can be borrowed against a nonowner-occupied property depends on how much equity the owner has in the property and the loan-to-value ratio that the lender is using. In most cases, lenders will lend between 70 to 90 percent of a nonowner occupied property's appraised value. For example, a lender making a second loan at a LTV of 80 percent, on a property appraised at $200,000, would lend $160,000 ($200,000 multiplied by .80 equals $160,000). The actual amount of the loan would depend on how much equity the owner had in the property. If the owner had a first loan balance of $105,000, they would be able to pull $55,000 out of the property ($160,000 minus $105,000 equals $55,000).

Few Commercial Lenders Are Willing to Fund Loans under a Million Dollars

Today, there's relatively few commercial mortgage or deed of trust lenders nationwide that are willing to fund commercial loans for under a million dollars. Most commercial lenders claim that there's too much risk and not enough profit in commercial loans under a million dollars and generally cite the following three reasons for not making them:

1. High cost of due diligence in relation to the small loan amount.
2. Higher risk of default by borrowers.
3. Lack of reliable market, sale, and income data on properties securing loans for less than a million dollars.

Information on Commercial Loan Programs Available Online

The following web sites provide information about the various types of commercial loan programs that are available nationwide:

C-Loans: www.c-loans.com

Lending Tree: www.lendingtree.com/stm3/loans/commercial

Lending Expert: www.lendingexpert.com

HSH Associates: www.hsh.com/comm-showcase.html

Commercial Direct: www.commercialdirectloans.com

Low Quotes: www.lowquotes.com

Freddie Mac and Fannie Mae Small Multifamily Property Loan Programs

Fannie Mae and Freddie Mac both have small loan programs that investors can use to purchase multifamily properties with five or more units. You can learn more about these small loan programs by logging onto the following two web sites:

Fannie Mae Multifamily Loans: www.fanniemae.com/multifamily
Freddie Mac Multifamily Loans: www.freddiemac.com/multifamily

FHA Multifamily Loan Programs

The FHA has the following multifamily property loans available:

1. FHA section 223(f) loans are for the purchase and refinancing of existing multifamily properties.
2. FHA section 223(a)(7) loans are for refinancing existing loans on multifamily properties.
3. FHA section 221(d)(4) loans are for financing the construction and rehabilitation of multifamily properties.
4. FHA section 221(d)(3) and section 221(d)(4) loans are for financing the construction and rehabilitation of multifamily properties consisting of single-room occupancy (SRO) rental units.
5. FHA section 207 and section 223(f) loans are for the purchase and refinancing of existing multifamily properties.
6. FHA section 203(k) loans are for financing the purchase and rehabilitation of owner-occupied rental properties up to four units.

What You Need to Know about Hard Money Lenders

So-called hard money lenders make true equity loans, which are based solely on the amount of equity that a borrower has in a piece of property. Little weight is usually given to the borrower's income and credit history because the loan is secured by the property that's been pledged as collateral. Typically, hard money lenders will not lend more than 70 percent of a property's appraised value. This way, in the event the lender has to foreclose, it has an equity cushion of 30 percent in the property to cover the cost of the foreclosure action. However, the problem with hard money lenders is that they charge above market interest rates and most have outrageous application, origination, and closing fees that would make a Mafia Don blush. Plus, most hard money loans are generally short-term loans that aren't assumable and have balloon payments due in three to five years. The following web sites have information about the various types of hard money loans that are available nationwide:

Kennedy Funding: www.kennedyfunding.com

Regatta Capital, Ltd: www.1hardmoney.com

Avatar Financial Group, LLC: www.avatarfinancial.com

Advanced Funding Solutions, LLC: www.advancedfundingsolution-sllc.com

Clarity Real Estate Corporation: www.clarityrealestate.com

How Private Lenders Work

As I briefly told you earlier in this chapter, private lenders are mostly professionals and small business owners who are looking to get a better rate of return on their money than what stocks, bonds, treasury instruments, and various types of investment funds are paying. Private lenders are usually very picky, and rightfully so, about to whom they lend their hard-earned money. For the most part, private lenders look for experienced real estate investors who have a proven track record of making successful investments. For seasoned investors, private lenders can be an excellent source of real estate loans at market rates and terms. Market rate and terms refer to the interest rate and loan terms that institutional lenders offer their borrowers. Unlike hard money lenders, who generally have very stringent loan terms that aren't negotiable, private money lenders are usually more flexible about the type of loan terms that they're willing to accept. One method that I've used to locate private lenders is to advertise in local trade publications such as county bar and medical association newsletters and local business newspapers. Another way that I've found private lenders is by sending the following e-mail ad to the members of various online real estate finance forums:

Seasoned professional real estate investor seeks private lender to fund the purchase and renovation of small commercial properties in the $250,000 to $500,000 price range. Loan to be secured by first mortgage on property. No hard money lenders, please. E-mail tjlucier@tampabay.rr.com for details.

One of the best web sites for real estate investors to advertise online, for all types of loans, is the Real Estate Finance Forum, which you can subscribe to at: www.dealmakers.net/sub_unsub.asp.

It's Not Easy to Find Money Partners to Finance Deals

I hate to be a spoilsport, but unless you have a real estate investment background, experience, and a successful track record, you're going to have a hard time enticing so-called armchair investors to act as money partners and help you finance the purchase of investment properties. A money partner is an individual who puts up the money to fund a real estate transaction in return for a percentage of the gross profit when the property is resold. For example, if I am supplying the dough in a deal, I want at least 60 percent of the resale profit, for putting my capital at risk. If you're an inexperienced investor, the best place to start looking for money partners would be family and friends. However, be forewarned that if a real estate deal that a family member or friend financed turns sour, the fallout could end up causing irreparable damage to your relationship with your relative or friend.

Don't Overlook Finance Companies as a Source for Real Estate Loans

Finance companies are usually considered a lender of last resort for a real estate loan, but if you've been turned down by every bank in town for a loan, you may want to consider borrowing from a finance company. Nowadays, finance companies make real estate loans that are kept in their own loan portfolios. However, when borrowing from any type of finance company, you must be prepared to pay through the nose in loan fees and interest. There's also a certain stigma attached to borrowing from a finance company. Don't ask me why, but, for some unknown reason, borrowers with loans that are funded by finance companies generally receive lower credit scores, as they're perceived to pose a greater credit risk than other borrowers. The following finance companies make real estate loans nationwide:

> Household Finance Corporation: www.hfc.com
> American General Financial Services: www.agfinance.com
> Beneficial Finance Corporation: www.beneficial.com

Don't Be Bashful about Asking Sellers to Help You Finance the Purchase

You may want to do what I do and only buy properties from owners who are willing to help finance the purchase by providing seller-financed mortgage or deed of trust loans on reasonable terms. This way, the owner lends you his or her equity secured by a seller-financed loan on the property, which allows you to purchase it without going through the rigmarole of having to:

1. Fill out overly intrusive loan applications.
2. Qualify for new mortgage or deed of trust loans.
3. Pay outrageous loan fees.
4. Pay above market interest rates.
5. Assume existing loans that have above market interest rates.
6. Pay rip-off third-party due diligence fees.
7. Deal with less-than-honest lenders.

Ask Owners to Accept the Down Payment in Installments

A seldom used method for financing the down payment on the purchase of a property is to ask the owner to accept the down payment in two to four installments. In other words, instead of giving an owner a lump sum down payment at the time the sale closes, you would pay them in two to four installments. For example, if an owner agreed to accept two $5,000 installment payments, six months apart, as a down payment, you would sign two $5,000 promissory notes secured by the property. Once each $5,000 loan was paid, the seller would record a release of lien in the public records to remove the lien from the property's title.

Request a Short-Term Moratorium on Repaying Seller-Financed Loans

Whenever I buy any type of run-down or mismanaged rental property with seller financing, I always ask the owner to give me a three to six month moratorium on repaying the loan. This way, I can fix up and turn the property around, without having to support its negative cash flow in the process. For example, I specialize in turning small mismanaged rental properties around, and almost all of the properties that I buy have vacancy rates that range from 50 percent to 100 percent. This means that there usually isn't enough rental income or cash flow to pay for the property's operating expenses and debt service. So instead of paying the shortage or negative cash flow out of my pocket, I ask the seller, during negotiations, to allow me to delay making loan payments until I can get the property turned around and fully occupied. I document my request for a moratorium on loan payments by showing the owner written estimates of all needed repairs along with a detailed repair schedule, which outlines how many business days—Monday through Friday—it will take to make all of the rental units ready to rent. If the owner agrees, the moratorium becomes a clause in the loan document. To date, 80 percent of the property owners I have asked for a moratorium on payments have agreed to give me one.

Don't Agree to Loan Terms That Could Hinder the Future Resale of the Property

First and foremost, never agree to any seller-financed loan terms that could hinder the future resale of the property. In other words, don't let the seller slip any type of due-on-sale clause or prepayment penalty into the loan documents. As a precaution against due-on-sale clauses, I have a clause included in all seller-financed mortgage loans that states: *This mortgage loan may be assumed by an individual with proof of a FICO credit score of 670 and above, or by a business entity under the control of an individual, with proof of a FICO credit score of 670 and above.* This clause prevents the lender holding a seller-financed mortgage from acting in an arbitrary manner when it comes to allowing a third party to assume the loan. To preclude sellers from trying to impose any type of a prepayment penalty at a later date, I have the following clause included in the loan document: *This mortgage loan may be paid in full at anytime without penalty.*

Use Low-Interest Lines of Unsecured Credit to Finance Deals

Most of the straight-laced professors, who teach finance classes at graduate level business schools don't like to admit it, but credit cards have been the source of the majority of the lines of unsecured credit that have been the financial lifeblood for most small business start-ups over the past 20 years. Contrary to what many so-called financial experts may espouse, there's nothing financially irresponsible about the judicious use of credit cards. The fact of the matter is that low-interest credit cards provide financially responsible adults with readily available lines of unsecured credit to buy appreciating assets, without having to first submit to a financial strip search or pay outrageous loan fees.

In this business, access to readily available sources of cash allows investors to take advantage of opportunities to buy properties at below market prices the moment they become known. I've found that low-interest lines of unsecured credit are the most cost-effective source of short-term financing available today. And I've been using low-interest lines of unsecured credit for the past 15 years to finance both the acquisition and turnaround of small, mismanaged rental properties. I use the cash flow from the property to pay the credit line balance off in monthly installments. Believe me, once you factor in outrageous loan fees and rip-off third-party due diligence costs that are required in order to obtain a commercial mortgage loan on a mismanaged rental property with an "insufficient cash flow," you'll quickly come to the realization that low-interest lines of unsecured credit make financial sense.

I currently use three fixed-rate low-interest lines of unsecured credit that come with credit cards issued through three national banks. As you probably already know, banks and credit card companies routinely offer low-interest lines of unsecured credit to customers with excellent credit in the form of so-called convenience checks. These checks aren't cash advances per se, as they carry very low interest rates, which remain fixed until the credit line is paid off. To me, the real beauty in using unsecured lines of credit, instead of secured credit lines, such as a home equity line of credit (HELOC) is that you don't have to put your home on the line and pay those exorbitant closing costs that lenders generally charge borrowers for the privilege of doing business with them. In fact, the most that I have ever had to pay when using an unsecured line of credit was a $50 transfer fee. I don't know about you, but I don't know of any mortgage or deed of trust lender where I can borrow $50,000 at 2.99 percent interest without filling out an intrusive loan application or pledging any collateral and have closing costs of only $50. When you use low-interest lines of unsecured credit, instead of having to run to some bank and beg for money whenever a bargain-priced property comes along, you automatically:

1. Reduce the number of inquiries in your consumer credit files, which could adversely affect your credit score.
2. Reduce the chances of your identity being stolen during the loan approval process.

How I Earned a Fast $57,000 Profit by Using Cash from Unsecured Lines of Credit

I once bought a vacant four-unit rental property in West Tampa by using cash that I had obtained from two low-interest lines of unsecured credit. The owner lived in Macon, Georgia, and just wanted out of the property. Luckily for me, she received a copy of one of my letters that I routinely mail to out-of-county property owners on the same day that she decided to throw in the towel and sell her property. She sent me an e-mail with the property's address along with the name and telephone number of her sister who was acting as her property manager. Five business days later, after I performed my due diligence, I was the proud owner of a rental property that I had bought for $62,500 cash, which was approximately 50 percent below its market value of $125,000. Six months later, after I had spent $5,500 upgrading the property, I turned around and refinanced it with a loan for $94,000, which was 75 percent of its appraised value of $125,000. I promptly repaid the $68,000 that I had borrowed to buy and fix up the property. The remaining $26,000 went into my savings account, and I still had $31,000 worth of equity in the property. I had made an initial profit of $57,000, simply because I had bought the property for cash. All told, I earned an $82,000 profit on the property, when I resold it 18 months later for $150,000.

Obtain Low-Interest Lines of Unsecured Credit

If you're creditworthy and have a source of income, you should be able to obtain low-interest lines of unsecured credit from banks and credit card companies that offer lines of credit with their credit cards. Credit card interest rates are tied directly to cardholders' FICO scores. And your initial credit limit will be based on your credit score, income, and the amount of outstanding debt that you have. But once you have a solid track record of making payments on time, you can usually get a credit limit increase every six months. If I were you, I would obtain your credit cards through reputable regional or national banks. A word to the wise: Don't go hog-wild and end up with a wallet or purse full of credit cards. I recommend that you limit the number of credit cards that you hold to four. I am telling you this because most credit cards have lousy terms and interest rates, which are clearly stacked against cardholders. When selecting credit cards, I suggest that you choose cards that offer the lowest fixed interest rate and avoid cards with zero and low-interest teaser rates that jump into the high teens once the teaser rate expires. The following web sites have information on credit card offers from numerous banks and credit card companies:

CardWeb: www.cardweb.com
CreditCards: www.creditcards.com
CardOffers: www.cardoffers.com

CHAPTER 22

How to Fix Up Your Property So You Maximize Its Curb Appeal and Resale Value

In this business, it's a fact of life that most property fix-ups usually end up costing more and taking longer to complete than what was initially planned for. Often, the fix-up proves to be the make-or-break phase of a real estate deal. That's because a lot of real estate investors, both seasoned professionals, who should know better, and inexperienced rookies, just starting out, routinely get carried away and go overboard when fixing up properties. They usually do this by making extravagant spur-of-the-moment decisions that wreak financial havoc on their profit margin and greatly increase the amount of time that's required to finish the fix-up. In the construction industry, this is known as being over budget and behind schedule. In this business, you can be an ace at putting deals together, but if you're not in control during the fix-up phase, you can end up blowing what was supposed to be your profit on unnecessary improvements, which you're unable to recover the cost of making. For example, I know an investor in Charlotte, North Carolina, who let a contractor talk her into tearing out all of the cabinets in a kitchen, even though deep down she knew that all that was really needed to update the kitchen was new cabinet doors, hardware, and countertops. But because she didn't stick to her guns and tell the contractor to take a walk, what should have cost no more than $2,500, tops, turned into a $9,500 cost overrun because she foolishly spent $12,000 on new cabinets, which were an unnecessary added expense that took a big bite out of her resale profit. In this chapter, you're going to learn how to maximize your property's curb appeal and resale value by giving it:

- An industrial strength cleaning.
- An exterior cosmetic facelift.
- An interior cosmetic facelift.

Fix Up a Property on Schedule and within Budget

Once you close on the purchase of a property, time is money and you can't afford to dillydally around with the fix-up. The key to completing a property fix-up on schedule and within budget is in knowing how to complete the following five actions:

1. *Plan:* Develop a property fix-up plan, which is based on the property's appearance and information that was derived about the property's physical condition, during your pre-buy inspection.

2. *Budget:* Calculate a budget by using a bottom-line mentality, which is based on exactly what needs to be done to maximize the property's curb appeal and resale value and nothing more. In other words, when you calculate your fix-up budget, use the bare minimum amount of money necessary to obtain the maximum return on every dollar spent fixing up the property.

3. *Schedule:* I use what is referred to in the military as backward planning to establish a work schedule timetable. I do this by calculating a realistic completion date, which is based on a six-day work week that takes possible unforeseen problems and local weather conditions into consideration. Once I've established my property fix-up completion date, which, for me, is never more than 45 days from the start date, I establish a work schedule for each stage of the fix-up.

4. *Hire:* If you don't have the tools, skills, knowledge, experience, time, or desire to do a top-notch professional job, hire competent tradespeople to do it for you.

5. *Supervise:* If you don't have the knowledge, time, or desire to supervise the fix-up yourself, hire a competent professional to do it for you.

Know What You Don't Know about Fixing Up Properties

Rule number 1 of my 10 rules for success: Know what you don't know, which you read about in Chapter 2, should be heeded by everyone reading this book, who doesn't have the skills, knowledge, experience, or tools necessary to complete professional quality, do-it-yourself property repairs. That's because over the years, I've seen a small fortune wasted by wannabe handymen, who didn't have a clue as to what they were doing and ended up having to hire a professional to straighten out the messes they created.

Buy a Copy of the *Builders Encyclopedia on CD-ROM*

I am a journeyman carpenter with over 35 years of hands-on experience, and as far as I am concerned *The Journal of Light Construction* is the absolute best how-to-do-it magazine for the construction building trades. They've produced a *Builders Encyclopedia on CD-ROM*, which has 11,000 pages of detailed information on everything that any real estate investor would ever need to know about any facet of construction in an easy-to-search format. Having this type of insider information at your fingertips can be very valuable, especially when you're getting bids from contractors who, as a group, have a tendency to exaggerate the extent of the amount of work that needs to be performed when putting job estimates together. This way, you'll be able to take a contractor's job estimate and compare the scope of the work being proposed to what the *Builders Encyclopedia* says it takes to complete the same type of job. But just as important, you'll be able to carry on an intelligent conversation with people in the construction industry, and this alone can save you money and make contractors think twice about trying to rip you off with shoddy work at exorbitant prices. To learn more about the *Builders Encyclopedia on CD-ROM*, log onto www.jlconline.com.

Spend the Least Amount Needed to Maximize a Property's Curb Appeal and Resale Value

My sole objective during the fix-up phase is to spend the least amount of money that's necessary to maximize a property's curb appeal and resale value. That's why, my cardinal rule when fixing up a property has always been, clean, repair, or replace as needed. In other words, first try cleaning it, and if that doesn't do the trick, try repairing, and if that fails to work, replace it with a preowned replacement from a reputable source or buy a new one at a steep discount. I am also a strict adherent to the principle, if it ain't broke, don't fix it. In other words, don't replace something just for the sake of replacing it. For example, I know an investor in Tampa, who, when he buys a single-family house, automatically replaces every air-conditioning unit that's over 10 years old, regardless of its condition. His rationale for doing this is that most air-conditioning units aren't made to last more than 10 years—which is false by the way—so why not replace the unit and eliminate any possible questions from prospective buyers about its condition. Here's is a listing of 14 areas and items that I clean, repair, or replace when fixing up a property:

1. *Walkways and parking areas:* Clean, repair, patch, and seal all walkways and parking areas as needed.

2. *Exterior doors:* Clean, repair, or replace all exterior doors, hinges, and locksets as needed.

3. *Windows:* Clean, repair, or replace window frames, glass, and locks as needed.

4. *Exterior lighting:* Clean, repair, or replace all exterior light fixtures and bulbs as needed.

5. *Interior doors:* Clean, repair, or replace all interior doors, hinges, and locksets as needed.

6. *Kitchen cabinet:.* Clean, repair, or replace all cabinet doors, hardware, and countertops as needed.

7. *Interior lighting:* Clean, repair, or replace all interior light fixtures and bulbs as needed.

8. *Plumbing fixtures:* Clean, repair, or replace all sinks, tubs, showers, faucets, commodes, and vanities as needed.

9. *Heating and cooling systems:* Clean, repair, or replace all heating and cooling systems as needed.

10. *Floor coverings:* Clean, repair, or replace all carpets and floor coverings as needed.

11. *Exterior and interior paint:* Clean, prepare, and paint all exterior and interior surfaces.

12. *Landscaping:* Prune, cut, trim, and mow the property's landscaping and lawn as needed.

13. *Gutters and downspouts:* Clean, repair, or replace all gutters and downspouts as needed.

14. *Roofs:* Clean, repair, or replace as needed.

Free Job Cost Estimating CD-ROM
Available at Home Depot Stores

The Home Depot has a free job cost estimating CD-ROM called the *Worksite CD*, which has a listing of building materials, along with estimating software designed specifically for construction professionals by the Craftsman Book Company. The *Worksite CD* allows you to create accurate estimates that can be automatically converted into orders and sent to your local Home Depot via the Internet. Plus, it exports invoices to QuickBooks accounting software programs. You can pick up a copy of the latest version of the *Worksite CD* at the contractor help desk at any Home Depot store.

Hire Retired Tradesmen and Contractors
to Fix Up Your Property

I recommend that you do what I do and hire retired tradesmen and contractors to fix up your property. There are numerous retired journeymen carpenters, plumbers, painters, plasterers, roofers, electricians, and heating and air-conditioning mechanics all across the country who are extremely competent and seeking part-time work. By hiring retired tradesmen, you'll cut your fix-up costs substantially because you won't have to pay the high hourly rates that most full-time tradesmen and contractors charge. Plus, most retired tradesmen know all of the money saving tricks of their particular trade, which can help to reduce your overall fix-up costs. In addition to hiring retired tradesmen, you can also visit construction job sites and ask tradesmen if they're interested in what's commonly referred to as "side work." Once you find a tradesperson, who wants to work for you, ask him or her for references from people that he or she has done work for in the past. Contact each reference, and ask if they'd hire this person again.

How to Avoid Being Ripped Off by Unscrupulous Tradesmen and Contractors

Here are three ways that you can avoid being ripped off by the many unscrupulous tradesmen and contractors, who make a living by taking naive real estate investors to the cleaners on a regular basis:

1. Hire only properly licensed and insured tradesmen and contractors.
2. Require written estimates for all jobs.
3. Require that everyone who provides labor and materials on your job, sign your state's version of a waiver and release of lien on final payment form.

Require Written Estimates for All Jobs

Require written estimates for all jobs that include the following information:

- Detailed description of the scope of all work to be performed on the job, including clean up.
- Detailed work schedule with commencement and completion dates.
- Specifications for all building materials to be used on the job.
- Listing of all building permits required to perform the job.
- Detailed payment schedule outlining the amount and time when payments are to be made.
- Warranties covering workmanship and building materials used on the job.

What You Need to Know about Your State's Construction Lien Law

Most state construction lien laws allow everyone who provides a service, labor, or material for the improvement of real property the right to file a lien against the property's title for nonpayment. In most states, if a contractor is paid for a job, and the contractor fails to pay the subcontractors, who supplied the labor and the material men who supplied the materials, the property owner is still financially responsible for paying them, even though the contractor has been paid in full. In other words, you could end up paying for a job twice, if you don't have legal proof that everyone was paid in full. The only way to avoid having this happen to you is to require that everyone who supplies services, labor, and materials on your job sign your state's version of a waiver and release of lien on final payment form on receipt of payment. This way, you'll have legal proof that everyone connected to your property fix-up has been paid in full.

Require Tradesmen to Obtain the Necessary Permits before They Start the Job

In most jurisdictions, not all repairs on nonowner-occupied properties require permits. The requirement to pull a building permit is usually based on the size and scope of the needed repair. When you hire a tradesman or contractor, you must have them pull any required building permits before they start the job. This way, their work will be inspected by your local building department to ensure that it meets the building code.

Give the Property an Industrial Strength Cleaning

The first stage in the fix-up phase is to give the property an industrial strength cleaning by having the building, all walkways, and parking areas pressure washed. A properly applied pressure washing job can dramatically change the appearance of any building's asphalt, shingle, or tile roof and flat surfaces such as concrete sidewalks and driveway. The two keys to a great looking pressure-washing job are state-of-the-art equipment and properly formulated cleaning chemicals. A professional pressure washer will have the right pieces of equipment to clean all types of washable surfaces and will use chemicals, which are specially formulated to remove soot, scum, mold, grease, grime, mildew, and rust from all types of washable surfaces. I've been able to pressure wash stucco and concrete block walls, which were coated with layers of grime, soot, mold, and mildew that had accumulated over the years and make them look like they were just built. I've also been able to clean asphalt shingle and tile roofs, which were filthy from mold and mildew and make them look like new, without damaging any shingles or tiles.

A Professional Paint Job Adds Thousands of Dollars to a Property's Resale Value

I am always amazed at the remarkable difference that a professional paint job can make to any building. In this business, a professional-looking exterior and interior paint job will literally add thousands of dollars to a property's resale value. On the other hand, the combination of cheap paint applied by an inexperienced painter will always result in an amateurish looking paint job that sticks out like a sore thumb. I use Behr brands of exterior and interior paint, which I purchase from the Home Depot. Behr paint costs more than most other brands, but it covers well with just one coat and is very durable. I use a three-color exterior paint scheme, which incorporates three tropical colors that people generally associate with Florida. I paint the body of the building one color, the fascia and exterior doors a different color, and the drip edge around the roof and window shutters another color. Interior walls and ceilings should be painted in light neutral colors, using quality interior flat latex paint, while interior trim and doors should be painted with latex semi-gloss enamel paint. I use a two-color interior color scheme: flat white paint on walls and ceilings and antique white semi-gloss on trim and doors.

Keep Track of Your Property Fix-Up Costs on a Daily Basis

The best way to avoid breaking the bank during a property fix-up is to keep track of your fix-up costs on a daily basis. The easiest way that I've found to do this is by maintaining a property fix-up cost worksheet, like Form 22.1, to record your material, labor, and miscellaneous costs on a daily basis.

FORM 22.1 Property Fix-Up Cost Worksheet

Date	Material Costs	Labor Costs	Miscellaneous	Total Cost

How to Package and Market Your Property So You Can Sell It for Maximum Profit

If you follow the advice that I've given you in this book and buy a piece of property at a price that is below market value, you should always make the majority of your profit on the day that you close on the purchase. But in order to realize your profit, you have to get paid, and to get paid, you must know how to package and market a property so that it can be sold for maximum profit. However, I want to warn you right up front that if your idea of salesmanship is to stick a "for sale" sign in front of a property, or to place a classified ad in your local newspaper, and then wait by your telephone for calls to come rolling in from eager buyers, who want to buy your property on the spot, you're going to be in for a big disappointment. The key to quickly selling property, in today's competitive real estate market, is to take an aggressive, hands-on, proactive approach, which puts your property on the radar screens of prospective buyers, who are in the market for the type of property that you're selling. The only way that you're going to be able to bring your property to the attention of the largest possible number of prospective buyers is by using the following four methods to market your property:

1. Internet.
2. E-mail.
3. Classified ads.
4. For sale signs.

How to Calculate a Property's Resale Value

The very first thing that you must do before you ever put a property on the market is to calculate its resale value. You can do this by using the step-by-step instructions that I outlined in Chapter 18 to estimate a property's market value. Just make sure that your sale price includes the cost of:

- Searching for the property.
- Acquiring the property.
- Putting the property in a marketable resale condition.
- Marketing the property for resale.
- Your time spent on the transaction.

What to Include in Your Property's Information Sheet

The first step in preparing to market a property for sale is to compile a comprehensive property information sheet. For example, if the property being sold is a single-family house, its information sheet should contain the following details:

1. Your name, web site and e-mail address, and telephone number.
2. The street address of the property being sold.
3. The asking price, sale terms, and existing loan information.
4. The year the property was built, along with the type of construction and architectural style.
5. The square footage of living space and the number of bedrooms and bathrooms.
6. Descriptions of the living room, dining room, family room, den, carport, utility room, garage, basement, and any other rooms.
7. The type of heating and air-conditioning system.
8. Descriptions of any fenced-in yard, sprinkler system, security system, swimming pool, spa, patio, deck, landscaping, or other special features that are part of the property.

Package Properties to Highlight Their Best Features

Your resale profit is ultimately tied to how well you're able to package the property that you're selling. The trick to packaging a property is to highlight or accent its best features so that the property appeals to the largest possible segment of prospective buyers. For example, when I am preparing a property package for a single-family house, I include the following four pieces of information:

1. Property's geographical location to include any special features or benefits about the area and neighborhood.
2. Size and shape of the property to include any unique architectural features.
3. Nearby sources of public transportation, employment, shopping, schools, recreation, and health care facilities.
4. Special features and amenities about the property and grounds, including lush landscaping, large shade trees, fenced yard, and home office.

How to Advertise Your Properties for Sale Online

If you already have a web site, you can create a "property for sale" web page to advertise your properties for sale online. If you don't have a web site, you should have an inexpensive one built so that you can take advantage of the Internet and market your properties on the World Wide Web. To see an example of a property for sale web page, log onto my company's web site www.homeequitiescorp.com and click on the "property for sale" button. Your property for sale web page should include the following information:

- Interior and exterior photographs of the property.
- Property location map.
- Driving directions to the property.
- Property site plan.
- Property features.
- Property's sale price and terms.
- Information on how to set up an appointment to view the property.

In Chapter 15, I explained how URL forwarding works for a "property wanted" domain name. The same principle applies when using URL forwarding for a property for sale domain name. For example, I own the domain name www.tampapropertyforsale.com that is forwarded to the property for sale web page on the Home Equities Corp web site at www.homeequitiescorp.com/propertyforsale.html. This way, whenever the domain name www.tampapropertyforsale is typed into a computer's browser window, it's automatically forwarded to the Home Equities Corp property for sale web page.

Where to Advertise Your Property for Sale Online

You can advertise commercial and residential property for sale online at the following web sites:

Craigslist: www.craigslist.com/about/cities.html

Biz Trader: www.biztrader.com

Loopnet: www.loopnet.com

Land Net: www.land.net

Realty Investor: www.realtyinvestor.com

Dealmakers commercial and investment property forum: www .dealmakers.net/ mail/index.html

Commercial Real Estate Listing Service: www.cimls.com

For Sale by Owner: www.forsalebyowner.com

Owners.com: www.owners.com

Buy Owner: www.buyowner.com

How to Compile a List of Prospective Buyers from Visitors to Your Web Site

The most efficient way that I know to compile a listing of prospective buyers is to have visitors to your web site, who are interested in buying property, complete a buyer e-mail notification form, and submit their name and e-mail address so that they can be notified by e-mail when you have a property for sale. To see an example of a buyer e-mail notification form, log onto my company's web site at www.homeequitiescorp.com/propertyfor-sale.html and scroll down the page to the buyer e-mail notification form.

E-Mail Buyers Information about Properties That You Have for Sale

To notify the prospective buyers on your list about a property that you have for sale, send each prospect a property information sheet via e-mail, which includes the following information:

- Property address.
- Description of the property.
- Estimate of the property's market value.
- Sale price and terms of the property.
- Location map of the property.
- Site plan of the property.
- Directions to the property.

Put a "Property For Sale" Ad at the End of All Your E-Mail Messages

Whenever I have a property for sale, I place an ad at the end of all my e-mail messages, which contains pertinent information about the property. For example, if I have a duplex for sale, my ad would read as follows:

> **Duplex for sale, $150,000.** Both units have 2/1. Owner financing is available to a buyer with good credit and a $15,000 down payment. Please send me an e-mail message at tjlucier@homeequitiescorp.com for further information about the property.

Run Classified "Property For Sale" Ads in Local Newspapers

In addition to using property for sale web pages, online advertising, and e-mail property information sheets to market your property, you should also place classified ads in local daily and weekly newspapers, which include the following information:

- The sale price.
- The amount of the down payment and monthly loan payment.
- Your web site and e-mail address and telephone number.

I suggest that you record a detailed outgoing telephone message on your answering machine, which provides callers with the property's features, sale price, sale terms, street address, and driving directions to the property. This way, prospects calling about your ad will be able to access information about the property 24 hours a day, seven days a week.

Place a Professional Looking "For Sale" Sign in Front of the Property

As part of your marketing strategy, always place a professional looking "for sale" sign, which faces the street in front of your property. I use four-foot by four-foot signs, which are made from ¾-inch marine grade plywood, and attached to 4 × 4 inch by eight-foot pressure-treated posts. I paint the plywood white and have my web site and e-mail address and telephone number painted in red and black colors by a professional sign painter. I use marine grade plywood because it's very durable and doesn't delaminate after it becomes wet. I also cover my signs with one-eighth inch Plexiglas, to protect them from vandals wielding cans of spray paint. This way, I can use paint remover to clean the Plexiglas, which saves the cost of having the sign repainted.

Consider a Flat-Fee Real Estate Broker to Help You Sell Your Property

If you don't have the time or the desire to sell your property yourself, but you don't want to pay an arm and a leg as a sales commission, your best bet may be to hire a flat-fee real estate broker, who charges a flat fee to sell property, instead of six or seven or ten percent of the sale price that traditional residential and commercial brokers charge. To find flat-fee brokers in your area, log onto the following web site: www.brokerdirectmls.com.

How to Avoid Wasting Your Time with Nonqualified Prospective Buyers

A lot of investors end up wasting their time with nonqualified buyers, who don't have the credit or income to qualify for any type of real estate loan. The only way to avoid wasting your valuable time with nonqualified prospective buyers, who are dead broke and have really rotten credit, is to ask questions that are designed to weed out the pretenders from the serious buyers who are ready, willing, and have the financial wherewithal to purchase your property. For example, whenever I receive a telephone call or e-mail from a would-be buyer inquiring about a property that I had advertised for sale, I ask the following four key prequalifying questions:

1. Do you currently have the money on hand to pay the down payment and closing costs?
2. Do you have the income to afford the monthly mortgage payment?
3. Have you been preapproved by a lender for a loan in the price range of the property?
4. Can you close on the purchase of the property within the next 30 days?

Have Lenders Prequalify Your Prospective Buyers for a Loan

I recommend that you find three reputable lenders to prequalify your prospective buyers. By using three lenders, your buyers will have a large selection of loan programs from which to choose. When you have a prospective buyer who needs to obtain his or her own financing, in order to purchase one of your properties, you can send him or her to one of your lenders to see if he or she is qualified to obtain a loan in the price range of the property that's for sale. This way, you'll know within 24 to 48 hours if the prospect is going to be able to obtain a loan and close the deal.

Ask Buyers for Verifiable Proof of Funds When the Sale Agreement Is Signed

Another way to protect yourself from having nonqualified buyers tie up your property is to require buyers to show you verifiable proof at the time they sign the sale agreement that they have the needed funds on hand to close on the purchase of your property. I do this by having the prospective buyer provide me a letter written on bank or credit union stationery, which states that the buyer has the amount of money in an account that's needed to buy the property. If for whatever reason, the buyer refuses to provide me with verifiable proof that he or she has the funds to close the sale, I kill the deal on the spot.

Require Buyers to Provide a Loan Preapproval Letter from a Licensed Lender

I won't show a property that requires financing unless the prospective buyer has a verifiable loan preapproval letter that's written on the stationery of a Florida licensed mortgage lender. I require loan preapproval letters because I don't want to have my property tied up by a wannabe buyer who doesn't have the income or credit that's needed to obtain a loan. Once I have a buyer's loan preapproval letter, I call the lender to double-check that the buyer's income and credit have been verified and that all is good to go. I verify the letter with the lender because many lenders issue loan preapproval letters without ever actually checking a borrower's credit or income, which makes the letters worthless and results in a lot of "preapproved borrowers" being rejected when they apply for a loan because of inadequate income and lousy credit.

Always Take Backup Offers until the Sale Closes

Whenever I have a property for sale, I take backup offers until the property is sold. I tell the buyer who's making a backup offer that the property is under contract to be purchased and that my acceptance of their offer is contingent on the pending sale not closing. And I have the buyer sign a sale agreement and give me a refundable $1,000 earnest money deposit. This way, if for whatever reason, the sale falls through, I have one or two buyers waiting in the wings to purchase the property.

How to Protect Yourself When Showing Your Property to Prospective Buyers

Showing property can be dangerous to your health. That's because in recent years, the criminal element has been targeting owners selling their property. In order for you to lessen your chances of being robbed, attacked, or murdered by a criminal posing as a prospective buyer, I very strongly recommend that you take the following seven precautions when showing your property:

1. Obtain the prospect's full name and telephone number when you schedule the appointment to show the property.
2. Conduct an Internet search of the name and telephone number provided to you by the prospect.
3. Carry mace or pepper spray on your person.
4. Carry a cellular telephone on your person.
5. Carry a concealed firearm on your person, if you have a permit to carry one.
6. Have a spouse, partner, or friend wait in your vehicle while you show the property.
7. Require prospects to provide photo identification before you show them the property.

Maximize Your Resale Profit by Minimizing the Amount You Pay in Income Tax

Another way to maximize your resale profit is by structuring a tax-efficient sale, which allows you to minimize the amount of income tax that you're required to pay from the sale of your property. I recommend that you consult with a tax professional, who's well versed in real estate tax matters to find the best way for you to conduct business as a real estate investor. You can download the three Internal Revenue Service publications that are listed below, from the following web site: www.irs.gov/formspubs /index.html:

1. Publication 537, *Installment Sales.*
2. Publication 946, *How To Depreciate Property.*
3. Publication 550, *Investment Income and Expenses.*

Real Estate Investor Resources Online

The following is a listing of over 100 real estate related web sites, which every serious real estate investor should bookmark on his or her personal computer.

Accessible Housing Information

Access Board, www.access-board.gov

Accessible Housing Resource Center, www.abledata.com

Fair Housing Accessibility Guidelines, www.hud.gov/library /bookshelf09/fhefhag.cfm

The National Accessible Apartment Clearinghouse, www.forrent.com /naac

ADA Standards for Accessible Design, www.usdoj.gov/crt/ada /reg3a.html#Anchor-17431

Attorney Locator Information

Martindale Hubbell Lawyer Locator, www.martindale.com/locator /home.html

Findlaw, www.findlaw.com/14firms

Lawyers, www.lawyers.com

Builders' Risk Insurance Information

Zurich North America, www.zurichna.com

International Risk Management Institute, www.irmi.com

Commercial and Residential Property Sale and Income Data Information

CoStar Exchange, www.costar.com

Loopnet, www.loopnet.com

National Real Estate Index, www.realestateindex.com

IDM Corporation, www.idmdata-now.com

DataQuick, www.dataquick.com

Real Estate Information Source, www.reis.com

Commercial Loan Information

C-Loans, www.c-loans.com

Lending Tree, www.lendingtree.com/stm3/loans/commercial

Lending Expert, www.lendingexpert.com

HSH Associates, www.hsh.com/comm-showcase.html

Commercial Direct, www.commercialdirectloans.com

Low Quotes, www.lowquotes.com

Fannie Mae Multifamily Loans, www.fanniemae.com/multifamily

Freddie Mac Multifamily Loans, www.freddiemac.com/multifamily

Construction Cost Calculators

Construction cost calculator, www.get-a-quote.net

Construction material calculators, www.constructionworkcenter.com /calculators.html

Building cost calculator, www.rsmeans.com/calculator/index.asp

Consumer Credit Information

Credit Info Center, www.creditinfocenter.com
Credit Net, www.creditnet.com
Credit Boards, www.creditboards.com

Credit Card Information

CardWeb, www.cardweb.com
CreditCards, www.creditcards.com
CardOffers, www.cardoffers.com

Credit Reporting Agencies

Equifax, www.equifax.com
Experian, www.experian.com
Trans Union, www.transunion.com

Demographic Information

FFIEC Geocoding System, www.ffiec.gov/geocode/default.htm
U.S. Census Bureau FactFinder, www.factfinder.census.gov/servlet /BasicFactsServlet
U.S. Census Bureau QuickFacts, http://quickfacts.census.gov/qfd
U.S. Census Bureau zip code statistics, www.census.gov/epcd/www /zipstats.html

Environmental Hazardous Waste Information

EPA superfund hazardous waste site search, www.epa.gov/superfund /sites/query/basic.htm
Environmental hazards zip code search, www.scorecard.org
EPA Enviromapper zip code search, www.epa.gov/cgi-bin/enviro/em /empact/getZipCode.cgi?appl=empact&info=zipcode

Finance Company Loan Information

Household Finance Corporation, www.hfc.com

American General Financial Services, www.agfinance.com

Beneficial Finance Corporation, www.beneficial.com

Hard Money Loan Information

Kennedy Funding, www.kennedyfunding.com

Regatta Capital, Ltd, www.1hardmoney.com

Avatar Financial Group, LLC, www.avatarfinancial.com

Advanced Funding Solutions, LLC, www.advancedfundingsolutionsllc.com

Clarity Real Estate Corporation, www.clarityrealestate.com

Insurance Information

Insurance Institute, www.iii.org

A.M. Best Company, www.ambest.com

National Underwriter Company, www.nationalunderwriter.com

State Insurance Departments, www.naic.org/state_web_map.htm

Independent Insurance Agents & Brokers of America, www.independentagent.com

Standard & Poor's, www.standardandpoors.com

Lead-Based Paint Hazard Information

EPA National Lead Information Center, www.epa.gov/lead/nlic.htm

Lead-Based Paint Disclosure Fact Sheet, www.epa.gov/opptintr/lead/fs-discl.pdf

HUD Lead-Based Paint Abatement Guidelines, www.lead-info.com/abatementguidelinesexamp.html

EPA Lead information Pamphlet, www.epa.gov/lead/leadpdfe.pdf

Loan Servicing Information

U.S. Loan Servicing, www.usloanservicing.com
North American Loan Servicing, www.sellerloans.com
PLM Lender Services, Inc., www.plmweb.com

Mapping Information

MapQuest, www.mapquest.com
MapBlast, www.mapblast.com
Yahoo Maps, http://maps.yahoo.com
Maps, www.maps.com/DriveSolo.aspx?nav=DD

Miscellaneous Real Estate Information

American Society of Home Inspectors, www.ashi.org
National Association of Public Insurance Adjusters, www.napia.com/search/index.asp
Municipal Code, www.municode.com/resources/online_codes.asp
Abstracters Online, www.abstractersonline.com
Flat-Fee real estate brokers, www.brokerdirectmls.com
HUD Section 8 Housing Program, www.hud.gov/offices/pih/programs/hcv/index.cfm
Federal Code of Regulations, www.gpoaccess.gov/cfr
United States Code, http://uscode.house.gov.
Garn-St Germain Depository Institutions Act, www.phil.frb.org/src/Garn.html.
Real Estate Settlement Procedures Act, www.hud.gov/offices/hsg/sfh/res/respa_hm.cfm
EPA Mold Resources, www.epa.gov/iaq/molds/moldresources.html
Comprehensive Loss Underwriting Exchange, www.choicepoint.net
HUD 1 Settlement Statement, www.thomaslucier.com/HUD1SettlementStatement.pdf

RESOURCES

Online Property Sales Information

Craigslist, www.craigslist.com/about/cities.html

Biz Trader, www.biztrader.com

Loopnet, www.loopnet.com

Land Net, www.land.net

Realty Investor, www.realtyinvestor.com

Dealmakers commercial and investment property forum,
www.dealmakers.net/mail/index.html

Commercial Real Estate Listing Service, www.cimls.com

For Sale by Owner, www.forsalebyowner.com

Owners.com, www.owners.com

Buy Owner, www.buyowner.com

People Search Information

Internet Address Finder, www.iaf.net

Pretrieve, www.pretrieve.com

Switchboard, www.switchboard.com

Skipease, www.skipease.com

Social Security Administration Death Index, www.ancestry.com
/search/rectype/vital/ssdi/main.htm

Street Address Information, www.melissadata.com/lookups/index.htm

Reverse Telephone Directory, www.reversephonedirectory.com

Property and Casualty Insurance Information

Property and Casualty Insurance Carriers, www
.ultimateinsurancelinks.com

Property and Casualty Insurance Buyer's Guide, www
.propertyandcasualty.com/buyersguide

Property Appraisal Information

Appraisal Foundation, www.appraisalfoundation.org
Appraisal Institute, www.appraisalinstitute.org
American Society of Appraisers, www.appraisers.org

Property Records Information

Public Record Finder, www.publicrecordfinder.com/property.html
Search Systems, www.searchsystems.net
Tax Assessor Database, www.pulawski.com
Public Records Online, www.netronline.com/public_records.htm
Public Records USA, www.factfind.com/public.htm
First American Real Estate Solutions, www.firstamres.com
DataQuick, www.dataquick.com

Property Valuation Software Information

Real estate investment analysis software, www.invest-2win.com/index.html
Z-Law real estate software catalog, www.z-law.com
Real Data real estate software, www.realdata.com
Marshall & Swift, www.marshallswift.com

Renters' Insurance Information

Geico Renters' Insurance, www.geico.com/home/renters
Insweb, www.insweb.com
NETQUOTE, www.netquote.com

Residential Loan Information

Fannie Mae, www.fanniemae.com/homebuyers/homepath/index.jhtml
?p=Homepath
Freddie Mac, www.freddiemac.com/sell/factsheets/frm.htm
Federal Housing Administration, www.hud.gov/fha/loans.cfm
Department of Veterans Affairs, www.homeloans.va.gov/veteran.htm

Residential Property Sales Data Information

DataQuick, www.dataquick.com
HomeGain, www.homegain.com
REAL-COMP, www.real-comp.com
HomeRadar, www.homeradar.com
Domania Home Price Check, www.domania.com

Tax Information

Internal Revenue Service, www.irs.gov
Internal Revenue Service forms and publications, www.irs.gov
/formspubs/index.html

Title Insurance Information

Old Republic National Title Insurance Company, http://orlink
.oldrepnatl.com/Underwriters/pages/Table%20of%20Contents.htm
Chicago Title Insurance Company, www.ctic.com/operations.htm
First American Title Insurance Company, www.firstam.com/faf
/reference/uwtools.html
Stewart Title Virtual Underwriter, www.vuwriter.com
Real Estate Lawyers, www.realestatelawyers.com

Thomas J. Lucier has been a real estate investor in Tampa, Florida, since 1980. Mr. Lucier is the author of seven books and three CD-ROMs on real estate investing and managing Florida residential rental property. He's also a Florida licensed mortgage broker, and an active member of the National Association of Real Estate Editors, and the Real Estate Educators Association. Mr. Lucier's real estate investment advice has been published in the *Wall Street Journal, Commercial Investment Real Estate* magazine, Real Estate Journal .com, Bankrate.com, and other financial publications and web sites. To read more about Thomas J. Lucier, log onto his web site at www.thomaslucier.com.

Unlike 99 percent of all real estate authors in America, there isn't a phalanx of gatekeepers between Tom Lucier and his readers. You can e-mail Tom directly at tjlucier@thomaslucier.com, or you can call him at his office in Tampa, Florida, at (813) 237-6267 to speak with him personally.

INDEX